YOU
ARE THE
ANSWER

About the Author

Michael J Tamura is a world-renowned spiritual teacher, healer, and clairvoyant. For over three decades, he has offered clients classes, seminars, and sessions in spiritual guidance and self-healing. He has been featured on radio and television, including CNN and NBC. More information can be found at www.michaeltamura.com.

YOU
ARE THE
ANSWER

Discovering and Fulfilling
Your Soul's Purpose

Michael J Tamura

Llewellyn Publications
Woodbury, Minnesota

First Edition
First Printing, 2007

Book design and layout by Joanna Willis
Cover design by Gavin Dayton Duffy
Cover image © Rudi Von Briel / Corbis / PunchStock
Interior illustrations by Llewellyn art department

Llewellyn is a registered trademark of Llewellyn Worldwide, Ltd.

Previously published as *You Are the Answer: An Extraordinary Guide to Entering the Sacred Dance with Life and Fulfilling Your Soul Purpose* (Star of Peace Publishing, Mt. Shasta, California) © 2002 by Michael J Tamura

Library of Congress Cataloging-in-Publication Data
Tamura, Michael J., 1953–
  You are the answer : discovering and fulfilling your soul's purpose /
Michael J. Tamura.—1st ed.
    p. cm.
  ISBN 978-0-7387-1196-6
  1. Spiritual life. 2. Self-actualization (Psychology)—Religious
aspects. I. Title.
  BL624.T367 2007
  204'.4—dc22
                                                    2007026016

Llewellyn Worldwide does not participate in, endorse, or have any authority or responsibility concerning private business transactions between our authors and the public.
  All mail addressed to the author is forwarded but the publisher cannot, unless specifically instructed by the author, give out an address or phone number.
  Any Internet references contained in this work are current at publication time, but the publisher cannot guarantee that a specific location will continue to be maintained. Please refer to the publisher's website for links to authors' websites and other sources.

Llewellyn Publications
A Division of Llewellyn Worldwide, Ltd.
2143 Wooddale Drive, Dept. 978-0-7387-1196-6
Woodbury, MN 55125-2989, U.S.A.
www.llewellyn.com

Printed in the United States of America

In Memory

This book is dedicated in memory of my mother,
Kei Tamura (1932–1996),
a beautiful, loving soul, who continues
to be an angel to many,

and

my beloved friend and teacher,
Lewis S. Bostwick (1918–1995),
an enlightened being who left an immeasurable gift to us all.

I am forever grateful. Without either of you,
I wouldn't have had the chance.

CONTENTS

FOREWORD

During your life, you may have the great fortune of crossing paths with an extraordinary human being who touches you so profoundly that you are never the same after your encounter. I would like to introduce you to such a person. The author of this book, Michael Tamura, a preeminent spiritual healer and teacher, is a man who sees life, the world, and you through his spiritual eyes. And his wisdom plumbs the depths of your soul. If you are just awakening to your spirituality, Michael will give you a solid foundation from which to embark upon your journey. If you have been on the path for some time, he will inspire you, provide additional tools you can use, and help you gain the certainty in yourself to renew your commitment to your spiritual growth. For the advanced soul, Michael offers a treasure chest of insights, validation, wisdom, and a comprehensive reminder of your soul purpose.

I had heard about Michael for several years. In fact, before I finally got to meet him, I had collected twenty-two pieces of paper with his phone number on them given to me by many of my clients. I was definitely getting the message that I needed to see this man, although for what purpose I wasn't quite sure. Some of those who recommended that I see Michael told me that he was a clairvoyant, while others described him as a spiritual healer. Of course, in my circle of friends, clients, and colleagues, there are many clairvoyants and healers. Why should I go see this particular person?

I received my answer immediately upon meeting Michael. As I arrived at the appointed place for my first reading and healing session, the door opened to reveal a short Japanese man with a welcoming and compassionate smile. I was amazed at the beautiful golden and blue light radiating all around him. And flanked on either side of him I saw his two brilliant spiritual guides. I knew I was meeting an extraordinary man.

In the private session that followed, I knew right from the beginning that Michael had reached a place deep in my soul. Without hesitation, he described accurately my nature as a soul, validating how I have always felt within myself. He communicated to me with a depth of understanding about the spiritual and psychic dynamics of my relationship with each member of my family and the karmic cycles we were here to resolve. With equal ease and clarity, he gave me insight into my career challenges, psychic condition, and what might help me in taking the next steps in my spiritual growth. And as he gave me an energetic healing, I could feel tremendous changes happening within me.

Right now, you are fortunate to hold these pages in your hands for they, too, will help heal your soul. When I first started reading this book, it evoked a memory of my first inkling of "purpose." It was 1966, and I was a young boy. In those days, Saturday mornings meant watching cartoons, then biking over to a nearby vacant lot to meet my friends and begin our weekend adventures. Like most kids, I looked forward to these times with a tingly anticipation of what the day might have in store for us. On one particular Saturday, we decided to go to the local pond to search out frogs. On our way, we stopped at a red light at the main intersection of town. When the light turned green, my friends pedaled quickly across the street, but I could not move. I had an overwhelming feeling to stay put. I remember feeling funny as my friends called to me to get moving. Then, the light turned red and it was too late to cross. Suddenly, an old man began to walk against the light, totally unaware of oncoming traffic. Without thinking, I immediately dropped my bike and ran to pull him back on the curb. He looked at me with a startled expression before he realized what had happened. He thanked me profusely for stopping him from certain disaster. When the light turned green again, I escorted him to the other side of the street.

Before I wheeled off to join my companions, the old man turned to me and said, "Young man, you have a great purpose in life."

I politely said, "Thank you," not understanding what he meant by that remark. I smiled and whizzed away. It wasn't until much later in life that I began to understand the meaning of the old man's words: "purpose in life."

Although I had many intuitive experiences or *feelings* during my youth, I often misunderstood these messages because, at the time, no one talked about such things. It was difficult, however, not to pay attention to them because these experiences were usually accompanied by specific physical sensations. Usually, I had a tingling feeling in my stomach, followed by a fluttery excitement throughout my whole body. As I grew older, I often referred to these episodes as *experiencing the energy of knowing.*

Eventually, I learned to trust these *knowing* sensations. I felt them mostly when I was quiet and undisturbed by outside distractions, especially at bedtime when I said my prayers. The more I listened to these feelings, the stronger they became. I can see now that when I prayed, I was having a relationship with my inner being or soul. These times with myself were the first steppingstones to uncovering my soul's purpose in life, leading me to the world of spirit.

Michael is a true spiritual messenger and he eloquently describes the nature of spirit and takes you on the journey of the soul from its conception to its fulfillment as seen through the eye of spirit. Many of us have been taught that the physical world is the end-all, be-all of existence. We might believe that "if we can't see it, it doesn't exist." This book, however, is not pieced together from academic research; rather, it is a book birthed from the heart and soul of one who has seen and experienced the truth of Divine Purpose. Ride the wings of his poetic vision to experience your deeper connection with your divine heritage.

Reading this book is such an experience and, once you read it, you will want to read it again. It is not a book to rush through. Savor the words and let them touch you on many levels. As you open up your heart and soul to their energy, you will discover truths you need to hear . . . and you will never be the same. We can spend lifetimes asleep, or we can choose to wake up. Michael provides the inspiration, motivation, answers, steps, and the tools with which to do just that. Don't miss this opportunity. It is time to fulfill your soul purpose and live the life you were meant to live—now.

James Van Praagh

APPRECIATION

No book is ever written by one person. The author dons the robe of the scribe who breathes deeply before putting pen to paper and, in that act, summons universal truths into life. Just as there is no inhalation of breath without there first being a living heart, there is no inspiration of truth without there first being a loving heart.

Writing tears us apart to reveal the true contents of our heart and soul. Any shred of arrogance that we possess within us that makes us think that what we write is solely ours is burned away by the fire of truth. Each writer becomes the crucible in which the prayers of humanity wrestle with the will and love of Divinity. If the author is successful, a drop of heaven is distilled and delivered into the hearts and souls of the readers.

The book you now hold in your hands is a culmination of years of preparation. The love and support and prayers of countless souls wrote its very pages. I am grateful to have been its crucible.

Little in this book could have been written without the miraculous years I spent with the late Lewis S. Bostwick. He was an extraordinary friend and spiritual master who taught and mentored me through my spiritual adolescence. Without his loving guidance and the gift of spiritual tools, I would not be where I am today. Thank you for everything you have given to me and to the thousands of others whom you graced with your wisdom. The psychic kindergarten that you created as a sanctuary for evolving souls has set off a ripple in a stormy sea that continues to this day, touching the hearts of many who seek a greater awareness. It was in your presence that I truly learned to walk in spirit.

I am grateful to my dear friend James Van Praagh, who supported me in this noble endeavor in so many ways. You are a true pioneer of the heart and soul. With courage you carved the trails through dense skepticism along the perilous mountainside of a global spiritual awakening.

To my editors, who gave me literary ladders with which to reach the shelves where now my book can be found, my undying gratitude:

Carroll Knowles, who was the first to help me toward publication and who taught me the secret to writing the first draft. She said, "We have professionals who can edit, but only you can write the stories and the teaching. Just write. We'll fix it up later." Without that sage advice, I would still be staring at a blank computer screen.

Heidi Schulman, who invited me to her home in the backwoods of New Mexico, read my first draft, and started me on the road to rewriting. Then, I knew I had a long way to go, but that it was definitely doable.

Doug Childers, who probably gave me a four-year writing course in a few months. Without your extensive coaching about structuring my writing, I would have rambled off of my first page.

Linda Thomchin, who helped me cut through the fog of countless rewrites with a clear outline to put me back on course to the book I set out to write.

L. T. (Laurie K. Turner), who gave me valuable professional and personal validation to take the next step.

Allan Silberhartz, a wonderful friend and founder of Bridging Heaven and Earth Foundation, who offered to read my manuscript and introduced me to Tony Stubbs and his publishing company, TJPublish.

Tony Stubbs, an extraordinary scribe of the wisdom of the ages, who provided me with the literary midwifery needed to bring this book into the world. Your heartfelt encouragement and soulful guidance were the wings that carried this book gracefully to its natural birth. Another editor/publisher without your spiritual and editorial understanding might have given us a C-section instead.

Carrie Obry, the kind and prescient Acquisitions Editor, who was the first at Llewellyn to see the potential in this book and who recommended it for publication. Thank you for your support and for helping me give this book its new life.

To the rest of the wonderful people at Llewellyn Worldwide, thank you for your dedication and expertise in making this and a diversity of great books available to many.

To Debra Katz, gifted psychic, author, and friend, thank you so much for introducing my book and me to Llewellyn.

To Leszek Forczek, preeminent artist with a beautiful heart, thank you so much for commemorating this book with such a soul-felt painting.

To James Twyman, peace troubadour extraordinaire and a true emissary of light and of love, my gratitude not only for your support but also for your selfless devotion to bringing peace on this planet.

And to all who were friends, teachers, and students during my almost twenty years at the Berkeley Psychic Institute, with whom I shared countless hours of growing pains and laughter, thank you and many blessings on your continuing adventures.

To my friends and current students, I am thankful for the chance to share what I have with you.

To my many friends who have cheered me on and patiently waited as I fumbled in the dark to prepare this book, I am truly grateful.

To all the guides, angels, and teachers in spirit who have guided, prodded, consoled, and cajoled me into writing this book, thank you for lifting me up with love and truth.

Our special angels B. J. and Rich Evans. Thank you so much for your love and support on earth as well as in heaven. Without the two of you, I would still be piecing my book together.

My mom, Kei, now in spirit, and my dad, Rey, have given me more love and support than I could have hoped for. Thank you for bringing me into your lives and changing my diapers.

Every day I count my blessings for the two absolutely wonderful souls I am proud to have as my sons, Greg and Nick. I love you both with all my heart. You light up my life and inspire me in everything I do.

And finally, Raphaelle, without whom this book would never have been completed. Your undying love and support, your constant encouragement and healing, and your wise feedback touch its every page. Thank you for letting me be the one to test your patience this lifetime. I love you, friend, partner, angel, and wife.

INTRODUCTION

This book is about your soul purpose. At first, when you ask about the nature of your soul purpose, you will uncover more questions rather than receive any definitive answer. Who am I? Where am I from? Where am I going? What am I here to fulfill? In fact, seeking the truth of your soul purpose will lead you on a profound adventure. At times, the fear, ignorance, doubt, and isolation you encounter along the way may seem overwhelming. Yet, if you are willing to explore and discover what lies hidden within your heart, soul, body, and mind, you will be treated to treasures beyond imagining. It is not an easy path, but you will find that there is nothing in the world worth exchanging for it. I pray that this book serves you as a guide on this extraordinary journey of spiritual healing and growth.

In the beginning of our spiritual growth process, most of us live life like shipwreck survivors adrift on the open seas. Constantly dashed around by the waves of fate, terrified, we might feel that "life is hard and then we die." Yet, when we choose to abandon our fears and make peace with those powerful waves, we learn to float over them. Then they no longer repeatedly slam us under. Our life begins to alternate between the pleasant and unpleasant. Sometimes we crest a large wave, see the beauty all around us, and even catch a glimpse of the shore. At other times, we sink into a trough and all is dark, with no hope other than to get over the next wave. With perseverance, we begin to realize we can learn to surf. When we do, those same waves, once menacing, become our allies. Riding on their awesome power and direction, we learn to surf homeward to the shores of our freedom. Just as a surfer must learn to dance with the vast power of nature, we must learn to enter into the Sacred Dance with Life to fulfill our soul purpose and experience the joy of our existence.

Since I was a child, I've loved to dance but have tripped and fallen many times. I have stepped on countless partners' toes as well as careened unawares into other dancers. There were also times when I was incapacitated and couldn't dance. Yet none of that can take away my love for dancing. And so it has been with my soul purpose. I love fulfilling my purpose, even though I have tripped and fallen many times.

I came into this lifetime to heal and teach. Healing and teaching, however, are not my purposes. It is through them that I am fulfilling my purpose, which is just like everyone else's: to fully become who I am.

My purpose always called to me and, as a child, I responded without question. Purpose was the magnet, and it guided the compass of my heart as to where to go, what to do. It was not at all about what I was going to be when I grew up. I felt for my purpose in the same way, for example, I felt for Mrs. Olsen, my kindergarten teacher. She was a beautiful, graceful woman with rich, full, black Spanish hair rolled up on her head as if to help her hold her head higher in the face of adversity. Her gentle kindness seemed somehow pulled down toward an unseen gravity. She was longing for something beyond her reach and it saddened her. Something inside of me wanted to reach out to her, to comfort her.

Somehow, I knew I had to shine her shoes. I knew it would lighten her heart. So, each day at story time when we would gather around her on the floor, I would gently take off her shoes as she read to us and spit polish them lovingly with some tissues. When she finished the story, I would slip them back on her feet. This always brought a smile to her face. After the first couple of weeks of this daily communion, she called my mother to tell her how much better she felt since I started to do this and how much happier she was. She asked my mother if it was all right with her if I could be allowed to continue for as long as I wished.

I was a healer then as I am a healer now. I didn't have to grow up to be one. The only difference is that now I know what it means to be a healer. As a child, I was just being it. All I knew was that I wanted people to be happy; I knew they didn't have to suffer. Whenever I had a chance, I wanted to learn how to help people feel better.

By the time I was seven, I was introduced to the *amma-san,* the blind Japanese massage healer and musician. During the Second World War, a Japanese medical doctor realized that, although blindness may be a handicap, it also heightened other senses of perception. So he established a school to teach the blind how to provide healing to people through massage and music. Even after the war, the healers so trained would set out to the residential streets playing their bamboo flutes to announce that the *amma-sans* were in the neighborhood and ready to be of service.

"Here's two hundred yen" (at the time about fifty-seven cents), my grandmother would say to me. "Go ask the *amma-san* to come over."

I would run out to the street in search of the healers, following the musical scent of the mysterious yet earthy melodies of their bamboo flutes. A quiet joyfulness bubbled inside of me when I was given the opportunity to bring home the *amma-sans.* On many evenings, I sat next to the healer as he or she massaged my grandparents' bodies, akin to a virtuoso pianist playing a rhapsody of healing. I watched the healer's every move and in my mind duplicated them. With eyes closed, I could even feel how they worked—sight was not necessary.

After the *amma-sans* left our house, I would volunteer my services to anyone who wanted more of the massage healing. My hands itched to try what I had learned that evening. In fact they not only itched but also began to blister. No one knew what was wrong with me. I was given all manner of medicines to no avail. Only later would I learn that I was channeling so intense a creative healing energy through my hands that I was burning them.

Without proper spiritual guidance, my healing abilities caused a variety of problems for me. So much so that I decided I had to become a doctor. After all, any time you have a serious problem, you go to a doctor. My image of a doctor was a person of great wisdom and compassion, who knew about life and its mysteries. The opening scene of *Ben Casey*, a popular doctor TV show of the time, said it all: "Man, woman, birth, death, infinity." Back then I didn't know what it meant to be psychic or a healer. I didn't know those words.

Elementary school was pretty tough for me. Nobody seemed to quite know what to do with me. I was alternately put in the "gifted" and the "retarded" classes. I was sent to the school nurses, psychologists, counselors, and doctors. As a child, I knew things about others because I saw the geometry of their lives, but that didn't help me communicate with them. I saw what I called "colored clouds" around everyone—at the time I didn't know the term "aura"—and that didn't help me relate to others either. I didn't understand what was expected of me. All I knew was that it wasn't okay just to be myself.

So, throughout most of my teen years, I worked hard not to be myself. I tried my best to be what others seemed to respect: intellectual, competitive, responsible, and accomplishment-oriented. It wasn't until a friend fell ill when I was twenty that I began to return to my true self. Conventional treatment was out of my reach at the time, but a miracle of healing occurred through my hands and I once again turned to the call of my purpose.

Answering the call, I returned to a world brimming with adventures in healing and spiritual growth. It is a world of miracles. Ever since, I have lived in a world opened to new truths and never-ending beauty. It is a magnificent world overflowing with love, with grace, with freedom.

Is it hard to believe that such a world exists? I don't think so. It's not that the world I live in has no pain or suffering. It does. It has plenty of difficulties and challenges, and trials and tribulations. But, in the world I live in, those things are transmuted into wisdom, like turning lead into gold.

Just how did I come to live in such a world as this? It's simple, but it takes practice. I learned to abandon fear and suffering, exchanging them for loving and being at peace with myself. Living in a world of miracles is living the life of spirit on this earth. It's being *in* the world, but not *of* it. When you become more your true self, you begin to live the miracle. It's simple, because you *are* that miracle.

It's easy to say, "Abandon fear and suffering, and love yourself instead." Yet, as with anything else in life, it takes much practice. If you practice singing, you become a better singer. If you practice basketball, you become a better basketball player. When you practice living the life of spirit, you become better at fulfilling your purpose in life. You become better at finding happiness within yourself, no matter what the circumstance.

Living the life of spirit in this material world, and healing, growing, and fulfilling your destiny, are not only possible, they are inevitable steps in human evolution. It isn't true that enlightenment and spiritual fulfillment take a lifetime of asceticism, discipline, and training. Your lifetime of living is the training. Your life is your school. They cannot be separated. You need only to choose to be aware and learn.

Nor is spiritual fulfillment or happiness reserved for the chosen few. You don't have to be of a particular religious denomination or lead a life of a saint. You don't have to be a college graduate. It's not necessary to be poor or rich, ambitious or successful. All that is required of you is to be who you really are. Simple, but often not easy. However, the good news is you can learn. Anyone can learn.

I have had many wonderful teachers who, whether they knew it or not, have guided me to my own truth. I always advise students to learn from everyone. But "learning from everyone" doesn't mean blindly believing what anyone says. Learning from others means letting them point out the truth already within you. Your friends often teach you about love and your enemies teach you about truth. Your friends cherish and nourish what is wonderful in you, while your enemies tear out of you the pain and lies you don't want to face. Love will lead you to truth and truth will lead you to love. Love without truth is not complete love, and truth without love is not the whole truth. Without both, we are not free.

You may want to think of your teacher as infallible. You may insist that your teacher be the best. After all, if your teacher isn't perfect and makes a mistake, what's going to become of you? You will, however, come to realize that as you relinquish the fear of trusting in your own inner being, you can learn from everyone and everything in your life. When you trust in yourself, you know you can handle whatever happens. Life itself will then become your teacher. I hope that this book will help you toward that eventuality.

This book can be a doorway into an adventure in consciousness, spiritual healing, and personal growth. The secret to opening that door is for you to approach it with openness. As you explore what is written in its pages, you may become aware that reading this book gives you not only information and understanding, but also an *experience* of spirit and of healing. Those who read the preproduction manuscript have reported experiences of expanded consciousness, flashes of insights, spontaneous healing, past-life recall, and other stirrings of awakening to their inner being. After reading through this book once, consider using it as a regular reference guide. You can turn it into a formal study aid, digest the contents of each chapter, and practice applying them in your daily life. Or you can pick it up as a daily meditation tool and just open to any page and receive a special message for the day. Sometimes you might want to flip through its pages until a phrase or sentence catches your eyes and then reflect upon its meaning. You may also discover that reading the same passage at a later time will give you new insights, inspiration, or validation.

Let this book be your companion as you navigate the river of your spiritual life. Along your way, there will be times when you experience the rushing white waters of inspiration, a leisurely float down a glassy stretch of calm, the occasional snag on an outcropping of resistance, and the respite provided in an eddy of forgiveness. Reading this book may take you on a similar journey. Know that underlying whatever you experience at any given time is the call of your purpose—learn to respond to it and enter into the Sacred Dance with Life.

ONE

WHAT IS YOUR SOUL PURPOSE?

Life has a purpose for us, a purpose that refuses to be ignored and makes us ache with such longing for fulfillment. We come into physical being to fulfill that purpose. And the life that lives within the borders of our physical existence yearns for us to return to the whole that is life. Everything plays a part in fulfilling life's purpose. Nothing exists without a purpose to bring it into being and that purpose calls until we respond. And when we do respond to the call of purpose, we enter into a Sacred Dance with Life.

Purpose is the energy and consciousness that exist within a seed that compel and guide it into a beautiful flowering plant, given the correct nourishment. It is the meaning and worth within the seed that mature into a fruit-bearing tree, and every type of seed has a definite purpose. The purpose of an apple seed, for example, is to grow into an apple tree and produce apples. It cannot produce cherries or watermelons or anything else. The human soul is also such a seed. It is, however, a God-seed. Just as with the apple seed, a God-seed cannot grow into anything but a God-tree whose fruit expresses the totality of Divinity. How much of what you know to be Divine within you are you cultivating now? And how far will this go? Just as a single apple seed can produce apples as well as entire orchards for centuries, a single human soul can grow to heal and enlighten generations of humanity.

There are many varieties of apples, but they can all become apple trees. Some are grown in private backyards whereas others are grown in large orchards. In the same way, each of us is a unique human soul and we will fulfill our purpose in diverse and original ways. Yet we all have the same purpose for being here: to realize, through fully incarnating as a human being, all that is God.

What does it mean to *realize* God? It means to make God a reality in our being, in our consciousness, and in our living. But what is this God that we need to make real? I personally like what the Sufis say about God: *La Illaha Il Allahu,* or "There is nothing but God."

God is the word I use to bring awareness to that ineffable transcendence that creates every atom of our existence, breathes power into life itself, becomes all that is made manifest, preserves every bit of it in memory, experiences all of it, gains wisdom, and grows. If you can be aware of it, think it, imagine it, be it, do it, have it, it is God. These very words are God taking form to express one view of Him. God is that which is behind everything, is involved in everything, and contains everything.

God is infinite, eternal, and immortal. Yet the moment we ask anything of God, He not only provides, but also becomes the very provision and gives Himself to us. He is limitless but makes Himself limited so that we may touch Him, see Him, know Him. He is all-powerful, yet He makes Himself helpless so that we can give help, helpful so that we can receive help. God is all-knowing and everywhere.

Although I write of God as "He" and "Him," any pronoun I use can be replaced with another, for God is neither he nor she. Yet God can be he, she, it, we, they, you, or I. And God is not separate from us, except that God will accommodate our illusions of separateness. God can appear as an old man with a white beard on a throne in the heavens if you so desire, or as the whole universe, or surprisingly like you.

To the extent that you impose your controls, limits, and conditions upon the free will of Divinity, in yourself or in others, God will be you in your life. The more you relinquish those conditions you place upon free will, the more you will be God in God's life.

Purpose Is the Asking; We Are the Answer

We are spiritual beings learning to become complete human beings. Far from being a liability, our humanity is truly our grace and fulfillment. When you view yourself as a kind of failing and say, "But I'm only human," you not only demean your worth, but you also insult all that is sacred. In order to discover the true meaning of your soul purpose, it is imperative to reassess what it means to be human. For it is only through your humanity that you can fulfill divine will.

If purpose is such a sure thing, why does it so easily elude our grasp? Even those who seem to live with great purpose can have difficulties defining exactly what it is.

A television reporter asked Mark McGwire during his record-smashing season if being the home-run king was his life purpose. I recall Mark's answer that it definitely wasn't. What I understood him saying was that he was certain he had a purpose for being here, but it wasn't setting world records, hitting home runs, or even playing baseball. He said that he felt God had given him an incredible talent: hitting more baseballs farther than most people. He was also committed to continuing to give it his best. Mark McGwire knew what wasn't his life purpose, but couldn't quite put his bat on what was. Yet he ended the brief post-game Q & A with a memorable testimony of his faith. I remember him saying that if he kept using his various God-given talents to the best of his ability, he believed that he would eventually fulfill his purpose—whatever that may be.

Knowing one's purpose in life is not an intellectual matter; its power and meaning are experienced within. To get a clearer sense of purpose, let's look at it on a personal level as well as on a cosmic scale.

Imagine that you finally accomplish a difficult task, realize a long-held dream, reach a hard-won goal, create a masterpiece, or finish a magnum opus. You are done! Or are you? What more could you want? The "want" has been satisfied. Now, you *have*. When you are completely fulfilled, what naturally arises is the *sharing*. This sharing is not a separate action, but the giving that effortlessly radiates out of being.

Now, imagine being all-knowing, all-powerful, all-loving, all-creative. There is nothing you don't know, nothing you can't do. In your limitless ecstasy, celebration explodes out of you in an infinite variety of forms. A universe is created that follows your laws and fulfills your divine commands. An omnipotent, omniscient, and immortal being containing the infinity of life, you created all that is. Complete in every way, free and self-fulfilled, what more could you possibly need or want? Only one thing: to share that living and joyful creation.

This giving is God's outpouring of love. In this divine outflow, everything is both created and unconditionally supported. Protons support electrons. The sun supports the earth. All of nature supports humanity. And everything serves life's own purpose. It is a sacred dance.

All of life is God's ecstatic celebration. This sacred dance to which we are called is life's own purpose. The universe is the ballroom. Nature provides the banquet and the symphony. And God made us in His image, a seed containing the whole of Divinity so that, in our flowering, life could have a partner in its sacred grand waltz. The celebration would then be complete.

For humanity to fulfill life's own purpose, God gave the human soul what nothing else in all of nature possessed: free will. This is what children seek from loving parents as they grow up—the freedom to go out into the world to explore, discover, experience for themselves; to exercise what they were given; to love and create their own families; to give as they were given to; to discover their own worth.

The test of every parent's love is giving their children their freedom—supported by undying love, unconditioned by fear—for them to venture forth on their own to make mistakes, to learn through their own experience, to fail as well as to succeed beyond their wildest dreams. They may flounder, get hurt, or even die.

What if you had the power to change anything in an instant, yet you had to stand by and cheer on the child you loved more than your own self to stumble along life's precipice? Would you be able to let him or her learn through pain, fear, and suffering as well as through joy and love? It takes love beyond measure. This is the love that gave the human soul free will. And this is the love that we each have to discover within ourselves to have our freedom as individual souls, full creators—to be one, at last, with God.

For it is from love that we are born. And to love that we must return. This is the journey of the soul we call Life. To be who we are, to have all that is within us and to fully express our divine heritage— that is our purpose for living and the destination of our journey.

Spiritual growth is the process of fulfilling this purpose. And as you answer to the call of purpose, you become its answer. Your journey to your ultimate destination is not one of getting *there* from *here*. Instead, it is one of returning *here* from *there*. And destiny chooses its own time with you. Our spiritual development is not in some distant future, and the fulfillment of our purpose is nowhere to be found but here, within us now.

Our destiny *is* our freedom. And the process of fulfilling our life purpose is to choose truth at every crossroads and act upon it with love.

You are the answer. Purpose is the asking. Now, let us discover the question.

TWO

THE SOUL'S JOURNEY

"It is hard to be born as a human being, and hard to live the life of one. It is even harder to hear of the path; and harder still to awake, to rise and to follow."

—Gautama the Buddha, *The Dhammapada*, 14:182

The incoming soul sees the world as an awesome display of creation. It is a world full of vibrant energies and opportunities for experience. We are fascinated and curious as we approach these dynamic forces in a cosmic dance. Although we begin our incarnation conscious of being spirit and immortal, often we end up mesmerized by these tremendous forces of manifestation. In the same way that we can become so involved in an exciting movie that we forget it is not real, we can give up the power and consciousness of our being to materiality. Then, we start to believe we are separate physical personalities in a world made up of independent objects. This experience can be so absorbing that many of us forget who we are and why we asked to incarnate. For some, only the shock of impending death awakens them from their reverie to rediscover the path they must follow. Even for those who somehow manage to awaken themselves fairly early in their lifetime, there is much territory to cover. For most of us, it takes repeated incarnations to fully awaken from this hypnotic "dream" and realize the totality of our being and fulfill our divine purpose.

Each earthly incarnation, however, is not a separate life into which we are born and from which we die. We live, in truth, only one continuous life, moving in and out of each incarnated "lifetime" as easily as we change our clothes daily. Wouldn't it be strange to divorce ourselves from our life yesterday because we wore different clothing or because the weather was unlike today's? We don't consider each day as a separate "life" because we have a continuity of memory from day to day. When you are able to remember from one incarnation to another, however, you will realize that it is but one life you have been living eternally. And just as you don't have to remember everything from yesterday to continue the same life today, you won't have to recall the details of previous incarnations to know you have lived continuously through them as an immortal spiritual being.

You incarnate into a variety of body personalities and diverse circumstances so that you can gain the experience necessary to fulfill your purpose here. You have been born male as well as female, poor as well as rich, of every color and race, of various nationalities, and of different faiths. Whether you were born pampered royalty or abandoned at birth, became a superstar or a housewife, lived as a Muslim or a Christian, or died a soldier or a peace activist, there is no comparison of worth between them. How can there be? They are all part of the same one life. All of them have been necessary to equip you with what you need to fulfill your purpose thus far.

Your purpose unfolds along a continuous road with ever-changing scenery. You drive a variety of vehicles over this life-path so that you can experience it from different perspectives. This time you could be driving a Volkswagen surrounded by huge eighteen-wheelers, and complaining of those road-hogging truckers. Next time, you may be behind the wheel of a semi-truck cursing the inconsiderate driver of the "bug" you're trying not to squash. To be in one or the other is no better or worse—each vehicle type serves a purpose. Sooner or later, you remember that you've been in the other's seat, and then you understand and develop more compassion. You begin to realize more of the oneness of life.

Experiencing the many perspectives of life through your various incarnations, you will ultimately come to realize that the life you are living is the same one life I am living. Those you love are living the same one life as those you may detest. It is the one life of spirit. We all share this life in the same way that we all breathe the same air on this planet. What I do to the air will eventually affect you as much as it will affect me. Although you can pretend that the air they breathe in Africa is separate from the air you breathe in America, in truth, it is one and the same.

We mentally divide up this one life into your life, my life, and their lives. In the same way, we divide it up into my current life, my past lives, and my future lives. This division of life is strictly political, as are the lines we draw on our maps to divide the earth into countries. Then, we start to believe lies, such as "My country is greater than yours," as if life in one country were more valuable than life in another. One portion of life is never worth more or less than another. Life is life.

Within each human soul is the whole of all that is life. And its purpose is what gives meaning and, therefore, value to existence. We can never put a price tag or judgment on that soul, for its worth is always 100 percent. No soul is worth more or less than any other. It is not in accomplishing something of greatness that you gain your worth. It is in realizing the true worth within you that everything you do becomes of great value.

Just as one soul's life is neither greater nor lesser than another's, one of your incarnations is neither more nor less valuable than another. It is only through your present life that you are the sum of all of your incarnations—past, present, *and* future. You were never greater than you are right now, nor will you ever be. Your worth is already complete and never changes; only your relationship to it evolves. You might say, however, "I'm just a housewife and can't even get a job, so how can this life be greatest? How can it have more meaning than a lifetime in which I was a pharaoh, a president, or a saint? And what is the worth of the lives of those who are murderers on death row?"

Does a mother love one of her children any less than the others? Is a child in third grade worth less than one in high school? Of course not. A mother may find it more difficult and challenging to raise one of her children than another, but her love is no less for that child. A father may express his love for one of his children quite differently than for another one, but the love is no less. A child may not be as educated or as strong as an adult, but the meaning of her life is no less. How then can God, who doesn't have the limitations we do, love one soul any more or less than any other?

From the human perspective, life can seem to be full of suffering and injustices. Yet, from our soul viewpoint, we are all enrolled in the school of life *by our own choice*. Some of us are in kindergarten, others in junior high, while still others are in postgraduate schools. In school, everyone has to learn some basic subjects no matter what their intelligence or aptitude. There are also electives that some choose to pursue while others do not. In one classroom, we may choose to sit in the front row, right in the action, while in another, we sit in the back. When we took the class on criminality, some of us went all out and lived a life of raging crime, others of us learned from the horrors of being a victim to it, while others chose to join the police force for yet a different perspective.

The school of life is one of experience and distilling what we learn from it into wisdom. Therefore, what is truly important in a soul's education is not what we are born into—our heredity, gender, environment, religion, or socioeconomic status—or what happens to us in life. It is in *how we choose* to respond to whatever happens in our life, in whatever condition we find ourselves, that we gain our immortal wisdom and everlasting freedom, and reveal the true worth of our soul.

Your journey as a soul began with the oneness of innocence. Like an innocent child, you were at one with God and free. In order to become conscious of your true nature, however, you had to be born into individuality, had to be given free will, and had to forget that you were one with God. Through the trials of choice and consequences, you have been distilling your experiences into wisdom. With each birth into the physical world, you have brought forth more of your spiritual self into it. You are now learning to awaken your consciousness out of the hypnotic lure of dualities so that you can become a complete human being, a human embodiment of divine being. This is the deeper meaning of the line from the Lord's Prayer: "Lead us not into temptation, but deliver us from evil."

One of the great challenges of incarnating is to remember our spiritual self and not be tempted into the polarizing forces of materialization. We are like the little girl saying to her newborn brother, "Quick, tell me what God looks like. I'm beginning to forget!" Yet, if given permission and a safe harbor, most children before the age of four or five remember at least aspects of their previous existence as souls. I know one boy, then age five, who piped up in response to his mother's loving remark, "I am so grateful to God for having sent you to me," by retorting, "But God didn't send me to you. I *chose* you."

Being a scientist and a Catholic, his mother faltered at not only *what* he said but at the authority with which he said it. When she asked what he meant by that, he began to patiently explain, "Before I was born, while I was in spirit, I decided that I wanted you to be my mother in this lifetime. At first, I couldn't find you. When it was time and I couldn't get to you, I almost chose to come through another couple in Germany. But I'm really glad that I did find you at the last moment and was born through you."

The little boy's sermon rattled his mother. "There's a lot more to tell," he continued, "but you aren't ready for it yet. When I'm seven, I'll tell you the rest."

Disturbed by her son's startling revelations of his conscious spiritual life before birth, the mother sought out more spiritual understanding. Soon after, her deceased father came to her in a dream and told her that death is nothing like what most people think it is. On another occasion, she noticed her son playing checkers with a friend. When she remarked how nice it was that his friend was teaching him to play, her son corrected her, "Grandpa (her father) taught me how to play."

"I guess Grandpa must have done that before he died," she replied.

Her son corrected her once again. "No, Grandpa taught me to play last night in my dreams!"

As he had promised, two years later, the boy continued his spiritual revelation. He told his mother, "I've lived many lives before," and chose five of his recent lifetimes to recount in detail his identities and personalities, where he lived, what his work involved, who his family members were, and how he felt about each incarnation.

When my younger son, who was eight years old at the time, overheard me relating the little boy's story, he offered his own experience of having a conscious life before his birth. "Before *I* was born," he told us, "I was in a bright, white room. On the walls were pictures of who I could have as my parents. Once I picked the parents I wanted, I slid down this tube and everything got dark. Then, I was born!"

With that, he ran off to resume playing. We are all conscious spiritual beings with free choice—before our birth and after our death. Now, we must remember to be that *during* our incarnation as well.

A Doorway into Immortality

It was during my first visit to Egypt, when I was thirty years old, that the door to my own immortality blew wide open. Although I had been able, since my early clairvoyant training, to consciously access past lifetimes on a need-to-know basis, the tangible and ever-present reality of the continuity and oneness of life had faded with childhood. One particular experience, however, restored my certainty that I not only have incarnated many times before but also that all of my incarnations live within me here and now as sparkling facets of my own being.

On one excursion, I found myself transfixed by the grandeur of the sheer cliff from which spilled the remains of a once-great temple. The glare of the unrelenting sun danced upon the massive stones of antiquity, those bearers of ancient secrets in varying stages of undress. Faint echoes of lives long lost came murmuring into my consciousness. I stood at the threshold between worlds.

An Arabic construction foreman shook me out of my reverie with a call for an extra hand. "Can you help us pull?" he asked, offering the end of a mammoth rope wrapped around a gargantuan block of stone, halfway up a stone incline. My gaze met the sun-scorched smiles of a dozen workmen all holding a section of the rope.

"Sure, why not?" I replied and also offered the services of my friend and fellow traveler. "Didn't we used to levitate these things before?" I joked with him.

Once we were all positioned around the behemoth, the foreman taught us an Arabic call-and-response chant, much like the boot-camp cadences of the Marine Corps. The rhythm of the chant, the effort of pulling the massive stone up the incline, and the scorching sun began to exert a strange but wonderful influence on me. Soon, I was no longer in the ancient Egyptian ruins of 1984 or aware of my current body or personality. . . .

I am a young servant, one of Pharaoh's personal attendants. I know Pharaoh is dead and that I am to follow him to the next world. Several men in white robes are preparing me to be buried with his mummified body. Rich herbal fragrances fill the air. I am receiving my final instructions on what to expect upon leaving my body. A priest explains, "Spiritual teachers and guides will meet you and instruct you upon your arrival in the spirit world."

I can't keep my eyes open. I am falling asleep. Then I am aware that I have died. I am standing, suspended, in a large open space. Before me appear three beings in an effulgence of golden light. As my vision clears, I can see that these beings of light appear as three men in flowing robes. The one closest to me is dressed in a white robe that covers him to his feet. He emanates a gentle, priestly presence. Behind and to the right of this being waits a man in a radiant saffron-colored robe. His face is full, soft, and smiling, a smile of understanding. Still further to the right stands a man of dark complexion whose face is etched with ageless wisdom. He waits patiently, attired in a majestic robe of royal purple adorned with gold.

The first being steps forward, arms outstretched. He holds a pure white cloth, neatly folded. "You have successfully completed your life of service, dear one," he says. His thoughts gently soothe my soul. "This white raiment is spun from the purity of your heart, cleansed by the life you dedicated to the service of your master. Welcome to your next initiation of the soul!"

As I bow my head, he places the unfolded white cloth of silken light over my shoulders. I feel the purity of this shawl-like garment flowing through my being as I witness scenes from the life I have just departed. I experience in my soul the consequences of my small daily acts of kindness as I watch my young self placing sandals upon the Pharaoh's royal feet. I feel the love radiating from my master's heart as I realize that not only was he Pharaoh but also a spiritual master of a high order of initiates.

I see the intricate agreements woven in spiritual dimensions prior to my birth. I see that I am to be given over into the life of service to the royal family and receive my secret training as an initiate. This short life of spiritual training was secret in that I was not to be aware in the physical incarnation that I was undergoing one of my initiations. By the very nature of this particular initiation, I had to agree to forget. This way, I could live the life of service out of my true desire and choice rather than from the knowledge of a reward at the end of my incarnation. I was not afraid to give my life in service to my master in life as well as in death. This was my initiation. For this, I received the grace to die in full awareness into a higher state of being.

Next, the being in the saffron robe, radiant with a quiet power, steps forward. "You have done well, my friend," he begins. "I bestow you with your next degree. This shall be of power so that you may make a change in the world to which you shall return."

With that, he places his hand on my forehead and I close my eyes. Images flow through my mind of a variety of lives into which I can choose to incarnate next. With each option, I become aware of the possibilities of growth and learning as well as the manner in which I could make a difference in the world around me. Each of the choices presents various forms of leadership. I understand that the best servant in the house will be the master of the house.

It doesn't take much for me to choose to be born into the royal household of a pharaoh. I loved my master during the life I have just left and constantly looked up to him. I desired to be like him, as a son desires to grow up to be like his father. With this, I am given the chance to be born, not only as a future ruler, but also as one who will be trained and initiated into the mysteries. I am to become an initiate and pharaoh, just as my former master was.

Following this decision and revelation, I open my eyes to behold the third being standing before me. For a moment, I feel a shiver of apprehension and confusion. Up to now, I have been in a continuous state of peace. Then, I hear inside of me more a feeling than a voice: "Let go of everything."

I step away from the confusion that is rising up in me. Then, I experience a kind of blankness. Nothing. Next, a light emerges from above me and descends into me. I know. Certainty emerges within me of spirit, of God. Beyond this, I cannot put the experience into words. I know that this is what I must take with me into my new life on Earth. I know that somehow I must learn to lead others from this space. This is my next initiation.

At this point, I seem to fast-forward, watching from above the family preparing for my birth. Then, blackness.

As if awakening from one dream into another, I am now my childhood self of this current lifetime. Although the memory of the ancient Egyptian afterlife still echoes strongly in my consciousness, I find myself feeling and thinking as I did as a child. I am in the fourth grade of an American school on a military base in Tokyo. It is Mr. Davis's class. He has given us the assignment of going to the library and copying a paragraph out of the encyclopedia about ancient Egypt. I am thrilled for some reason and plunge into my project headfirst. In my excitement, I forget about the actual assignment. All I want to do is to make a large model of the Nile Valley, with its temples, pyramids, Sphinx, and the people of ancient Egypt. I work through the night on my project and am pleased with the card-table-sized model, complete with sand dunes. I even write my story about ancient Egypt on a fake papyrus pamphlet I make, bound with leather strips.

The next day, the rest of my classmates turn in their one paragraph copied from an encyclopedia at the school library, but I receive a D-minus for my assignment and must even stay after school to be chastised by my teacher. My joy turns quickly into confusion, for I don't know what's happened.

Then, as when becoming lucid during a dream, my consciousness steps out of my fourth-grade self and I am now aware of being my current adult self, observing my childhood dilemma. Then I understand. The assignment was about research skills! Technically, I failed the assignment; I never even looked anything up in a book. All I heard was "Egypt" and was flooded with enthusiasm and information. As a child, I couldn't understand why my teacher went all out to punish me, with no regard for how much I put my heart and soul into my version of the homework assignment. Now, I can see that his extreme reaction was fear. He couldn't handle the fact that a fourth grader, who had never previously studied about ancient Egypt, could know so much about it without referring to any books. It was beyond his comprehension and control.

"Okay!" yelled the construction foreman and suddenly I was myself, back amidst the present-day rubble of ancient Egyptian ruins. I had no recollection of pulling the massive block of stone to the top of the incline but somehow it was there, with me right beside it. Sweating and smiling, the foreman thanked us. I looked around at the stones, once new, now ancient. A door had opened within me and I had walked through it to immortality. Since this experience, I have become more intimate with the oneness of Life and the eternal love, within which our patchwork of "lifetimes" is a seamless tapestry.

Seen through the eyes of a soul, death is but a transition. Through our dying, we shed our outer garments of flesh and blood, and our judgments, isolation, and pain. Arriving after our physical death, we find that we are neither "on the other side" nor in an "afterlife." Our consciousness has merely expanded and gone more deeply into our own being and the oneness that is life. We become more aware of what has always been within us but which we'd forgotten in all the "busyness" of physical incarnation.

When our consciousness settles more into our spiritual self, we examine in vivid detail every thought, feeling, word, and deed that we put forth in the physical personality we have just shed. Not only do we experience their repercussions in what we believed to be "us" in the oneness that is Life, but we also realize we *are* those whom we had assumed to be "them." We fully experience, as recipients, the same condemnations we so self-righteously hurled at others. And we suffer the hurt and humiliations that they endured from our words and deeds. In the same way, we also bathe in the loving compassion we offered our loved ones and share in the healing of their hearts and souls. Then, we begin to appreciate what Jesus knew when He taught: "Love your neighbor as yourself."

During this phase of our spiritual journey, we meet with friends and family as well as with our teachers and guides. It is our *consciousness* that "travels" to spaces of healing and learning. As in the physical world, we have created places of higher education, healing, the arts, and much more in this inner dimension of reality. Here we prepare for the next leg of our journey. Just as we reviewed the incarnation we have left, we preview the life lessons we are to embody in the next incarnation. We plan out our next birth into a physical body based on:

- the nature of our soul personalities;
- our propensities and values;
- any unfinished karmic cycles from prior incarnations;
- any agreements we may have with other souls;
- what we have in abundance to offer;
- what we need and desire.

The extent of our prebirth planning isn't hard to imagine when we consider all the expert advice we get and the planning that goes into starting a new career, a business, or a family. Could there be any less when planning for a whole new incarnation, one that your life totally depends on?

Incarnation literally means "being in the flesh." The long sojourn of the human soul begins in the infinite, eternal, and limitless potential of spirit. And since there is no time or space in spirit, there can be no memory, consequence, responsibility, or the experience of growth. In order to experience the totality of what we may call God, the soul must incarnate in the physical dimension, into time and space. Hence the soul will have the capacity to experience mortality, responsibility, and the opportunity to exercise and develop its free will. What we call the human soul has one foot in nothingness and the other in everything. And in between lie all the limitless possibilities of experience that bridge the two into one. During our embodiment, when we learn as souls how to awaken from the addicting lure and hypnosis of the ever-materializing world, we discover that we no longer must wait for physical death; we can cross that bridge to our homecoming . . . now.

THREE

MAKING SPACE FOR SPIRIT

Frequently, I see people struggle to have their spiritual growth while living everyday life. For most of us, balancing the two is not easy. We have families to care for, job and financial responsibilities, career-building, personal dreams, and our health to maintain amidst myriad other demands. Many people end up merely penciling-in their spiritual life between the day's more pressing obligations. Often, they cancel their date with spirit because "there's one more thing to do."

I meet many people who conduct the business of their regular lives each day and then nourish their spirituality at religious services one morning a week, at metaphysical seminars, at weekend intensives, or annually at a spiritual retreat. Some may even squeeze in a spiritual practice such as yoga, tai chi, or another type of meditation exercise once a day, or pray at appointed times throughout the day. Yet once their allotted period of spiritual reflection, meditation, or worship is over, well . . . it's over. Then, for many, it's back to the busyness of business, family, relationships, and so on. Soon, spirit is forgotten.

It's not difficult to stray from our spiritual path in our increasingly fast-paced, high-tech lives. With cell phones, pagers, fax machines, TVs, computers, PalmPilots, Internet access, and e-mail, there's always one more thing that grabs our attention before we can quiet our mind and turn inward. Then, our lives become such a chaotic jumble of needs that we begin to try to create a semblance of order by compartmentalizing it: we make life a series of individual events to fit into our schedule . . . and our spiritual growth gets put on standby. So many of us have done this for so long that, in the world, our lives have become mere case numbers in court dockets and government agencies, medical charts in hospitals, and sound bites in the media.

Yet life isn't a series of unrelated events, and we cannot afford to pigeonhole our spiritual growth into an available slot in our Day-Timers. Spiritual growth is how we fulfill the purpose of our lives. It is the very underpinning of life, providing the theme and the meaning that pervade and sustain every aspect of our existence. But when we fail to nourish and heal spirit, the thread of meaning and continuity wears thin and disappears into the chaos ruling our daily existence. As a result of this, we may experience:

- isolation;

- loss of our sense of purpose and worth;

- a feeling of powerlessness;

- unbearable psychic pain.

Only our return to spirit can restore the purpose-filled spiritual life with which we were born into our day-to-day existence. We must develop this spiritual awareness and certainty so that we can navigate through the ever-changing conditions of life in the world and fulfill our purpose.

Perhaps the most common lament I hear from people who struggle to return to their spiritual path is, "I have too much to do. I don't have enough time." All their attention and energy get swallowed up by everything they *believe* they must do and there is not enough time for spirit at the end of their day, week, month, or year.

They may not realize that we all have twenty-four hours each day. No one has any more or any less. Lack of time is not an objective reality; it just appears that way to our senses. When you feel that you don't have enough time, what you're lacking is not time but *space*. You've lost your space to be *who* you are, *where* you are, *how* you are, *what* you are in the here and now. Whenever the demands become overwhelming and you're running out of time, it's time to make space for spirit.

Martin Luther, the leader of the Reformation, understood this well. He said that he prayed one hour every morning, but on days when he knew his "plate would be full," he would spend an extra hour in the morning "on his knees." To the logical mind, this makes little sense. On a day when he needed more time to handle the extra workload, he spent twice as long in prayer. Most people tend to do the exact opposite. For them, the time they allow for inner spiritual reflection diminishes in direct proportion to the demands of the outer world.

As Luther did, I found that the more space I made for spirit each day, the more able I was to face the challenges of the day. Instead of having less time to do things in the day, I would have more. And what at first seemed to be insurmountable challenges became manageable by the time I got to them. Thus dealing with them took a lot less time and energy. Why does it work this way? To understand this, we need to look at exactly what spirit is.

First, "spirit" has become a loaded word that for most people conjures up all sorts of images and feelings. For some, the word brings up religion, whether reverence for the sacred, forced solemnity, or fire and brimstone. For others, it's horror stories, ghosts, and demonic possessions. If you've been hurt or disappointed by religion, the word may have become your antidote to dogma and oppression. In some psychic circles, it could be another word for "entity." Still others may carry the word around as a kind of membership card required of New Age peer pressure. And, of course, avowed skeptics will swear that it doesn't even exist. Yet, if we could set aside all that for the moment, "spirit" is a word that validates existence and its true nature, i.e., being, consciousness, and energy.

So, first, spirit exists. Those who believe that it does not exist do so because they think of spirit as something separate from what they consider the form of existence. Spirit is being the form, creating it and experiencing it. Spirit *is* existence.

Next, spirit is consciousness. If you are reading this, if you are aware of any thoughts or feelings, you must be conscious. That consciousness is spirit.

Finally, spirit is energy. If you need some sort of external proof, scientists have already recognized that everything is *energy*. So you exist, are conscious, and are made of energy: *you* are spirit.

You are a conscious energy being. Spirit is not a *thing*, but it can become anything. In fact, everything in the universe is spirit *being* that thing: a tree is spirit being a tree; a chair is spirit being a chair. You are spirit being all that you are. Only when spirit is neutral—having no positive or negative charge—does it remain itself. Otherwise it interacts with the charges in the world around it and becomes them.

Spirit is like water. At higher temperatures, water turns into vapor. We can hardly see it, yet it is everywhere. Similarly, when spirit vibrates at a higher frequency, it is less visible to the naked eye, yet it is omnipresent. When the frequency of water vapor falls, it becomes liquid. We can see it and touch it, but it doesn't retain a definite form. Then, when it cools down even more, it becomes frozen into a solid form. In a similar way, spirit slows down its vibration to materialize into denser form. Spirit has the limitless capacity to become whatever existing conditions require of it. Spirit fulfills nature's needs.

It is said, "Ask and you shall receive." This is essentially how everything manifests in the universe. When you ask in spirit, whatever it is you ask for is instantly given in spirit. To the degree that you make space for it in yourself and in the world around you, what you asked for can then manifest in your physical life. Spirit as consciousness-energy transforms into the very atoms that make up the material world. Only when we turn our attention toward our inner spiritual being can we begin to receive what it is that we need to fulfill our life.

If you feel you don't have a minute to spare just keeping up with your workload, and you don't make space for spiritual awareness, then what you already find challenging becomes even more unmanageable. Whenever you choose to turn your attention toward your inner being and give spirit room to breathe, however, you would soon discover that you steadily become more capable at solving problems, managing relationships, attaining your goals, and fulfilling your purpose. Your perception of a lack of time is only that you are unable to meet all those challenges by forcing your will on nature. And it isn't time you lack; you just haven't made enough space for spirit, your existence as a conscious energy being in a physical body.

You are spirit and, in an ideal, pure state of being, you are infinite and eternal, unbounded by limits of space or time. Potentially, you have limitless comprehension and power. You are immortal. Yet, if you are like most of us, your life doesn't come close to reflecting that. The more you are able to give yourself the space to be spirit, the more of your unlimited potential you will manifest in your life.

How do we give up our space for being spirit and end up straying from our spiritual path? We forget who we are, and the dynamic forces of materialization, which are continuously manifesting the world, hypnotize us. We become part of the world instead of being in it and experiencing it. It's as if we're standing on the edge of the ocean of spirit and, as we look inland at the shore, we become mesmerized by its beauty as well as by its potential threats, and we forget the huge waves of power behind us. Soon, a wave knocks us down and we struggle to keep from drowning. Then another wave smashes us against the hard sand and we believe that the *beach* is beating us up instead of knowing that the culprit is our mismanagement of our own power. If we were to turn around and look seaward to spirit, we would see the waves and learn to swim over them, under them, or go out to sea and ride them back to shore.

The challenge facing every human soul while incarnating is this: can we remain true to our spiritual nature *and* fulfill our purpose, or will we succumb to the pull of energies of our bodies and the material world and forget our true nature? Remember, spirit is free when it is neutral. When you build up a charge, whether positive or negative, it engages and becomes whatever it engages with. This means that when you decide to engage in a desire, you charge your inner spirit energy. The desire of wanting to bring something to you has an attractive (+)

charge, the desire to avoid something has a repelling (–) charge. If you choose to disengage your energy and consciousness from a desire, you return to neutral. *Neutrality* is "the straight and narrow way" referred to by Jesus; Buddha called it "The Middle Path." So important is neutrality to spiritual growth that we devote an entire chapter later in the book to the concept.

You *Have* a Body

Whenever you lose your space to any degree, then in order to return to your spiritual nature, you must first realize that you *have* a body but are *not* the body. You are a spiritual being incarnated into a physical body. The "gravitational" pull of the energies of your body is so great that it is easy to *become* the body instead of *having* it. We have clothes, houses, computers, and cars. To you as a soul, your body is actually all of those things and a lot more. Your body clothes you; houses you; provides a computer so you can analyze, compute, memorize, and communicate; transports you everywhere; and so much more. However, you are not the clothes you wear, the place you live in, or the car you drive, are you?

Being a body is quite different than *having* one. When you become the body, you act as the body, and your consciousness and energy become severely limited. *Having* a body, on the other hand, allows you not only to be yourself with all your intrinsic abilities, awareness, and power of spirit, but also to have all the tools and benefits that having a body confers upon you, so that you can fully realize yourself. You will develop your healing ability, your creative genius, past-life recall, clairvoyance, intuition, and much more. As you develop spiritually, you will reassess the value of your body as an evolving soul and have a much greater appreciation for it—whatever condition you might think it is in.

As long as you are *being* the body, you will be deathly afraid of death. The body knows that it is going to eventually die and is programmed to do everything to survive. The more you start to *have* your body—and function as a spiritual being in lovingly taking care of it, educating it, and growing it—the more your awareness of immortality, of infinity, and of eternity can become the property of your body as well. First, however, you must learn to resurrect your spiritual self from your physical body. Then, you will be able to learn how to resurrect your immortal body and take it with you. (A later chapter will revisit this topic.)

How to Tell When You Are Being the Body

The more you are being your body, the more you will be a "victim." As the body, you will invariably feel that things happen *to* you. That's because things always happen to the body. The body is always the *effect*, not the cause. *You* are the one able to cause. Your body can never do anything new without your conscious, creative direction. Your body is always the effect of where you are, consciously and unconsciously. The choices you make in spirit will eventually become the effects in the body.

If you're listening to your radio and don't like the music you hear, would you kick the speakers? Of course you wouldn't. That wouldn't change the music but only damage the speakers. Nothing you can do to the speakers will change the music you hear. You must instead change the station the radio is picking up. The same is true with the body. The body feels what it feels and hears what it hears. If you don't like what it's feeling (hearing, seeing, knowing, etc.), you must tune it to a different frequency. You must *change the channel*.

Changing the Channel

If you're being the body and don't like how you feel, you'll feel as if there's nothing you can do about it. You feel how you feel and that's that. The same thing happens in terms of hearing or seeing, or any other sense perception. If you are being the body, you can't change the thoughts running through your head just because you don't like them. You must become the operator of the body as much as you are the operator of your radio, television, telephone, or computer. So, if you don't want to feel like a victim or act like one, then it's just one more reason to wake up to your spiritual self and become more of the cause in your life rather than its effect. You are spirit and you have a body in which you live—and give life to. The quality of the life you live is up to *you*, not your body.

The more space you make for your spiritual self, the more you will realize how much of how you feel or think is neither yours nor your body's. There are a variety of energies from others that your body-mind receives continually. How often have you rubbed the bridge of your nose to try to clear your mind of unwanted thoughts? It's so noisy and crowded in there that there's no room for *you* to think. When was the last time you regretted what you said or did while under the influence of uncontrollable emotions? Or do you often encounter emotions you can't resolve and stuff them down until you can't feel them anymore?

As with your television set, your body-mind constantly receives broadcasts from anyone anywhere and from everyone everywhere. Each one of us is also a major broadcasting station, transmitting our pictures, thoughts, and emotions twenty-four hours a day, whether we're aware of it or not. This incessant psychic bombardment can become a major challenge in finding our way back to our spiritual self. Because, if we misinterpret the thoughts, emotions, and other psychic energies we're picking up from others as our own, we won't be able to solve, fulfill, or change them in any way.

As an example, let's say your husband gets angry about something at work. He radiates this anger all afternoon but, of course, you're not aware of what happened. However, because you are tuned in to him, you start picking up more and more of his broadcast anger in your body-mind. You, too, begin to feel angry and frustrated, and start having thoughts about punching someone out for no reason at all. You even find yourself snapping at your children. "What's wrong with me?" you ask. There's nothing wrong with you, but the more you try to solve the problem of *his* anger and its accompanying thoughts, the more you become mired in them. This is not your energy, so you can't solve it, but, for as long as you stay tuned to your husband's broadcast and he remains angry, you're going to feel his emotions and think his thoughts.

Once you give yourself permission and the opportunity to be spirit instead of being the effects of your body-mind receptions, you can choose to change the channel. Ask your intuition, "How much of what I'm feeling (or thinking) right now is not mine?" Perhaps ask for a percentage figure. Just know off the top of your head. You might get an answer-sense such as "Eighty percent" or "Most of it." Be glad, for it isn't up to you to solve. Decide to let it go and consciously choose what *you* want to tune in to instead, such as your own feelings and thoughts. When you practice this regularly, you'll find a great difference between what you feel (or think) and how you feel (or think). Often *what* you feel is what you're picking up from others and *how* you feel is your true feelings about something, which comes from you consciously making space for spirit instead of being some reaction.

Discerning Truth

We begin this process by giving ourselves permission, certainty, and the opportunity to discern what is true for each of us. And truth is energy. Each one of us has a unique relationship with God and this relationship sets the basis for our spiritual growth. It's the tuning fork with which we must measure our pitch. Are we ringing true? Is this energy true for us?

Our relationship with God establishes what each of us needs for our spiritual growth. So, what is true for you must ring true to your individual relationship with God's love. A correct choice and response for one may be incorrect for another. And what is right for you one time may not be right the next time.

If you fall into competition and try to walk another's path, you will not reach your destination. No matter how good something looks or feels or how much it may work for someone else, if it's not from within you, it's not for you. If you cling to it, it will limit your space to be you. Put simply, any energy that is not from within you diminishes your space. And energy that is not generated in your unique pattern with God is not yours. You must always measure the pitch of truth by your own tuning fork within.

Our trials of discerning the truth of what is and isn't ours begin immediately at physical conception. In the womb, even before we're born into the world, we encounter the joys, hopes, dreams, expectations, fears, and dread of our parents-to-be. Relatives, neighbors, doctors, nurses, midwives, and ministers may also throw in their opinions, blessings, judgments, anxieties, and reassurances.

I'm finally going to be a mother!
Oh no, I'm pregnant!
What am I going to do with it?
If it's a boy, he's going to be a _____! If it's a girl, she'll be
  a _____!
What if there's something wrong with him?

How many parents actually give their child the name that the incoming soul wishes to be known by? When our first son was nearing his arrival date, a very psychic little girl walked up to his mother, touched her belly, and proclaimed, "Oh, that's my friend Gregory in there!"

How often do we as parents, teachers, ministers, doctors, babysitters, and relatives impose upon the little ones what *we* want for and from them instead of learning who *they* are and what *they* need in order to fulfill their purpose in life? We may view our children as gifts from heaven, but they are on loan to us and not for us to possess. We are given the chance to be their temporary guides so that they may fulfill *their* destiny, not ours.

In one way or another, as children, we all experienced being invalidated. As much as our parents and others may have loved us, more often than not, we were regarded in childhood as perhaps a living lump of clay that was to be modeled and molded to accommodate their expectations, hopes, dreams, and fears. The love of our parents and others fell prey to their fears of losing their beloved child, and we became the unsuspecting beneficiaries of their powerful and often misdirected will. The sensitive and giving nature of the divinity we cradled within our souls recoiled at the assault of violent tempers and unkind thoughts.

Like threatened amoebae, our soul retreated into a shell formed of our defenses. We gradually became spiritual amnesiacs. The more we forgot our spiritual nature, the more we became the body and all that happened to it in the world.

Use Every Day as a Spiritual Reminder

In order to reverse this spiritual degeneration, as adults we must make more space for all that is spirit to be. Spiritual retreats, cloistered meditation, praying in church, and ascetic practices are needed in different levels of our spiritual development, but the spiritual enlightenment gained through these practices is only half of fulfilling our purpose in life. The other half is the challenging adventure of realizing every aspect of our enlightenment in our worldly life. From the perspective of the soul, each challenge we face in our everyday life provides the crucible in which we distill wisdom into our own being. Every crossroads we face provides us with the golden opportunity for spiritual growth by asking the following:

- Do I intervene or look the other way?
- Do I speak the truth, lie, or remain silent?
- Do I stay in this relationship or move on?
- Do I stay true to my purpose or hold on to what is secure and familiar to me?
- Do I become a victim to these emotions that I'm feeling, or do I choose to change the channel?

The measure of our evolvement is not in what happens in our lives but in how we *respond* to all that happens. It's not about controlling outcomes but about consciously responding to what life presents. That choice is always completely ours to make.

Birthing Spirit Back into Our World

God was to be born into this world and there were no rooms available at the inn. In our society, Divinity often finds little breathing room to be. Instead of welcoming spirit into the world with the birth of every child, many of us begin to dictate to spirit the limits to which it must conform if it is to receive our approval and love. By the time we're four or five, most of us begin to forget our divine heritage. Then we begin seeking anything that might ease the pain of separation, isolation, and loneliness. We try to fill the void we feel with someone or something in the world.

Often, it isn't until someone we love dies that we are shocked into searching our hearts and souls to explore whether God is with us or has abandoned us. Don't wait. Start making more space today for spirit in your heart and in your mind, so that all that is divine in you can be born into the best suite in your house.

FOUR

FULFILLING YOUR SOUL PURPOSE

In the heart of your soul, you carry the seeds of Divinity. Fulfilling your true purpose means growing those seeds into an orchard of sacred trees. Every aspect, quality, and capability of Divinity can be produced by the variety of trees you grow in your life. Although we were each given all the same seeds making up our soul purpose, we will find different ways of planting and caring for them, and growing them into our own unique orchards.

Nature reflects all that is God, and the life cycle of a tree clearly expresses fulfillment of purpose. It begins as a seed containing all the potentiality of its full existence. When it is planted and nourished, it matures into a tree, which blossoms and bears its fruit or offspring.

In fulfilling your soul purpose, you will go through much the same process. Your individuality does not blossom because you have a different purpose to fulfill than others, but it blossoms from the unique way *you* use your creative awareness and imagination in loving each seed into maturity and fruitful expression of Divinity.

How do you know when your purpose is fulfilled? Is it complete when all your seeds grow into mature trees? In the life cycle of a tree, where does it all end? When a fruit tree matures, for example, it can produce fruit for years to come. Its fruit also bears seeds, which can give rise to future generations of trees. And so it continues. When you grow all the divine seeds in your heart into a full orchard and become a complete human being, you will continue to express all that is divine, for you are an immortal soul. Your purpose never stops growing; its fulfillment becomes your everlasting dance with life.

In the previous chapter, we explored the process of *making enough space for spirit* in our conscious awareness and daily life. This is the first step in fulfilling your soul purpose, in which you must till the hard ground, perhaps fertilize it, and make the space in which you can plant the seeds. The following sections of this chapter examine the stages of fulfilling your soul purpose, starting with planting your soul-seeds into the fertile soil of your body. Although each seed must go through the same stages of germination, you have a variety of seeds to grow within your soul purpose. So, at any given time in your life, you will be shuttling back and forth, tending to the various plants in their respective phases of growth. You may be making more space for spirit in order to plant a new seed while reaping the harvest of ripe fruit from a tree you planted years ago.

Remember, your spiritual growth wilts in competition, whether with yourself or with others. So fulfill your purpose with joyful cooperation, humor, compassion, and detachment.

Embodying Your Spiritual Self

You have been making space in your awareness and in your life for your spiritual self. You're paying more attention to the fact that you are a spiritual being and that you have a human body-mind. Now you're ready to plant your purpose-seeds in the fertile ground that is your body. Since those seeds are within your spiritual self, *you* must come into your physical body in order for them to sprout and take root. You must *embody your spiritual self.*

Does this mean that you are not in your body? Not very much if you're like the majority of people I see every day both in my practice as well as out there in the world. I feel that our bodies are the greatest natural wonders in the world and that it takes very little spiritual awareness and energy to keep them working fairly well for a while. If you knew the awareness and power you hold within your soul, you would understand how little of you it takes to live what seems a "normal" life. Where, then, does the rest of you go? And not only can you be some*where* else, you can be some *time* else, as well. In fact, you are a spiritual *being* and you have the infinite capacity to *be* any*thing*, any*how*, any*where*, and any*time*.

For example, suppose you have an important date tomorrow evening at your favorite restaurant and you're worried about how it will turn out. You are *being* the "dater" (something), worried (somehow), at the restaurant (somewhere), tomorrow evening (sometime), and you're clearly *not* fully here, now. But your body, on the other hand, can only be what it is, how it is, where it is, and when it is. If you merely have a passing thought about your date, you'll only be a little out of phase with where and when your body is. But if you're intensely worried, you'll be way out of your body. How much of your spiritual awareness and energy is centered here and now determines the degree to which you are in your body.

Whenever you're trying to be something other than *who* you are, in a condition other than *how* you are, somewhere other than *here*, and at sometime other than *now*, you're going to be out of your body. The good news is that the choice is entirely yours. Most of the time, however, you don't *consciously* choose to be out of your body. You go out as a means to avoid pain. Nonetheless, you must consciously decide to return to your body if you are to fulfill your purpose. Every time you're unhappy and choose to blame, judge, criticize, hate, covet, cling, or resist in some way, you leave your body's space-time continuum. As you can see, there are many ways to leave the body, but there is only one way to be *in* it. You must learn to enjoy being *who you are* under all the present conditions.

What is it like to be out of your body? Many books and even movies have depicted various extraordinary kinds of out-of-body experiences. People have found themselves out-of-body during surgery, watching the surgeon from the ceiling of the operating room. Or, during near-death experiences, people leave the body and go into a space of brilliant white light. And there have always been people who can consciously travel beyond the confines of their physical bodies and visit places in this world or in other dimensions. Sound exciting? Well, it is. Yet most people are out of their bodies to some degree most of the time and never even know it.

Being out of your body doesn't have to be a mind-blowing experience of sound and light. In fact, we all go in and out of our bodies all throughout our daily lives. Of course, when we sleep, we go out more fully. Some of us are aware of it as we do it; others may remember the experience in dream form upon waking. Many don't remember a thing. When we "space out," we are, to varying degrees, out-of-body. What are some common examples of being out of your body?

When the alarm clock blasts you out of bed and you stub your toe on the door frame on your way to the bathroom, you're not quite back in your body. You're late for work, driving in commute traffic, and you start concocting excuses to tell your boss at the same time as trying to figure out how you're going to finish your projects. As you reach over to pick up your cell phone to call in, you look up and realize you've missed your exit. You just "spaced out" of your body. Or, you have a little too much to drink at a party and get rambunctious. When confronted about your behavior the next day, you don't remember a thing—you were way out of your body at the party. No matter how you go out of your body, unless you leave in order to fulfill a certain purpose, most of the time you go out to avoid pain. (There's no pain in spirit, only in the physical body, something that later chapters will explore further.)

The more you're in your body, the more alert and aware you will be, for awareness is an essential attribute of your spiritual self. You'll have more energy, too, since that's also an attribute of spirit. The kind of awareness and energy you will experience depends on what aspect of your spiritual self is most present. For some, the awareness and energy will be focused on a physical level, so they're attentive to things around them and respond quickly to physical conditions. For others, it may be more in the psychic dimensions, where they respond better to psychic energies and interactions between people. Still others may find that they become acutely aware of all the sensations in their bodies.

Two conscious practices will help you enormously in embodying your spiritual self:

- *Ground your body to the earth.* Just as firm roots enable a tree to stand tall and strong, grounding provides the root system for your body and a solid foundation in the physical world upon which to cultivate your spiritual life. Grounding, as in the electrical sense, also helps you discharge the excess and negative psychic energies that you pick up from others and the environment. Literally, grounding will help you better stand on your own two feet instead of being buffeted by other people's energies and beliefs.

- *Center your spiritual awareness behind your eyes,* in the center of your head. This differs from when people say, "You're too much in your head," which refers to over-intellectualizing everything. Centering your awareness behind your eyes means you are taking up residence as a spiritual being in the driver's seat of your body.

As spirit, you can be anywhere, but this space behind your eyes in the center of your head is where you can have access to all the capabilities of the body that you need to fulfill your soul purpose. This is why it has been said since ancient times that "The eyes are the windows to your soul." When you look into the eyes of one who is spiritually centered behind them, you look into forever. (Your Spiritual Toolkit at the end of this book offers further instructions for grounding and centering your awareness.)

As you begin the practice of being in your body more, give yourself much encouragement and develop your certainty that, as you know in spirit, so it will be in the body. At this point, your purpose-seeds are buried underground and cannot be seen. Approach this part of your soul fulfillment as a child—playful, adventurous, full of wonder and willingness. Don't go into it full of expectations of certain results. This is not a time to play "prove it" with yourself but an opportunity for fun, exploration, and discovery. Let yourself be pleasantly surprised.

Fully Incarnating as a Human Being

When you're grounded in the earth and you bring your spiritual awareness into your body, your purpose-seeds begin to sprout and new plants emerge. Now that you can see them growing, you must also learn to work with their changing needs. How much watering do they need? Do they need protection from the wind, excessive sun, or animals? Do any of them need support stakes? Do you need to repel the bugs off them or pull the weeds that might choke them? Here, as you take care of your spiritual well-being, you must learn the ways of the human body and mind and, as a spiritual being, forge a new relationship with them.

Now, fulfilling your purpose means learning to *fully incarnate as a human being*. Your task, as a spiritual being, is to befriend your body and form a cooperative partnership, not coerce your physical body into becoming spirit. One of the great challenges for you is that the body requires air, water, food, shelter, and sleep, all of which are foreign to spirit. Your existence as spirit is infinite and eternal, while your partner is confined in time and space. You are immortal, yet your body will die sooner or later. The inherent differences between the two of you are at polar opposites.

Fully incarnating requires a loving, successful marriage between two disparate, yet ultimately complementary, partners: you (spirit) and your body. Imagine being a super-athlete genius (immortal, infinite spirit) married to a wheelchair-bound, illiterate partner (mortal, limited body). Imagine further that your spouse, though severely limited in areas you are not, loves you unconditionally and you need him or her in order to fulfill your life purpose. Divorce in this marriage is not really an option since it would mean the premature death of your spouse (the body) and failure to fulfill your purpose. If that happens, you will have to reincarnate, except with an even more karma-laden partner next time. To become a complete human being and fulfill your purpose for your incarnation, you must make this marriage work.

I remember having difficulty incarnating as a human being at my first Easter egg hunt. I was a six-year-old Japanese-American kid going to school on a U.S. military base in Tokyo. I didn't grow up with the Easter bunny and had no clue what an Easter egg hunt was. So, when we all lined up at the starting line, I was prepared to race but had no idea why I'd been given a colorful basket to hold. At the bang of the starting gun, I ran as fast I could, basket in hand, across the field to the finish line. Imagine my ecstatic joy at having won my first race ever.

My joy was short-lived, however, for suddenly three men swooped down, yelling at me. I felt as if I'd done something horribly wrong and was being scolded for it. *But how can this be?* I wondered. *I won the race.* The men became increasingly exasperated with me and started to pull me toward some bushes. Everything became a blur of confusion and I found myself out-of-body, looking down on the scene from fifteen feet above. I watched as the men pushed my body toward the bushes where all the other kids were on their hands and knees looking for something. As a spiritual being, I didn't know quite how to handle the inundation of everyone's energy in my body. This energy said, *What's wrong with this kid? Why isn't he going to find the eggs? Doesn't he know what an Easter egg hunt is? What kid doesn't know what an Easter egg hunt is? Go over there! Why aren't you looking for eggs like you're supposed to? It's fun!*

How was I to know that I was expected to find hard-boiled eggs hidden in the bushes? What a strange custom! Yet it was a way of life for everyone else. That's what Easter egg hunts were. Everyone else knew that!

By the time the pressure eased off of me and I could return to my body, it was on its hands and knees in the bushes trying to copy the other kids. I felt wretched, lost, discouraged, and humiliated. I felt out of context. I didn't fit in with anything that was going on. I was stupid. I'd messed up and, above all, the joy of winning the race had been ripped away from me. There, at the Easter egg hunt, there was no space for a soul who didn't know that Easter bunnies laid colored eggs in the bushes. The funny thing was that I didn't have a problem with the out-of-body part, for that to me was natural. I did have a hard time, however, being a human child, invalidated and confused in a very human event.

After several other childhood experiences in which I was expected to know or do something and was punished or humiliated for not knowing, instead of learning to incarnate my spiritual self more fully as a human being, I got smarter. I learned to be a step ahead, to always know what was expected and do it better than everyone else did. As long as I was the best at everything, I was safe. It made me successful in everything I did, of course, and I rarely did anything I wasn't going to be best at. Then, soul purpose no longer defined my life direction; competing to be the "best" and most "perfect" human became my life's compass.

You can be a highly evolved soul but, until you fully incarnate into your current body, you're more like a teenager who knows everything but hasn't lived it yet. You know the theory, but you haven't put it to the field test. I see many people who are evolved souls with great degrees of enlightenment who struggle to live their spiritual knowing in their human relationships. When they learn to function more spiritually with their body-mind, their lives begin to reflect the awareness and energy they had already developed as souls in former lifetimes.

Fully incarnating spiritually as a human being means integrating the awareness and energy you have as a soul with that of your body-personality. For most people seeking spiritual growth, their soul's consciousness is more developed than that of their body-mind. The good news in this case, however, is that since you already have the awareness and ability developed in spirit, you just need to learn how to integrate it into your body.

You don't have to start from scratch, however. For example, take the soul we know as Mozart. The incarnation that that soul made famous as a musical prodigy wasn't by any means its first as an accomplished musician—it had already attained a high degree of musical enlightenment in several previous incarnations. He needed to finish bringing that earlier musical genius into his body and express it. The lifetime as Mozart was for him his *magnum opus*. As with most great beings, what he introduced as art and entertainment to humanity during his lifetime took over two more centuries to realize its full potential as an innovative tool for healing, therapy, and education in our society today. Yet Mozart, though intimately in touch with aspects of divinity, had great difficulty fully incarnating as a human being. He freely expressed divinity through his music, but he often felt limited by narrow-minded, less-creative people in other arenas of life. Although spirit moved him to share his wealth, he often suffered the consequences of his extravagance, gambling proclivities, and general financial mismanagement. Nor did Mozart understand how the intensity of his spiritual involvement during his near-obsessive composing streaks affected his physical and emotional health. As we all learn, it takes more than genius, extraordinary talent, or miraculous powers to be human.

In my work, I regularly see people fighting unsuccessfully to overcome what they believe to be their human weaknesses. Yet, with the vast majority of them, what they believe to be their liabilities turn out to be the areas of their greatest spiritual power. For instance, I know a woman who has repeatedly failed in marriages. Yet, as a soul, her greatest ability is in healing relationships, so why couldn't she have at least one decent relationship? She's a wonderful healer and teacher in the affairs of the heart, so whom does she naturally attract? Those who are severely relationship-challenged, of course, and perhaps even completely relationship-disabled! Combined with her unawareness of her own power and abilities as a soul, she struggles to make marriage work with the very people who are supposed to be her patients and students, not her partners.

Another woman's greatest power lies in her ability to express her creativity. She was meant to be onstage, addressing large groups of people. Instead, not realizing the purpose for her creative power, she focuses it all on trying to love and make one person happy. Though well intentioned, her energy overwhelms him and she blows him away. If she learned to channel more of her creative energy as a performer, seminar leader, or minister, for example, her power would then be hailed as great stage presence or charisma instead of being blamed as "a problem." Your strengths are not problems to be solved, but talents to be developed and used.

I also knew a young man who, as a soul, loved freedom more than anything—not only his own, but everyone's freedom. He had such compassion for humanity that, in several lifetimes, he had sacrificed his own life to bring freedom to his family or country. He wanted to share with everyone the joy that he felt in his heart when he experienced freedom, yet people criticized him constantly for rocking the boat, for not leaving well enough alone, and for being too rebellious. He was even labeled antisocial by some. He often felt rejected and isolated by those he loved dearly. He didn't realize that he is a freedom fighter, here to transform the way people think and live. But most people are afraid to change, or at least shy away from great change happening too quickly. When he offered his greatest gift to people, they felt as if he were attacking their security.

One of the difficult lessons for this young man as a soul and a leader is to learn the humanness of fear and people's needs for comfort and security, and that, even if he has shaken off those fears and needs, those around him have not. If he could learn to accommodate those human traits with deeper understanding and harness his love of freedom into a viable teaching tool to inspire greater awareness for everyone, then he would be able to move on with his spiritual goals.

Turn your attention inward to discover what really moves you, and it will lead you to your greatest soul power and abilities. Learning to use them correctly in your human relationships is one of the challenges of fully incarnating as a human being. And the first human relationship you must learn to manage is the one with your own body. Avoiding human frailties and trying to transcend the body by denying its limitations won't work in the end.

Great meditation practices invented by ancient masters will, if practiced, help you to blast out of your body and attain awesome levels of bliss and light. However, once you attain them, you must still come back into your body and become a human being—in this lifetime or another. To fully incarnate as a human being, seek first what you already know and have within yourself, and practice what you discover in life instead of looking for what you don't know and don't have.

Learn to love yourself completely: who, how, and what you are, here and now. Love and enjoy yourself, whether you are divine or human, wealthy or poor, happy or sad, angry or content, healthy or sick, a doctor, an artist, or a bum. Then, all things will change . . . for the better.

Building a Temple of the Soul

Your purpose-plant is growing into a strong, well-rooted tree. A magical transformation is taking place in which nature turns a still-green sapling into a mature, majestic tree. In the beginning of your incarnation, nature (God through your parents) provided you with a new body. Now, fulfilling your purpose means transmuting that mortal body of karma into an immortal body of wisdom.

It has been said that the body is the temple of the soul. Yet the true temple in which the soul resides is not the outer physical shell that most people call the body, but the immortal body that the soul builds on the inside through incarnation after incarnation. The outer biological body you were born into was created from the karmic patterns of your soul and what would best suit your needs for their fulfillment. Hidden within it is the key to your true immortality and freedom as a soul—a perfect template for your immortal, radiant body, through which you can eternally experience and express the totality of Divinity.

The opportunity for the human soul—and its challenge—is to incarnate into the mortal body needing karmic fulfillment, and develop the wisdom needed to build an immortal body matching that holy template. Once the true temple is complete, the soul can resurrect the divine body out of its physical shell and take its true place with God, both God the manifest and God the unmanifest. Without completing this immortal, radiant body, the soul can only return to God the unmanifest, without free will, and forever remain His *un*begotten child.

The body you were born into is truly God's grace. Within it is everything you need as a soul to fulfill your purpose, even if you were born with a disease or other extraordinary limitation. Your mortal body was shaped by *karma*, i.e., unfulfilled desires and incomplete cycles of action. And not all of the karma forming it is yours. Some may be genetic, some may belong to one or both of your parents, some to race, nationality, or gender. Yet, even if some of the actual unfulfilled cycles or desires aren't of your making, you choose to take them on to fulfill those that *do* belong to you.

An oversimplified example might involve you taking on some of the suffering of your parents, thinking you could heal it for them. But the sublimely intricate living tapestry woven by the threads of karma are beyond intellectual description or comprehension.

When you took the first of your numerous incarnations into mortality, you started with a mass of unformed energy around your heart. Over the course of many physical embodiments, through trial and error, through desiring things and attaining them, through suffering the consequences of destructive action and learning to forgive, you shaped this amorphous mass of life-energy more and more into a human body-mind. If you were to see reality as the energy that it is, you would see a soul that has not matured much, having a "body" that looks somewhat like a sack of potatoes or a giant amoeba.

On the other hand, a being of great enlightenment and wisdom would have a fully formed human body with all the trimmings, radiant in its magnificent splendor. When a soul completes building this holy temple, that being will be able to travel between universes, go between the highest heavens and the lowest hells, and sit with the Absolute or materialize a physical body on earth at will. This is the true destiny for the human soul: to have its full freedom, and to be or not to be.

As you become more conscious of shaping your immortal body, you will come to know that every part, every organ, indeed every cell of your physical body reflects a divine ideal, experience, and meaning. It is the dynamic aspect of God—what Christians call the Holy Spirit—that incarnates as each cell and forms the template for our immortal body. Thus, if we refuse to see some aspect of truth, then, over time, our eyesight may fail. When we harbor hatred against some aspect of our self, we begin to leak vitality out of our life-giving blood supply as well as compromise our immune system. Every cell in our body and every experience in our life are given to us as God's love. And the only way we can receive that love is in loving.

The first time I experienced my true body and the world as it really was, I was walking with my teacher through his backyard. Suddenly, I found myself standing in awe, speechless at the scintillating, silvery, shimmering glory of existence. The tree so solidly rooted in front of me just moments before now vibrated and pulsed with life, sending out wave after wave of light, giant silver ripples dancing in total abandon in a pond of glittering sunlight. The waves of energy cascaded like a cool waterfall through my whole being in a symphony of thousands of tiny silver bells and a homecoming of feelings. Existence sang and danced its ecstasy through the birds, the insects, the trees, the flowers, and even the rocks. My body, as well as that of my teacher, was radiant and also made of brilliant light. Everything in the world was connected with a beautiful luminescence, as silvery threads of light penetrated everything. My teacher looked at me, smiled, and said, "Everything's talking to you, isn't it?"

When I nodded, he told me to say hello to the tree next to me. When I did, I saw my voice as ripples floating toward the tree. The tree then opened itself up and greeted me in kind.

Since then, through twenty-eight years of giving spiritual healing and clairvoyant readings to thousands of people, I learned little by little what truly makes up these bodies of ours. I sought to understand their divine purpose.

During that search, about ten years ago, a series of experiences culminated in a moment of profound revelation. It began one morning while I was taking a strolling meditation in my neighborhood. I was greeting the trees and flowers, the grass, and its tiny inhabitants when suddenly it seemed the universe opened up. Or perhaps it would be more correct to say that I opened up to the universe. The very sky parted and the opening filled with a magnificent blaze of fire. The entire world around me sparkled in glorious golden speckles of light. I felt the universe flow through me and I became as large as the universe. In that moment, I understood the grace of my body. All the snippets of understanding I had gained over the years and the missing pieces came together in an instant of comprehension. Then, the sky closed up to a brilliant blue and, for a while, everything in the world shimmered with a renewed golden brightness.

The understanding I brought back was this: the body is created through an intricate tapestry of karmic desires and actions. When we are born into it, it is the embodiment of the sum of our previously unfulfilled desires. It contains everything, from the original seed of desire for the fulfillment of our destiny to the myriad desire-thoughts conjured up in our minds out of ignorance and fear. Every wish, longing, and unfulfilled want are taken into consideration in the formation of our body. This includes the kind of parents we need, not only to provide the right genes but also the experiences, environment, and opportunities that they will provide. The gift of the physical body is given to the human soul for its ultimate freedom and total realization of its own divinity.

When a person dies, all the desires left unfulfilled become as seeds within the heart of the departing soul. From these seeds, the soul creates its next life and the body through which those desires can be fulfilled. Upon the selection of parents, conception can take place. The sexual attraction between a man and a woman, especially in the presence of a soul desiring incarnation through them, can be immense. This is desire-in-action to bring about various levels of fulfillment in all three souls.

Usually about four months after birth, the karmic seeds carried by the soul are planted in the heart. There, the seeds lie dormant until the appropriate energies nourish them. Then, the seeds sprout. They can sprout on contact with another with whom they have an unfinished karmic cycle or even just in the presence of someone with a similar karmic pattern. Once sprouted, the karmic patterns are released into the bloodstream and pumped throughout the body by the heart. These living geometrical energy patterns of cause and effect travel to every cell of the body as the blood nourishes the cells. Depending on the nature of the karmic pattern, different cells receive different information.

Thus, the body of karma continues to be shaped according to the dictates of these patterns. The effects may be largely physiological or they can manifest more on the emotional or mental levels. When the heart becomes purified as the karmic patterns are fulfilled, transformed, or transcended, the blood is also purified and the cells of the body receive increasingly more light.

This body of karma can be transmuted more and more into the immortal body of wisdom in one of three ways:

1) The slowest method is to go through each karmic cycle, over and over, until it is fulfilled and a balance is achieved.

2) Once a soul in an incarnation awakens more, it begins to realize that there are much more efficient ways to fulfill one's karmic debts. Instead of going through the agonizing slowness of "an eye for an eye," the soul creates a plan of action to resolve a great deal of karma more quickly and effectively. For example, a soul who in a life as a ruthless military leader may have killed, raped, and maimed thousands, after realizing the karmic consequences, may choose to dedicate his life to being a doctor, building a hospital in which he treats and saves many thousands of lives.

3) The fastest means of resolving karma comes from the soul choosing to fully forgive. By doing so, the soul reclaims all the energy it invested into the karmic pattern and discharges all power out of it. Complete forgiveness allows one to transcend the unfulfilled desire or incomplete cycle of action. Many of Jesus's miraculous healings were through this kind of forgiveness and the one healed had his or her self-imposed karmic sentence commuted.

Expressing the Totality of Divinity

Once a tree is mature and begins to blossom, it can bear fruit. As you transmute your karmic body more and more into your wisdom body, you will better *express the totality of Divinity* in your unique way. Every time you express some aspect of Divinity, your orchard offers Life another fruit. That potential of God becomes manifest in the world. The more you develop the marriage between your spiritual self and your body, the more you bring heaven onto earth. Expressing all that is God here on earth requires that you gain your spiritual freedom within physical limitations and experience the oneness in polarities.

Every time a soul is born onto the earth, God dies giving that life. Entering the material world to give that soul a body, Spirit must relinquish infinity for the finite, eternity for the terminal, and immortality for the mortal. Can anyone give up more than that to give you life?

Yet God, entering your heart, gave it all up for you because you asked—just as you would gladly give up your meal to a starving child or a few minutes of your time and attention to a soul in distress. And how great is your joy when that child returns to you years later as a thriving adult to thank you for the meal that kept him alive? Or when the person you comforted confides in you that your kindness kept her from jumping off a bridge to self-destruction?

Love begets life with these words: *I gladly give you my life so that you may live. All I ask of you is that you take this seed of life, take good care of it, and grow it into the beautiful tree it is meant to be. Let the roots take deep into the earth so it grows strong and tall. Let the trunk be a pillar to the community so that children can climb up and play on it while the weak can lean on it for strength and the young can look to it for solid wisdom. Let the branches grow wide and full of leaves to give shade to the weary pilgrims needing rest along life's difficult trails. Let the leaves be for the healing of the whole community, bringing peace, cooperation, and camaraderie. Let the flowers bloom fragrant and bright to lift up the heart of every soul who beholds them. Let this tree bear sweet fruit to nourish the body and mind, heart and soul of everyone who wishes to grow. And let its seeds scatter far and wide to give new life to all that seek it. My life is now in your hands, my beloved child. Give to life as I have given my life to you.*

When we are born into our body, God enters the world with us as the consciousness of the field that is our body-mind. To the extent of our unconsciousness, God becomes dormant to us, akin to a seed in the field overshadowed by tall weeds. As we awaken our consciousness and grow in this field, so too our God-seed grows until we finally harvest the totality of Divinity from this field. In a sense, we resurrect God with our expanding awareness and love, little by little, from our unconsciousness.

To express the immortality of Divinity, you must face death. If you cling to fear of death, you cannot host immortality. To express the infinity of Divinity, you must relinquish containment, possession, and limitation. To express the eternity of Divinity, you must sacrifice the past and the future. You cannot cling to past hurts that you didn't forgive, blame for things done, or future expectations or worries. Only in the present moment does eternity reside. These are some of the fruits of Divinity that we must share. Expressing aspects of Divinity means taking care of God in ourselves and in others.

Entering the Sacred Dance with Life

A mature tree producing fruit continually fulfills its purpose. It serves life, and life provides the tree with all that it needs to flourish. And so it is when we begin to express more of the divinity within our being into the world around us. When we begin to ask how we can serve life's own purpose, we open ourselves to the abundance and flow that is Life Divine. We *enter into a Sacred Dance with Life.*

As you replace fear and doubt as your guides with loving and trusting awareness, you will find how much life has been providing you with your every need. Many times, you may have missed it because you were dwelling on something other than what you truly needed at that moment. And life gives, moment by moment, step by step. When you were afraid that you didn't have enough money, life may have been showering you with opportunities for learning so that you could eventually earn a better income, or sending you people to help you with your difficulties. Life always gives what you need most now, but it's always up to you to heed its call and accept it.

What makes us hesitant to enter this dance with life is that when we open to life, life opens us up even more. When we open the curtains to let in the sunlight, we often discover, for the first time, how dirty the room is. Entering this dance requires courage to explore the darker recesses of your heart, mind, and soul. You must first love yourself and be sufficiently committed to yourself to risk the consequences of your discoveries. The Sacred Dance with Life is full of love and light, yet it is love that breaks your heart until your heart is free of judgment, and it is light that threatens your mind until it is empty of possession. Be bold! You have all you need within you to realize your happiness, and anything you can lose is not worth holding on to anyway.

As you enter this continual flow of asking and receiving, you will become more self-sufficient, more complete within yourself. Then, *what* you ask for begins to change. Your asking becomes more attentive to the needs of life itself instead of centering on your personal needs. You begin to ask, "What can I give to life today?" And you will discover that the more you share the divinity within you, the more you will share in the divinity that *is* life and abundance all around you.

I have a delightful memory of this dance with life from a retreat that my wife and I led in Hawaii. We were asking what could bring a more joyful experience for the participants in this retreat. We had already arranged to take the group on a day's sailing cruise to provide an opportunity to see dolphins and swim with them if they came. We also considered other possibilities, such as recommending that people visit the sacred sites in the area on their own. So, I decided to refresh my memory of how to get to them in order to give accurate directions. The morning before our scheduled dolphin sail, I drove out toward a couple of my favorite spiritual sites. When I reached a crossroads on my way to one of them, however, I felt a pull to go in the opposite direction. "The dolphins want to see you," I heard in my head.

I turned right instead of left and headed down the road ending up at a large bay. I hadn't intended on swimming out but took my mask, fins, and snorkel just the same. On my way to the rocky shore, an old Hawaiian man approached me. "I wouldn't swim out there today," he said. "Roughest I've seen out in the bay in a long time. Very dangerous."

I thanked him for the caution and reassured him that I wasn't planning on swimming. "Besides," he added, "no dolphins out there. Haven't seen any in several weeks."

When I walked down onto the rocks, I realized the old man was right. Six- to eight-foot waves crashed violently against the rugged shore. In all the times I had been to this bay, I had never seen waves like these. And there were no signs of dolphins. I sat away from the wave action and decided to meditate.

During my brief meditation, I asked why I had been called there. "Come in and swim with us!" I heard-felt the dolphins. I laughed. "I don't think I can," I sent my thoughts to them. "Not in these conditions."

Suddenly, something changed. Everything quieted down and a hush of calm settled around me. Opening my eyes, I saw that the waves had disappeared and the bay had turned into a swimming pool as if someone had flipped the switch on the thundering waves. "Now you can come and swim with us," I heard-felt the dolphins once more. What could I do? I went in the water.

Within two minutes of swimming out into the bay, I was greeted with the unrestricted outpouring of joy of about a hundred dolphins. Some swam beneath me while others circled around me. Several treated me to a beautiful aerial ballet. We cavorted in delight for the rest of the morning until I told them I had to go teach a seminar. Before taking my leave, I asked them to come play with us the next day when our group would be sailing along the coast north of the bay. They gleefully accepted my invitation.

The following day, the cruise, led by a good friend of ours, was met with over forty dolphins immediately on leaving port, and they escorted us throughout the whole sail. And all who wished had the chance to swim with them. Later, our friend told us that, in all the years she's taken people on these cruises, she'd never encountered such an immediate response from the dolphins and that they had *never* escorted the boat throughout the whole trip.

Life is always there, giving; the only question is whether we are there to share in it. At this stage of fulfilling our soul purpose, our needs become the needs of fulfilling life's own purpose instead of our personal needs. We begin to realize that, if we ask life to provide us with what we need to fulfill life's purpose, it will provide us first with all that we need personally. After all, if we don't survive, we wouldn't be able to fulfill any other purpose, would we?

Learn to cultivate the orchard that is your relationship with God's love, harvest its divine fruits and share them with life. In this way, you *will* enter the Sacred Dance with Life.

FIVE

WAKE-UP CALLS

Every moment, our purpose invites us to join in its fulfillment. Sometimes it calls us to appreciate the beauty of a sunset, a rose, or the song of a meadowlark. At other times, it may ask us to throw a party in celebration of our lives. Often our purpose encourages us to dig deeper, discover the truth of the situation, bring in new awareness, and change our ways. But, whenever we fall asleep at the wheel of life and repeatedly ignore its prompts, its gentle appeals become urgent wake-up calls.

When my older son was fourteen, two local gang members tried to gun him down for no apparent reason. As he waited for his mom to pick him up after school, they drove by him and opened fire. It was no movie. This was real—he was running for his life between the spray of bullets.

Later he shared a revelation with me. "When you walk away from a close call, where you could've died, it's because you have a purpose for being here. I don't know what it is yet, but I know I have a purpose in life."

Coming within heartbeats of losing our life or the life of a loved one, we bolt upright from our ignorance-sleep. Our awareness instantly expands, we return to the present and appreciate how precious life is. Then, as we glimpse the sacredness of life's own purpose, we may catch our breath. With time, the intensity of our gratitude may fade, but somewhere in the background of our awareness, we retain the ineffable sense that life truly has a purpose for us. We may not be able to explain it, but we know we have a purpose for being here.

Crises are sent to shake us out of our slumber, to re-awaken a sense of purpose. Too often, we become so preoccupied with our vested interests that we forget why we are here. We fall asleep. Then life gives us a wake-up call. We've all had them. Whether they've been life-threatening situations, financial disasters, emotional upheavals, or relationship conflicts, they remind us that we are ignoring, or have forgotten, what is most important in our lives. They make us ask again, "What am I here for?"

If ignored, these "I could've been hurt" wake-up calls may grow until tragedy actually strikes. Failing to heed the warnings of a gathering storm, we find ourselves thrown ill-prepared into a tempest. Such a wake-up call broadsided Rich, a friend of mine.

"You have cancer," the oncologist told him. Three simple words we hope we never hear. Then, he delivered an official death sentence to Rich: "You have perhaps three months left."

A wake-up call stops us dead in our tracks and commands our attention. It rattles us out of our mind-ruts and fixed behavior patterns rooted in ignorance and unconsciousness. If we've been selling our soul piecemeal to our fears and insecurities, burying ourselves ever deeper into trenches of resistance and denial, we can be certain the call will come again and again until we finally heed it.

No matter what form it takes (even a death sentence is a wake-up call from life), this call is reminding us that we need to embrace some important aspect of our soul purpose. And when the call comes, how we respond to what happens is more important than whether or not we "caused" or "deserved" what happens. Life never dials a wrong number.

An unfulfilled soul purpose becomes a restless sleep, or even a nightmare in life from which we long to awaken. And since we all fall asleep in our purpose from time to time, wake-up calls are necessary and, unfailingly, they come. They call us to realign our life's priorities to our soul purpose. And to do this, we must *choose* to wake up.

Waking Up: A Choice Between Life and Death

"Do you agree with my doctors that I'm going to die?" Rich asked me.

"Yes, I agree," I answered. "Just as I'm going to die; just as the doctors are going to die. What I don't agree about is when. That's entirely between you and your Maker. I have a feeling, however, that it's not going to be as soon as your doctors predict. You have too much to learn yet."

"That's for sure!" Rich laughed. "Well, I think I'm ready to learn. Can you enlighten me on what I should do next? The doctors are telling me that I'm going to die whatever they do, so should I seek out a naturopath or should I have spiritual healing from you instead?"

Naturally, the prognosis of imminent death shook Rich to his core. When the wake-up call comes, we often bolt upright in shock and react instinctively. A panicked survival response usually precedes a deep inquiry. We want to know what to do to "fix the problem."

"However you're approaching your healing, Rich," I said, "no matter what modality you pursue, it won't be right for you. You've been taught that if you do all the right things, you'll be okay, so now you believe that if you do the right things to your body, you can be cured and won't die."

"You mean that's not so?" he asked.

"No," I answered. "Although you're seeking the truth, you're seeking it outside yourself. You won't find it there because truth is within you. And besides, the cure is not the healing. But sometimes the healing will bring about the cure."

Rich was a gentleman and a scholar, a certified public accountant, an outstanding human being, well liked by all who knew him. His financial future was secure and he was happily married to a beautiful and loving wife. At sixty-nine, he looked like an athlete. He swam a mile every day and hiked regularly. He neither smoked nor drank and his diet was a model of healthy eating. He was conscientious and had done everything right. It would be easy for any of us to ask, "How could he of all people have cancer? Where did he go wrong?"

When faced with a threatening situation, we tend to criticize or blame ourselves, others or some condition. Yet a wake-up call is not an indication of some "wrongdoing" in a conventional or moral sense. Whatever symptom or circumstance snaps us out of our reverie, it is the cause or underlying purpose to which we must awaken. A wake-up call is a call to turn our awareness inward, to seek a deeper truth than we have been living. Truth, healing, and all our "answers" ultimately live within us. As long as we seek them outside our own being, no amount of being "good" or "right" or even being "the best" is going to lead us to our true fulfillment.

For Rich, the time had come to turn within and examine his life until he achieved a shift in perspective that showed him how to make life-affirming changes in the face of impending death. He needed to discover the areas he had been neglecting all his life in order to do all the "right" things he had been doing.

There were questions to ask: To what degree had he been living for the needs of others while leaving his own authentic needs unattended? (Selfishness is an act of taking away, while tending to one's true needs is an act of giving that benefits not only oneself but also everyone else as well.) How had he been treating his inner self, his heart's dreams, his intuitive knowing and soul purpose while doing all the "right" things for all those years? To what degree had he been focused on his own and his family's material welfare while neglecting his spiritual development in the process? These were the kinds of questions that needed to be asked.

We often bury ourselves in the graves of other's ignorance, illusions, and fears long before we are dead. Faced with a cancer diagnosis, Rich was now called to resurrect himself from that premature burial and tend to his own spiritual welfare.

Yet Rich had not yet chosen *life*; he was still desperately avoiding death. To begin to awaken, to be able to choose life and begin true healing, he had to first confront and accept a simple truth: we all die. Then he could ask the question, "How do I want to face my death?"

This naturally led him to, "How must I live?" This profound inquiry enables us to choose life at the deepest possible level. When

Rich asked that question, he realized that he had been looking outside himself to the "experts" for the answers and that, no matter whose advice he followed, it was still he who had to make the decision. He realized that in his avoidance of death, he had been looking for what he didn't have, and that, in order to choose life, he needed to start with what he had, what he knew. So, he started with his area of expertise—accounting. He decided that he had to face death squarely. He would first take care of his business, prepare his will, and settle all his financial affairs. He was no longer running from death.

Once he had gotten his business and finances to where he was able to let go of them, he seemed a new person. He knew he was going to die—not when, but ultimately. Now he was living each day. Next he tackled his healing program. He realized that, in his fear, he had given an enormous amount of power to the doctors and health practitioners. He decided to take it all back and be the conductor of the symphony. After thorough research and listening to expert advice, he chose to trust his intuition and defined each step of his healing process. He was no longer asking whether he should follow the nutritionist, the doctors, or the spiritual healer, but was culling what he felt he needed in each step. At some times, he refused certain invasive procedures, while at others, he opted to have surgery. He carefully set up a nutritional program with a natural health practitioner and a program of spiritual education with a spiritual teacher. No longer did he try to enforce the "right" regimen on himself.

Rich lived not for three months but for two more years. Until his final days, he swam and hiked regularly. He renewed old friendships and forged new ones. He meditated and reflected on his spiritual growth and soul purpose. When the day arrived for his departure from this earthly existence, he took his leave with dignity and grace, radiating the peace he found within himself to all present.

After his physical death, Rich's spiritual growth accelerated and to this day, he stays in close communication with his wife, myself, and many other spiritually aware individuals. Since his death, he has been instrumental in his wife's spiritual growth and she is quite aware of it. Rich has taught many around him both in his living and his dying.

Shortly after his death, Rich visited me in spirit while I was work-ing on an earlier version of this chapter. I asked him to hold on a minute while I finished putting down my train of thought. Just then all the electricity in the house shut off for a moment. Naturally, the computer turned off as well. He laughed and said he didn't mean to short out the electricity but just wanted to make sure that I wrote about what he had discovered on the "other side" about his cancer. He validated that a major part of it had to do with the anger he had suppressed during his life while doing all that was "right" for every-one else. He wanted people to know the power inherent in our emo-tions and the kind of damage it can do if we unwittingly stuff them into our bodies. "It was mostly anger toward myself from my early life," he said as the lights in my study flickered.

And so even from behind the veil, we learn that blame and criti-cism, of self and others, are the first contraband that we must surren-der if we would cross the border from survival into truth, healing, and living fully. All blame and criticism stifle the clear, quiet voice within us, the voice of our soul purpose that guides us, like a North Star, to our ultimate destiny.

Our waking-up process is the same as our dying process, for dying is an awakening to spirit. Whether we physically die or not, we each must face death in order to live and grow spiritually. A wake-up call is a death notice, but what do we have to let go of in order to awaken to spirit? What in the world are we holding on to?

A wake-up call is always a crossroads where we choose between life and death on a spiritual level, whether or not our physical life is threat-ened. It gives us an opportunity to make needed course corrections. And any decision we make in response to this call—whether we answer the call and awaken, or groggily hit the snooze button again—will pro-foundly impact our spiritual well-being, and our future.

The wake-up call also presents a paradox: to choose greater Life, we must be willing to face our death.

Author Gregg Michael Levoy tells us in his book, *Callings: Find-ing and Following an Authentic Life*, that in the Afghani language, the verb meaning *to cling* also means *to die*. Facing our death shifts our perspective on life, and consequently our relationship to it. It reveals to us all the lies that we are living, all that we are clinging to with a "death grip." Most of us don't want to die. Yet few of us are truly living. We tend to be sleepwalkers, attached to illusions, people, beliefs, and things that become substitutes for living. Choosing life involves a loosening of our death-grip on our attachments: we must surrender the world of illusions in which we tend to snooze.

Establishing New Priorities

The severest wake-up calls usually do change our priorities, at least for the moment. But it takes patience and perseverance to make these new priorities our solid foundation. When our child is seriously injured, or we're going through a painful divorce or a health crisis, all our "important" agendas may fade into insignificance. Yet unless we truly heed the call, we may slip back on "autopilot" once our child recovers, the divorce is behind us, or our health is reasonably restored.

Or we may simply give up. But a wake-up call is never a punishment sent by God for our past sins. Rather, it is a loving reminder to make positive changes toward fulfilling our purpose. The painfulness of a wake-up call is not inherent in the call but in how much suppressed pain we are clinging to that it stirs up in us. And the more reluctant we are in responding to the call, the greater the degree of pain we end up enduring. So a seemingly minor incident may provoke an intense reaction from one person while another person may take in stride what we would consider a major catastrophe. Also, the enormity of the wake-up call doesn't necessarily signify how asleep a person is. Sometimes a soul may choose to endure great ordeals and sacrifices not only for its own growth but also to serve as examples to others. Some have been great statesmen, such as Martin Luther King, Jr., and Nelson Mandela, or spiritual leaders such as Jesus, Mother Mary, and Buddha, but many have also been children who have been born with a variety of illnesses or other restrictive conditions, who show us the true priorities of life.

A Wake-Up Call Request

When I spend a night at a hotel prior to giving a morning workshop, before I go to bed I always arrange for a wake-up call. I know that I have a purpose for which I must awaken. Often I awaken myself long before the call. Sometimes, however, I need the help of the hotel operator. I always find that putting in an advance request for the wake-up call before going to bed is good insurance just in case I'm not wildly enthusiastic about waking up in the morning.

So remember, a wake-up call is a reminder *that you arranged for yourself in spirit.* Before you were born, you made a request of Spirit: "Please, don't let me waste this incarnation. Wake me up if I fall asleep!" And whenever you're asleep in this life, a part of you, the deepest part, sends out a wake-up call request.

Enjoy Waking Up!

Once each year, under a brightly lit tree, special gifts wrapped with love lie waiting to be opened with joy and delight by children who don't need *anyone* to wake them up on Christmas morning. Children are sufficiently aware of their purpose on Christmas day and, in fact, on most days. Being alive is childhood's purpose. And being in touch with this purpose, they tend to wake up bright and early, full of energy.

But, as we grow older, life becomes filled with obligations and demands, the multiple "purposes" foisted on us by others and by the world at large. Eventually, we cease to jump out of bed the way we once did as children. We become overburdened, harried, and confused. We buy alarm clocks. And when the wake-up call comes, we tend to reach for the snooze button.

But when we find our soul purpose again, when our life is an answer to its call, we again become like children who jump out of bed on Christmas morning. We choose to awaken with joy.

Just What the Doctor Ordered

Each wake-up call is uniquely tailored to our specific soul-character and spiritual needs. It may be a call for us to love and empower ourselves or those around us, to serve Life in some more meaningful way or even through some particular vocation or career, to develop some untapped gift or potential, to devote ourselves to some spiritual path or practice, or to pursue any of innumerable other worthy purposes. Its primary function is to turn our attention to our spiritual self and remind us of the soul purpose for which we are here on Earth.

And this call may take any conceivable form. We may require a grave illness to relinquish our total identification with the physical body and quicken our spiritual growth. We may need a miracle to remind us of the limitless power of Spirit. We may find in the experience of an abduction an opportunity to reclaim our power and faith in the face of terror. Or we may require a financial catastrophe before we discover the true treasure of our spiritual self.

Such was the case with Jim, another friend of mine. He was an enthusiastic entrepreneur and politician whose wake-up call to life was a devastating financial ruin. I met him for the first time shortly after his bankruptcy. Not only was he financially exhausted, he was careening toward emotional bankruptcy as well. "I don't know what I'm doing wrong," he said.

As a soul, he was already a spiritual healer and teacher. He was here to bring awareness and healing to all around him. Yet all of that had been buried in a casket of childhood invalidation and lack of family support. What was made important to him early on in his family life was to make it in business and in the world. To add to his confusion, Jim was naturally talented in business and politics, and as with Rich, he had done all the "right" things for everyone else. Then a series of inexplicable setbacks pounded him to the ground.

His call to awaken was not a choice between being a spiritual healer/ teacher or a businessman/politician. Instead, he needed to put his soul purpose *first* in his life and then to use his entrepreneurial talents to help in fulfilling that purpose. He had forgotten how much of a healer he was. When I brought it up to him, he started to recall all the times as a child when he would simply place his hands on sick people and they would get well. Unfortunately, no one at the time realized his potential.

Once he changed his priorities, however, Jim applied himself to intensive spiritual and psychic training for several years and developed his long-forgotten abilities. Then he went on to establish a successful spiritual healing center of his own. Once he put his soul purpose first, his sideline health business also blossomed.

Sometimes a wake-up call can come as a sudden awareness of the conditions you have long been enduring. For example, a starving artist might realize that she wants to be an artist but doesn't want to remain poor. Ana was such an artist. Talented, energetic, and beautiful, no matter how much she invested herself in her artwork, neither she nor her paintings were being recognized. And just as with Jim, she was very psychic and a natural teacher. She, too, had to first tend to her spiritual calling before she would find success as an artist. She enrolled in a psychic development program and went on to become a teacher. Putting together her love of art, her desire to reach out to other women, and her psychic nature, she started giving psychic development workshops for women artists. Sixteen women artists, ranging from the struggling to the famous, arrived for her first workshop. After the workshop, one of the participants, a well-known, highly successful artist, so appreciated what she'd learned that she wanted to know more about Ana. When she discovered that Ana was an aspiring artist herself, she insisted on seeing her artwork. Impressed, the woman offered to show Ana's work at her galleries in New York and Florida.

Of course, not all wake-up calls require you to develop your psychic abilities and become a teacher. But the true meaning of "psychic" is "of the soul" and, one way or another, we each rely on our psychic abilities to experience our soul purpose. And as a spiritual master once said, "If you want to learn something, study it; if you want to master it, teach it."

Wake-Up Calls Are God's Love in Action

My personal favorite wake-up calls come in the form of Magic, our cat. Her teachings are elegant and impeccable. First, her faint meow comes floating through the ethers, usually when I'm occupied with something "more important." Often, I choose to ignore it. So she increases her volume, prowling the house, seeking me out. Having secured my office door against intruders, I hunch over my computer (trying to finish this book!) and continue to resist her call. Soon it takes on a heart-rending and somewhat annoying quality, so I focus more grimly on my task. Her decibels increase, now coming down the hall. Then, she is at my door, her poignant but irritating yowling now accompanied by a light scratching.

"I know you're in there," she calls.

As I ignore her and continue my "all-important" work, the scratching becomes frenzied. It's a full-scale battle of wills. I know I'm outmatched, but I refuse to give in. I wonder if I'll need to repaint the door. Suddenly, the scratching and yowling cease. There is an ominous silence . . . the calm before the storm?

Too late, I realize that I have mismanaged my priorities. I should have heeded her earlier wake-up calls. Will there be heck to pay? Will I live to snooze another day? There it is, the loud "thump!" as Magic leaps up and body-slams the door, pawing the knob on her way down, as usual. The knob turns and the door flies open. Unruffled, she breezes in and leaps onto my lap to purr and massage me with love. (Why was I so resistant? Love was her soul purr-pose all along.)

This is the perfect analogy of a wake-up call. It is God's love seeking us out when we are lost in our illusions. Its purpose, ultimately, is love.

Love gives us yet another opportunity to receive love. She whispers softly in our hearts, first as dreams and intuitions. If we ignore them, she speaks louder in our thoughts and emotions. Then, she gets louder still by the aches and moans in our bodies. We may think that she is demanding. But love never demands, she gives. And she never stops giving of herself. Yet often we resist because we are afraid. When invalidated in life, we tend to harden ourselves against love. There is too much pain in our heart, too many disappointments, too many losses. It is too painful to dream when we cannot imagine any way of ever fulfilling our heart's dreams. And when love tugs at our scabs to heal the wounds that lie beneath them, that hurts as well. So, we close the door to our heart and we listen to the incessant thumping of love giving life. And no matter how much we turn against her, love never gives up on us.

Become Your Own Wake-Up Call

No need to wait passively for the next wake-up call to come. Be pro-active and choose to wake up on your own initiative. (That's why you're reading this book, right?) Make waking up a spiritual habit, a way of life, a long-term priority. This doesn't mean you'll never receive another wake-up call. But you'll notice the calls sooner, and you'll know how to respond when they come.

SIX

EXPERIENCING YOUR PURPOSE THROUGH INTUITION

Your soul purpose is the power and meaning that guides your life. You can find it neither in the world nor in your mind, for it resides within spirit. Unless you tap into its energy, you cannot experience the reality of your life purpose. And when you fail to discover the meaning that purpose gives to your life, you cannot know your true worth. Ultimately, any unhappiness and lack of fulfillment we feel result from our separation from purpose. Reclaiming your relationship to your soul purpose begins with finding answers, and you must know *where* to look, *how* to look, and *what* to look for.

Where Are You Looking?

How often do you look for answers in all the wrong places? If you believe that you don't already have the answer within you, you end up looking elsewhere. You look to experts and authorities, you look to the future and the past, and you look everywhere and anywhere but right here, right now, inside of your own being.

We are often like the old woman in a Sufi parable, on her hands and knees under a lamppost looking for her lost house key. When asked by her neighbors where she thought she had dropped her key, she replied, "Oh, in my house, of course."

"Why then are you looking for it outside?"

"Because it's a lot brighter here under the lamppost," the old woman said. "It's too dark in my house to find anything."

"That doesn't make any sense!" her neighbors said. "If you lost your key in the house, the only place you'll find it is in the house."

To their amazement, the old woman laughed. "You are so clever when it comes to little things in the world," she said, "but all of you have been doing the same thing with your inner life. You are always looking outside of yourself for what you forgot inside."

Especially when you are in doubt and in fear, you tend to seek the comfort of well-lit familiar territories rather than venture forth into the dark, uncharted waters within. It's also easy to assume, *If I already knew the answer, I wouldn't be in this mess in the first place.* Furthermore, you might believe that if you had the solution within you, you wouldn't be afraid. Instead, you'd know what to do. You wouldn't be confused and feel as if you were falling apart, would you? So you come to believe the answer couldn't be within you. You might even expect that if you already possessed the answer, you would at least have a sense of control over the situation.

Quite to the contrary, however; merely having the answer within you doesn't necessarily change anything. As with all the powerful programs you have in your computer, until you type in the correct code, your answers remain dormant as if they're not there at all. They are also like seeds. You must plant them and nourish them before you can eventually harvest their fruits. All your answers are within you, but you must first choose one, grow it, and then learn to apply it in your life. It may seem that we get lucky at times and stumble upon an answer, but mostly it takes practice in asking for it, learning to receive it, and knowing what to do with it once we have it.

When you've been taught to go ask your mother, that father knows best, to look it up in the book, that you need to listen to the teacher or the preacher, and that only the doctor can treat you, it may be difficult at first to be certain about what is true for *you*. Yet when you think about it, where did you find all the answers that ever truly mattered to you?

For instance, have you ever taken a problem and "slept on it"? You ponder a question and hang out with it for a couple of days. It's similar to taking a weekend trip with a friend. You get to experience facets of that person in ways you couldn't have imagined from just casual conversation. Then, you come up with a much more complete answer you can live with. Where did it come from? Sure, we've gotten facts and figures and recipes and theories from books and authorities, but the answers that fundamentally change our lives and help us grow always come from inside us. Even when someone teaches you a profound lesson, what that teacher offered rang true *inside you*. The answer you could use was a truth lying dormant within you. The teacher's words simply provided the keystrokes to activate it.

Jesus taught us not to be anxious and worry about our life, but to seek first the Source of all creation. Then, He said, all things will be provided us. After all, don't we go to the faucet when we need water or step outside when we need a breath of fresh air? We naturally seek the source of what we need. The problem only arises when we forget who actually provides what we need. Many of us have, at one time or another, wrongly associated a particular teacher with the source of our truth just because he or she spoke the words that guided us to our inner truth. Then, we end up seeking the teacher for the truth instead of turning our attention toward its real source. Another example is when we panic upon discovering our bank account showing a low balance, as if the bank is the source of our money. Or, if we feel the powerful love within us only when we fall in love with someone, we may mistakenly see our partner as the source of this love. Then, if anything should take that person away from us, we might feel as if our heart was torn asunder and that we would never love again. *All of our suffering begins when we lose sight of our inner divinity.*

Sometimes a crisis, in which conventional solutions are out of reach, helps us turn our awareness inward to spirit and our purpose. A turning point in my life that woke me up to my path was just such a crisis situation. One evening, a friend suddenly doubled over in pain. Being a nurse at the time and not able to rule out the possibility of a critical condition, I prepared to rush her to the ER. She, on the other hand, made it perfectly clear that she was *not* going to any hospital. Not expecting such a response, I was at a loss as to what to do. It was then she commanded, between her groans, "*You* heal me."

I knew that she *wasn't* saying, "You're a nurse. Get me some medicine. Patch me up." Not knowing what else to do, I put my hand on her to try to comfort her somehow. Then, as if it were the most natural thing to do, I closed my eyes. I remember consciously deciding that I could help her heal this way. It was then that my hand started to vibrate and heat up. I could feel energy surging through my hand into her and noticed that, after a few minutes, she had visibly calmed down. After twenty more minutes of this, she jumped up and exclaimed, "I feel better than I have in months!"

My friend may have received a healing, but I had discovered that the answer I was seeking about my path was already within me. I just needed to learn how to better access that inner space and develop my abilities as a spiritual healer to begin consciously fulfilling my purpose.

How Are You Looking?

By the time of my healing experience with my friend, I had already known that pursuing a career in medicine was not to be my path. That wonderful experience showed me that the healing that I wanted to give people came from within. At the time, however, I knew nothing consciously of how to heal spiritually and energetically. If I were to embark upon a path of healing, I knew I would have to learn to reproduce *consciously* whatever it was that I did that night. Now, I knew without a doubt *where* to look for my answers—within me—but I didn't know quite *how* I did it that time.

I realized that, at the time, I had just relaxed into myself since I couldn't think of anywhere else to look or anything else to do. I had surrendered, having decided that it was okay not to know what to do and I wasn't trying to be in control of the situation. Nor did I hold any judgments or expectations on how things should or shouldn't be. I only desired my friend to be well. In effect, I had decided just to *be*. Inadvertently, I had set aside my rational mind and, when I was no longer trying to figure everything out intellectually, a space opened for me to have my certainty in Divinity. I had accessed my soul consciousness and energy through intuition.

It is through the use of your intuition that you realize the profound truths in life and receive your inspiration, insights, and miracles. When you have certainty in your inner Source, you intuit your own truth. Your intellect can help get you to the doorway to truth, but intuition is the key you must use to open the door and experience the reality of your soul purpose.

Your intellect works with form: the external appearance of things or objects. It can analyze the letter of the law, but it cannot experience the spirit of the law. On the other hand, it is through your intuition that you can experience the energy of spirit and *know* its reality. If you use your intellect to try to figure out your soul purpose, you will become confused and be in doubt. This is due to the intellect's capability being limited to grasping structures while soul purpose is always evolving and is not static. If you arrive at an intellectual conclusion about your soul purpose, it means that your mind never opened up to allow you to experience the real answer. We often end up intellectualizing by asking why we got the answer we got, without ever stopping to discover what the answer is really telling us. It is part of the way our ego avoids the pain we do not wish to face. Purpose brings about form, but is not form itself. You must learn to use your intellect to formulate the correct question, but allow your intuition to experience the answer.

Awareness is the natural state of our being, so when we choose to look within, we become more aware. This process of awakening presents us with a challenge: the more awake we become, the more aware we become also of the pain and darkness we have so carefully buried in our psyche. And as the light of our awareness shines upon that pain, everything we have built around it to protect ourselves from it begins to fall apart. And, often frightened, we turn away from it. It is as if you've awakened from a deep sleep and the dreams you were dreaming fade into oblivion. At times you must choose a seemingly harsh reality over a pleasant anesthetic dream.

We've all experienced our leg "falling asleep." It gets numb, but when the circulation returns and your leg starts to "wake up"—yeow! It's quite unpleasant, isn't it? Waking up spiritually can be similar to this. While your awareness is asleep, you are unconscious and numb. You don't feel, hear, or see much. As you begin to awaken, however, you get the "pins and needles." Long-suppressed pain, emotions, and thoughts surface into your conscious mind.

The good news is you have a choice. You can choose to resist this psychic detoxification process and, with effort, continue to bury the pain. Or you can choose to willingly face the trials—and the rewards— of this psychic adventure into the depth of your being. Usually, the fear of anticipating what you might find is worse than its reality. And the gold to be found on this journey is not at the end but in the going. "The attentive man," taught the Buddha, "looks on wakefulness as his greatest treasure" (*The Dhammapada*, 2:26).

When your leg awakens from the numbness, it's painful, but you know it'll pass. The more you can relax and let the sensation work its way out, the more quickly it passes. The same holds true for the pain that emerges with spiritual growth. You must let it all pass. Resistance is not only futile, it also adds powerful fuel to the fire. Your cozy campfire can turn into your funeral pyre.

Letting go of pain, whether an old heartache, physical trauma, or mental anxiety, doesn't mean you have to try to get rid of it. Letting go of something means first letting it be. You may not like the problem, but you must be okay with the fact that it's there. Then, and only then, will the condition start to change. When you are willing to give it space to exist instead of trying to eliminate it, it will begin completing its own cycle. And everything seeks its own kind of fulfillment and fights for its survival.

Why is it so hard to let pain or a problem just be? Most often, it's because we're afraid that if we don't do something about it, we'll be stuck with it forever. You might think, *I can't stand it one minute more. It's making me sick. It's hurting me.*

If we give it so much power and seniority, it will control our lives. Fortunately, the truth is that you don't have to do that. No matter how bad the situation seems to be, when you're willing to turn inward and face whatever challenges you might find, the healing begins.

What Are You Looking For?

Once we start looking within, what answer do we seek? There is only one way to find the right answer: ask the right question, for every answer lives within the question. No question, no answer. Not sold separately. To find an answer that works for you, you must first learn to formulate the correct question. You can't go on hurling questions born of frustration and panic against your mind and expect to find good answers.

Confronted with a painful situation, we tend to fire away questions that lead us away from the answers we need. We might ask, for example, "What's wrong with me?" But when crises arise in your life, they aren't due to something being inherently wrong with you. So this question will not harvest a usable answer.

Another question we often ask is "Why me?" Although you may take them personally, situations in your life don't happen *to* you. They just happen and you are involved in them according to the way you respond to them. You might ask, "What am I supposed to do?" but that question assumes that you are *expected* to *do* something. It takes your power and control, and puts them into someone else's hands. Whose expectations are you going to fulfill?

The question "How can this be happening?" tries to establish by what conditions the events are occurring. Everything that happens is a tapestry woven of myriad threads. What are all the conditions responsible for it? Are you seeking a catalogue of them?

Still another question is "When is this going to end?" When is what going to end? What would you say signifies such an end? Would all your trials be over when the white owl calls your name? Is that what you wish to know? In the meantime, you still have to deal with what's happening and where you are with it.

"How much more do I have to endure?" What is it that you're enduring? Is it even yours to endure? "Why does it have to be so painful?" Once again, any intellectual question brings about only intellectual answers. You can collect a compendium of reasons for the degree of pain you're feeling, but is that going to relieve you of it? Of course not. But when we are afraid of feeling the pain, we repeatedly ask intellectual questions to avoid all feeling. If we are to heal from pain, we must be willing to face what it is that we are refusing to face.

On one of the many opportunities I was given to accept this challenge, I was lying in bed in agony. I tried everything to get rid of the pain or to escape its fury, but to no avail. *Oh please, God, make it go away! I can't take this much longer.* Then, somewhere in between the black thunderclouds passing through my mind, I found a ray of light: I realized I wasn't asking the right question. But while writhing in pain, it is difficult to think clearly. Then I asked myself, "What is the question I need to ask?" The answer I received was that I need to first ask myself what I want the answer to give me or do for me. This will transform an answer from an intellectual construct into an action and an experience.

"Okay, what is it that I want the answer to give or do?" I asked. The answer came immediately: "I want it to give me relief from the pain. I want it to give me comfort. Now, what do I need to ask for so that the answer can give me that?"

"God," I asked, "please help me be whole, to be well."

With that, I let go of my resistance to the pain and all the effort of trying to control and subdue it. In my asking, I surrendered. Within seconds, I felt a gentle and loving blanket of compassion come over me. Starting from my head, it moved down my body toward my legs and feet where I was feeling the greatest pain.

While this healing force moved through me, in my mind's eye, I saw many people who were suffering and calling to me for help peel away as if their clutching fingers were gently loosened from my ankles. Set free as well was my past anger, self-blame, and the remorse I felt for failing to heal everyone's suffering. I realized I had been holding on to this failure even from a prior lifetime when I was a physician who, after having saved countless lives, was in the end impotent to save the lives of his own beloved wife and child.

Within a couple of minutes, the intensity of the pain fell off by at least 75 percent. It became bearable. By the following morning, I felt no more pain. I was well. The answer had definitely fulfilled its mission.

In another circumstance, a businessman I knew kept asking himself, "Why isn't my business working?" The more he asked that question, the more his business failed. Finally, he changed his question. He asked, "What is it that I want from the answer?"

He realized he wanted prosperity, not only for himself and his family, but also for his employees and customers. He started asking a new question: "What can I do in my business to bring more prosperity to my family, my employees, my customers, and myself?"

He kept on asking his new question and, each time, received new insights as to how he could improve his business operation toward that end. He also felt inspired and motivated with each asking. His business started to produce exactly what he had asked for.

My teacher was a master of asking productive questions. The questions he raised would inevitably lead to someone's spiritual growth, healing, and improvement in the quality of his or her life. Instead of seeing a difficult situation or an adversary as a problem, he would ask quality questions such as: "What can I learn from this experience? How can I use this situation to teach my students what they need to progress? What can I do to turn this conflict into a resolution?"

In a sense, he was always asking a variation of the question: "How can I *seize* this opportunity for the good of all concerned?"

Love provides all the opportunities of life, and love shows us how to make use of them as well. But love also always honors free will so, unless you invite her in with welcoming questions, she remains silent, ever faithfully yours in the wings.

Asking the right questions will give you the right answers. Asking effective questions will produce effective results. Asking compassionate questions will deepen your compassion. Asking beautiful questions will make you more beautiful. Asking uplifting questions will surely inspire you and others. As the Sufi mystics say, "God makes us, using our prayers." With the answers to our questions, we fulfill our purpose.

Remember, to formulate the question, you must first ask: "What do I want the answer to give or do?" Then, once you ask a question, how do you get an answer?

Intuition: Asking and Receiving

Ask, and it will be given to you; seek, and you will find; knock, and it will be opened to you; for everyone who asks, receives. . . .

—Matthew 7:7–8

Everyone who asks receives. This is an unconditional statement. You don't have to work for it or earn it. You don't have to deserve in someone else's eyes before what you ask is given to you. This is a threatening concept for anyone who wishes to punish or control others. After all, how can someone punish or control you if you could just turn around and ask for what you need and receive it? The only way people can hold you hostage is if you agree to be limited by their self-made rules. *You didn't do this or do it well, so you can't have your reward. I don't like you that way, so I won't love you. You didn't suffer as much as I did, so you don't deserve as much.*

The Divine Law of asking and receiving cuts out all the middlemen. When you truly find your own space to be who you are, you will discover that there is only one relationship: the one between you and your All-Giving Maker.

Many masters have attained their enlightenment through repeatedly asking of themselves the question "Who am I?" They examine every answer that floats up into their consciousness in response to the question and then let them go. When every identity, every attachment to a belief about who they are, and every expectation and fantasy of who they might be is exhausted, they experience the truth of their being.

When we type a mathematical question into our computer, we don't try to figure out the calculations ourselves. Instead, we wait for the computer to do it for us. Then we go about the business of using the answer. Intellectualizing is like being in competition with the computer, not trusting that it can do the job we ask it to do, and becoming so absorbed in doing the calculations by hand according to all our rules that we fail to see the answer blinking on our monitor.

If you are in effort, trying to figure out what the answer is supposed to be, you provide no room in your mind for the answer to emerge from within. Often, a scientist or an inventor might throw in the towel after days of trying to figure out a problem and take a short nap. Upon awakening, the answer is right there flashing in his or her mind's eye. This happened with the noted German chemist, August Kekulé, while researching the structure of organic molecules. He dozed off and dreamt of a snake biting its own tail. When he awoke, he realized that organic molecules are circular arrangements of atoms.

Those who meditate seeking enlightenment find it when, instead of filling their mind with desires and thoughts of attaining enlightenment, they empty it. What they had asked for, the light, can then enter and fill that welcoming receptacle they provided. Asking a question, we must become a willing vessel in which the mystery of the answer can mature and blossom. Unless we clear out the clutter from our house, we cannot expect to welcome our guests.

Once a question is asked, all answers are actually intuited. Intuition is not an ability that only a few gifted people possess. It is working in you all the time. If you assume it is separate from you, you will have a difficult time "tapping into it." Realize that every time you think of a question, an answer pops up from nowhere. Granted, not all the answers we get are readily user-friendly. When we ask a question such as "Why can't I do this?" we may receive immediate replies such as "Because you're stupid" or "You're good for nothing and you'll never be able to do it." These are thoughts your mind collected at one time or another from someone. If you ask a question intellectually in this manner, instead of intuitively, your mind will rummage through all your memory drawers to provide intellectual answers to your questions. And on this level, any "reason" that your mind comes up with as an answer would be just as untrue and ineffective as another!

When you formulate a well-thought-out question, sit back and relax. Don't empower all the mind chatter that you may notice at first. Be still with the question. Let it go to work for you. You have already typed in the codes to activate your wonderful computer program, so trust that it will do the job it was designed to do. Be willing to be surprised. Be as an innocent child, without prejudice or expectations. Let the answer emerge into your consciousness whichever way it will. You may know, hear, think, feel, sense, or see it. When you intuit the answer to your question, you are not competing against it to try to control it or to figure it out intellectually. As with a toaster, when the question is toasted enough, the answer pops up!

Asking a question and receiving the answer are not always a one-shot deal. Each time you ask a certain question, you need to examine the answer. But you may need to ask it many times before you get the full answer or the answer you could truly use. It's as if you sat in a restaurant and said to no one in particular, "I would like a drink." Your friend sitting next to you may offer you a martini. A child passing by may offer you a soda. As you evaluate those answers, you learn from each one. Each answer is a step in getting you to the answer you can really use. Often, the earlier answers help you clarify what it is you need to ask next. You don't want alcohol or sugary bubbles, so you ask again. Finally, the waiter arrives and asks you, "What would you like to drink?" You realize that you need to hydrate yourself, so you say, "Water, please."

Every answer you receive through your intuition will help you pave the path to your fulfillment. Don't give up. If you have a quality question that is well thought-out with clear purpose, your perseverance will ultimately reward you.

A key element in receiving the answers to our questions is our willingness to accept the answer we get, evaluate it without defensiveness, make use of it, be grateful for it, and let it go when it has served its purpose. Some answers we receive are seemingly negative answers, such as "You must be kidding! It can't be done." Don't resist it just because it's not the answer you want to hear. Accept that that is an answer. Accepting an answer doesn't mean agreeing with it or resigning to it. It's a tool to take your next step in fulfilling your purpose for asking the question. Evaluate the answer by asking questions of it. "What is great about this answer? What can I learn from this answer that will help me take another step toward my goal? How can I use this answer to help me? How can I use this answer to formulate my next question?"

When you ask, you will receive—*that* is a certainty. Why many people don't realize this truth is that they cannot see, or they refuse to see what is being given to them as a result of their asking. When you ask a question, the asking of it puts your attention on the elements comprising the question. At the same time, it takes your awareness away from what is not being asked. When you ask, "Why am I feeling so horrible?" your attention goes directly to the horribleness you are feeling and eliminates your awareness of all the beautiful and wonderful experiences of life that are also in you. The "why" in the question seeks out reasons for the horribleness of your feelings that pile up inside of you, which intensifies those horrible feelings while shutting out your attention from all the great things you could be feeling in its place.

When you ask a "taking" question, such as "Why can't I get him to love me?" you narrow your awareness down to the single object you wish to "get" and all the reasons why you can't. When you ask a "giving" question, such as "What can I do to fulfill my purpose for being here?" or "How can I best benefit my community?" then your awareness opens up to greater possibilities, more opportunities, creativity, and energy.

At times, you may be so overwhelmed with what you're already dealing with that you may be afraid to receive an answer. You don't want one more thing to be responsible for. Don't worry. Just because you receive an answer doesn't mean you stop everything else in your life. Life goes on. You work, pay your bills, wash dishes, and take your kids to the park. Meanwhile, you incubate the answer. Let it age a little. Like fine wine, a good answer needs to mature and reach its full bouquet.

How do you know when it's time to use an answer? Well, from the time you received it, the power of that answer has already been working behind the scenes. Just don't invalidate that power with your worries and negative thinking. When you are willing for it to work, it begins to work. As with a seedling that hasn't yet broken the surface, you might not be able to see it, but it is already growing. Have faith. Keep watering it. While you aren't able to jump in and start doing everything the answer requires, incubate the answer. Nourish it with love, and it will grow into a more complete and powerful answer. Harvest your answer when it is ripe enough to serve the purpose for which you asked for it.

If you keep trying to make the answer more perfect, you may over-water it and never put it to use. It's as if you need to write down some great insight and any scrap of paper would do, but you decide to wait until you can buy beautiful, monogrammed, hand-embossed stationary. By the time you get some, you've probably forgotten what you were going to write down.

If you're hungry and want a snack to tide you over, don't spend hours scouring the town for a five-star restaurant with a view. That will defeat the purpose of your asking. On the other hand, if you're setting up the most romantic dinner possible for the purpose of proposing to your sweetheart, what are a few weeks of searching for that ideal spot? The true standard by which to evaluate the ripeness of an answer is to see how well it fulfills the purpose for which you asked for it. After all, there is a great deal of difference in the meaning of "accuracy" for a giant crane operator and a neurosurgeon.

In the bigger picture of life, purpose is the asking and you are the answer. You answer to the call of your purpose not by what you do, but by whom you become. You answer by being the answer.

Let us now ask, as did the sages of old, "Who are you?" What kind of an answer have you become so far? The answer you are now is the sum of how you have used all the answers to the questions you've already asked. As you seek that which gives everything, you turn within. And the *quality* of the prayers that you offer become the radiance of who you are.

SEVEN

VALIDATING SPIRIT

Saying "Hello" to Spirit

In America, we regularly greet each other with "Hello, how are you?" It's the way we begin to validate one another. *Hello. I am here and I confirm your existence.* Similar greetings are exchanged all around the world. Whether you greet someone in Japan and say, *"Kon'nichi-wa. Ikaga desu-ka?"* or in France and say, *"Bonjour. Comment allez-vous?"* it still means "Good day. How are you?"

We often forget how a simple "hello" from someone can be a spiritual healing when it validates our inner existence and we feel accepted just as we are. Some of the more ancient greetings still in use today in a few places serve to remind us of our spirituality. In India, for instance, the greeting of *Namasté* says, "The Divinity within me honors the Divinity within you."

Although today people often ignore much of its true meaning and power, this greeting still serves as a daily reminder of our sacred heritage for those who can hear it. Another example is the Mayan greeting *In Lak'ech*, which translates as "I am another you." It validates the soul purpose for which we have incarnated, which is to discover and realize the divine oneness of our true self. In Hawaii, we come and go with *Aloha*, a simple greeting with the underlying meaning, "Our joyous sharing of spirit/life energy in this moment."

If we are to fulfill our purpose, we must remember that, in whatever language we may communicate that purpose, we are here to validate the existence, consciousness, and energy that is spirit.

Without validation, even in the most mundane situations, conditions easily get worse. One example of this that many of us have experienced occurs when we get into a crowded elevator full of strangers. If you were to merely stare at the floor, counting the seconds until you can get out of there, you would feel the tension mount between everyone. Everyone's unease at having body space intruded upon becomes palpable and everyone leaves the elevator even more uptight than when they entered. Next time, try entering an elevator, looking each person in the eye, smiling, and greeting them with a warm and sincere "hello." See how much better everyone feels. It will brighten up the cramped quarters and dissipate the stale energy. Any validation at all enhances our state of being.

Once I was in a crowded elevator and someone surreptitiously passed gas. No one could escape the unpleasant, clinging odor or the growing embarrassment of the secret culprit. The tension built toward a crescendo when a little old lady blurted out, "Well, don't blame *me*; *I* didn't let it out!" As she looked defiantly at the rest of us with a twinkle in her eyes, we all started laughing and joking with each other. The cat was out of the bag, so to speak, and all the pressure of denial was off. As people got off at their respective floors, they were smiling and wishing the rest of us well. The old lady reminded us of the truth: no one really cared who did it; we all just wanted to be more comfortable with one another.

Even a little validation goes a long way. Once, when I was standing with my wife in the immigration line at a Mexican airport, I observed one weary traveler after another in the line ahead of us submitting to the scrutiny of an angry and unyielding immigration officer. He glared at them and slammed the entry stamp onto their passports, with not one word passing between them. Smiling, my wife whispered in my ear, "I don't think he's too happy."

"That observation, my dear," I told her, "is definitely in the 'no shit' category. I think he needs a little validation."

Just then, like a bullhorn, he summoned us to step forward with "Next!"

We walked up together and presented our travel documents. Both of us smiled and looked right into his dark, hard eyes. *We have nothing against you, amigo,* I thought. *We know you must be stressed, tired, and bored. We just want you to have a little break from it. We're enjoying being here; you can too.*

"Buenos días, señor," I said.

His head snapped back in surprise at having been addressed. After a moment, he mumbled back, "Buenos días." Then, as he opened my wife's passport, he beamed like a child opening a present. "Ra-pha-elle!" he exclaimed, pronouncing each syllable of her name. "Like the archangel," he added.

"Yes," she replied. "And my husband is Michael, like the archangel."

He looked at me, his face brightly lit with a toothy smile. "My name is Gabriel," he announced proudly, pointing to his identification badge. "Like the archangel."

"We could have an archangel convention," I joked.

"Sí!" he laughed, carefully stamping each of our passports and handing them back to us. "Gracias. Welcome to our country. You have a very nice visit here," he said as he nodded and smiled his blessing.

The little pebble of validation we had thrown into the pond began to create its magical ripples, and we were to share in their blessings. All we did was offer a simple but kind "hello" to cheer up an angry, bored, and frustrated government official, and we ended up being welcomed into a new country with a smiling benediction from an archangel's namesake. And we will never know how those ripples affected the people in line after us, or the man's family when he went home that night.

Leaving the immigration building, we were revitalized. And not only the quantity but also the quality of that energy propelled us through the rest of our day. Our baggage handler turned out to be named *Angel*; our cab driver was *Jesus*; we were met at our hotel by its manager, another *Rafael*; and served at the restaurant by who else but *Arcangel*. Needless to say, we had the full support of angels on that trip.

Validation begins when we say "hello" to spirit. Then it can become our spiritual passport out of old cramped quarters and into bold new frontiers. Validation always brings about an improvement in your condition. On the other hand, if you invalidate, or neglect to validate, your condition will degenerate. Nothing in the universe stays put; the condition of existence always moves toward more wholeness or toward more destruction. This is the way of Life. And validation is the secret key to all learning and healing; without it, you cannot have your spiritual growth and the fulfillment of your purpose.

When You're Feeling Stuck . . .

When you feel stuck, powerless, and isolated, you are invalidated and disconnected from the source of your truth, love, power, and purpose. It may come as a result of experiencing a great loss, such as the death or other departure of a loved one from your physical life, the failure of accomplishing a major goal, or enormous criticism from others. However, the real invalidation of your being comes from you forgetting and denying your true nature as a powerful, loving, immortal spirit.

But why do we do that when things go sour in our life? Ultimately, it boils down to one thing: we believe that we failed to fulfill someone else's expectations. Then, we attach shame to the pain we feel and to the one whom we believe we failed, be that God, someone else, something, or ourselves. We weren't "perfect" or the way we were "supposed" to be. And the bigger the discrepancy between the expectations of how we should be and the way we are, the greater the invalidation and stress we feel.

Most of the time, we tend to be somewhere between totally invalidated and fully validated. So what do we need to do, and how do we need to be, in order to have more validation in our lives and step out of whatever invalidation we are in? To answer that, let's first explore the actual definition of "validation."

What Does It Mean to Validate?

To *validate* means "to ascertain the truth or authenticity of something." Its multiethnic root can be traced back to Latin, Old English, Germanic, as well as Slavonic origins, and they all express the spirit of giving strength, power, and rule. When we explore the meaning of the word further, we find the definition of *ascertain* to be: "to discover with certainty, as through examination or experimentation." And finally, *authenticity* could be defined as: "the quality or condition of having true authorship or being from the true source." So in order to validate other people, we must discover, with certainty, their true source, and become aware of, appreciate, communicate with, and treat them as spiritual beings.

I frequently witness one woman going up to another and sincerely taking delight in her new dress, hairstyle, necklace, or whatever. "I love your new outfit," she might say. "That color goes so well with your eyes. And have you been working out? You look so trim and healthy!"

The validation is not in how nice the dress is or exactly what the woman is saying. It's in her communicating her awareness and appreciation for the creativity, care, and work that went into the choices the other woman made in buying and wearing that dress, as well as her efforts at the gym. The first woman is validating the other's spiritual qualities, abilities, and accomplishments as reflected in her clothes and fitness. And through this validation, both women are energized, inspired, and motivated. The one who offers the validation becomes inspired to take care of her own health and gives herself permission to have a new outfit with which to enjoy and celebrate life.

Men tend to emphasize accomplishments when they validate one another: "Hey, Jack, congratulations on your promotion" (or the new contract, golf score, etc.). Yet the validation, once again, isn't so much about the new status, business success, or winning score but that someone notices you, is happy for you, and appreciates the hard work you've put into accomplishing your goal. How and what we validate may be quite different between men and women, but who gets validated and how it affects us are pretty much the same. Validation confirms the existence of our being and uplifts the spirit.

So, to validate our spiritual nature, we must:

1) be aware that we are spirit;

2) be aware of and appreciate the attributes, abilities, and energy of spirit;

3) empower those qualities with our certainty in them;

4) express those qualities in our dealings with others.

Whenever you validate any aspect of spirit, you validate spirit. For example, when you are aware of truth, have compassion, are giving, express enthusiasm, forgive, love, or laugh, you are validating spirit. Each time you validate spirit in yourself or in another, healing takes place.

Once, a friend of mine, Sherrill, also a spiritual healer, and I went to visit a young woman in the hospital who had been in a coma for over eight weeks. Although the doctor said she had not responded to anything during that time, my friend decided to speak to her. "Cindy, I know you're scared to come back to your body, but if you don't come back real soon, you're going to lose it."

Moments later, Cindy opened her eyes and looked around, perplexed. "Where am I?" she asked. "What am I doing here?"

Before Sherrill did, no one had truly spoken to Cindy's *spirit*. Either people didn't bother communicating with her at all since her body was unresponsive, or they spoke *only* to her body, trying in desperation to resurrect it from the coma. Sherrill, on the other hand, validated Cindy's *being*. She recognized and respected Cindy's true spiritual existence and empowered her to make the decision to return. And that she did!

Healing Invalidation

The more you are validated, however, the more any invalidation you've held within you will begin to surface into your awareness. Often people refuse validation in their misguided attempt to avoid this emerging awareness of the pain of past invalidation. When they do, however, they miss their opportunity for profound healing. It is important to remember that the thoughts and feelings of invalidation (failure, hopelessness, depression, isolation, loneliness, etc.) that surface are part of healing past invalidation, and not the result of the new validation. Validation doesn't cause those feelings and thoughts in you, but rather it detoxifies those invalidating energies. Therefore, you must practice stepping out of those old energies so that you can heal them.

To do that, first, do not put any more energy into them. Let it be okay that you're feeling or thinking the invalidating feelings and thoughts. Neither try to stop them nor add to them. As an example, let's say your boss criticizes your work performance, humiliates you in front of your coworkers, and dismisses you without a chance for you to respond to his charges. You feel hurt, ashamed, and angry, but most of all, you feel like a failure. You want to tell him where to shove the job, you feel sorry for yourself, and you have a good cry. All sorts of justifications, excuses, and defenses may come up in your mind. Instead, here are some more healing steps you can take:

- First, disengage your energy from all of it. Choose detachment. Step back with your energy and awareness.

- Don't add more fuel to all the reactions. Let it be all right that you are having them.

- Remind yourself that you are spirit. Become aware of your energy as spirit.

- Recognize that the spirit you are is infinitely more spacious, intelligent, and powerful than the individual thoughts and feelings you're having. Appreciate that.

- Enjoy yourself being spirit. Even enjoy the fact that you're not enjoying the state you are in.

- Be grateful that you are spirit and have been given this opportunity to free yourself from the influences of the interacting energies of the world.

- See the humor in the joke of invalidation—that you supposedly cannot have what is eternally yours already.

- Choose to have compassion for yourself as well as your boss. Express some of the qualities and energies of spirit. Smile, laugh, show kindness, and forgive.

- Choose to relinquish your resistance and the holding on to of the thoughts, feelings, and energies of judgment and invalidation. Imagine them floating away from you in colorful helium balloons that pop.

Invalidation tells you that you cannot have or do not have what is inherent in you spiritually. Healing the various invalidations in your life requires you to develop a conscious relationship with your spiritual self.

Practice Validating Spirit in Your Daily Life

To incorporate the practice of validating spirit into your daily life, you must start where you are. In fact, where else *can* you start? You don't have to be any better or any more than who and how and where you are right now. You don't have to *do more things* in your life either. You are not required to shoulder any more responsibility or obligation. (No cosmic salesman will call.) Yet we often resist the next step of our spiritual growth because we're so busy already. *How can I possibly add one more thing to my day? I can't even get to what I already have on my plate. I don't get enough sleep, so how can I find the time to meditate or do spiritual practices?*

Don't worry or stress yourself. Learning to validate spirit becomes a profound meditation and prayer practice. But do not make it a separate activity to add to the life you are already living. It doesn't require more time and physical effort on your part. It only requires the willingness and commitment to pay attention as you live your day.

As you live each day choosing to ascertain the truth of your experiences, you will find that much of what you thought was indispensable in your life really isn't. You will discover that you begin to have more time and energy than you ever thought possible. The more you pay attention to the qualities of Spirit, such as timelessness, power, intelligence, compassion, patience, and myriad others, the more frequently and deeply they will visit you.

Whenever I anticipate a more demanding day than normal, I take extra care of my spiritual self. The more I am able to validate the various aspects of spirit within myself, the greater the ease and effectiveness with which I can manage my day's business. On the other hand, if I choose to shortchange spirit on account of a busier day, in the end I find I have toiled and labored needlessly. "What if a man gain the whole world and lose his own soul?" asked Jesus. When you are more mindful of your spiritual self in your daily activities, you will naturally end up having more time for meditation, prayer, and other spiritual practices each day.

Agreement as Validation

In the beginning was the Word, and the Word was with God, and the Word was God.

—John 1:1

I give you my word. That word is "agreement." Everything in the world begins with agreement, and nothing happens without it. Agreement exists in a relationship. It is the oneness between the two. The first relationship you have is with yourself, and within you is the Word, which is with God and is God.

Agreement brings about wholeness. It heals division. It brings forth all that is inherent in the oneness that is spirit. When someone calls you stupid, you can agree that that's what he's saying, but you don't have to agree that he's speaking the truth. When you're in agreement, you cannot be divided. A person insults or criticizes you to divide you against yourself, to try to invalidate your oneness and power of spirit. If you resist it, part of you wonders whether you are stupid and the other part defends that you are not.

Every condition in life exists as the result of agreement. When you feel the emotion of sadness in your body, you might agree that you are indeed sad. With that agreement, you become the sadness. If, instead, you agree that you are only *feeling* the sadness, you won't *be* sad but just *feel* sad. If you also agree that you have a choice to be aware of spirit, you can begin to experience more of the energy of spirit. Then, you could be happy while feeling the sadness. Even though it is the same sadness, you can agree to relate to it differently. What you agree to completely changes your state of being.

When your friend gets angry and says, "I hate you," you can agree, disagree, or ignore it. Agreement brings validation and oneness between the two of you, while disagreement or indifference brings invalidation and division. Agreeing with your friend doesn't mean you want to be hated by her or that it is correct for her to hate you. You are agreeing that that's what she's saying and that's how she feels right now. If you disagree with her in judgment of what she is saying, you might end up saying, "Don't say that" or "That's a bad thing to say." Then there is division between you. You'll find that destructive energy drops off enormously when there is some level of agreement. By saying, "I know you feel that way," you are agreeing with the state of her being, not the goodness or veracity of her statement.

The key in agreement is what to agree with. First, agree with the truth of the situation, even if you disagree with what someone is doing with it. Agree with the truth of the other person's state of being. He is angry, hurt, or afraid. He is spirit being those emotional states. Also agree that what he is doing is what he is doing. Always *agree* with the truth. Never fight *against* the lies.

Prosecuting attorneys were my best teachers in this. Whenever I was involved in some sort of litigation, whether it was against me or I was a witness or representative of an organization, the opposing attorney would always try to engage me by throwing lies as fact. "Isn't it true that you were _____?" or "Didn't you say earlier that _____?"

I learned to return to the truth instead of challenging the lies. "This is what I said," instead of, "I didn't say that." My agreement with the truth always brought out the power of the truth. Whenever I went against the lies, they would swallow up the power and spit it back at me. I would fall divided against myself. When Jesus was tried and stood accused of heinous crimes He did not commit, He always replied, "That is what you say." He would validate who He was and the truth, and never agree with the invalidation.

A few years ago, one of my students, Judith, crashed her car head-on into a car that was passing a truck on a blind curve. She didn't have her seat belt on and later told me, "Michael, when I went headfirst through the windshield and was flying through the air, I asked for you to come and help me. I knew you would heal me and help me be all right."

She continued, "Then I let go, and you showed up in spirit as a bright light and carried me to the ground. I knew I would be okay. At that point, I passed out."

The operating room surgeons discovered that, among her many injuries, the nerves keeping the facial muscles in place had been severed on her right side. As a result, the whole right side of her face had literally fallen down to her jaw and just hung there. She also suffered multiple fractures and contusions, yet was up and about just a couple of days after surgery! When I saw her the following week back in class, she had no visible signs of having survived such a traumatic accident.

How often did Jesus say, "Your *faith* has made you whole"? *I* didn't heal Judith. She *was* healed. I only provided the agreement, validation, and spiritual contact that she needed to have the healing she so desired. I didn't even need to consciously know of her exact condition. When I "felt" her spiritual call for help that night, I put my body down for a nap and went out in spirit to work with her. Our agreement with spirit opened the floodgates of healing. "Whenever two or three are gathered together in my name, I will be there among them" (Matthew 18:20). When there is validation and agreement, the truth, love, and power of spirit have the space to enter our lives.

Imagination as a Tool for Validating Spirit

Your imagination is a powerful tool for developing your ability to validate spirit. Imagination is what brings agreement into reality. Once you agree that you can have a new home, you imagine what that would be like. Once you have imagined your home clearly enough, you can describe it so that a Realtor can help you find it or an architect can design it. Once you agree that you are spirit, you can more clearly imagine the attributes of your spiritual self and begin to manifest them.

The key to working with your imagination rests in the present, the here and now. Most of us have had our imagination severely compromised by such regular invalidation as, "Oh, that's just your imagination. It's not real." Not all the products of your imagination are fantasies, however. Imagination used in the present provides the building blocks for our reality. When you apply your imagination to the past or the future, they are not real. A common example is what we imagine after a brush with an accident: "I could have been killed!" In this case, we are applying our imagination in the past. Or, when we worry that we may not come up with the funds to pay our mortgage in time and say, "We're going to lose our home," we're using our imagination in the future. Both are fantasies and are not real.

When applied in the present, we use imagination to start *real*-izing our spiritual truths. Most of the world-class athletes use their imagination as much as their bodies to perform at their peak. Again and again, I have heard champion pitchers, quarterbacks, golfers, and basketball players talk about using their imagination to "see" the ball go to its intended mark before they actually throw it or hit it. Day after day, world-record swimmers and runners practice visualizing every step of winning the race, sometimes for years before they actually compete in it. It is always in spirit first that a record is broken, and then it can be made real in the flesh.

Just as an athlete can imagine what winning a race looks and feels like, you can imagine what the energy of spirit looks like, feels like, and acts like. It is in our imagination that we begin to communicate with and experience spirit. The Sufis teach us that God builds us through our prayers. Buddha taught us that with our thoughts we make the world. Without the molds cast in our imagination, spirit cannot become manifest in the world. To the limits of our imagination's flight, God can be made real on earth. To the extent that you can imagine it here and now, in neutrality and truth, you can validate the omniscience, omnipotence, and omnipresence of Divinity.

Dare to ask intuitive questions that bring about direct experience of spiritual qualities; then ask for the experience. For example, ask, "What does my spiritual energy feel like? I would like to feel it now." Then, be still and let the awareness of this emerge from within you. Does it feel spacious? Expansive? Light? Pay attention to your inner experience. Imagine that you *can* see spiritual energy in your mind's eye. Imagine what your energy looks like right now. Then relax, close your eyes, and let your imagination "show" you what your energy looks like right now. See, sense, or feel what appears in your mind's eye.

Imagination applied in the present opens the door to spiritual experience (intuition, clairvoyance, telepathy, clairsentience, clairaudience, etc.). Remember what the Maid of Orleans (in George Bernard Shaw's *St. Joan*) said when a skeptic dismissed her visions and voices with, "They only come from your imagination."

"Of course they do," she replied. "That's how the messages of God come to us."

To talk to God, you must be willing to meet Spirit on Its own terms.

Having Your Certainty

When you discover some aspect of the nature of spirit, be willing to have your certainty in your own experience. Know that what you are feeling right now *is* what you are feeling right now; that what you know right now *is* what you know right now. It may be quite different tomorrow, but know with certainty that what you are experiencing is what you are experiencing in this moment.

Having certainty is not the same as wishful thinking or being hardheaded and clinging to a belief you have about something. Nor is having your certainty being right about something. It's about being honest with, trusting, and honoring yourself. Having your certainty means you know what you know within yourself and don't have to prove it to anyone. You may be certain of an answer you get intuitively to a question today and you can be certain of a different answer you get to the same question tomorrow. Truth is absolute in spirit but expresses itself relatively in the physical. The same single truth may be experienced in myriad ways depending on the changing conditions.

Many people have had a certainty of an inner prompting that led them to persevere against all odds and ultimately reach their goal. In fact, it is your certainty in Divinity that brings about your intuitive knowing. When you have certainty, you can face and relinquish the doubts that creep up into your mind instead of invalidating yourself with them.

Once, going sixty miles an hour, I hit a long stretch of black ice on a narrow mountain road in the dead of night. Instantly, I was hurtling down the icy pass in a two-ton derailed carnival teacup, the ghostly-lit world around me spinning wildly out of control. Yet, despite a solid wall of rock to one side and a sheer cliff to the other, I experienced a total certainty within myself that I was going to be all right, regardless of whether I lived or died. The left front tire went over the edge of the road on the cliffside, grabbing some gravel along the way and throwing the momentum of the car back toward the road. The car skidded toward the solid rock wall and came to a grinding halt four inches from it. Certainty doesn't rely on whether it's going to turn out a certain way or not. Certainty knows that you can deal with whatever happens, that this is the way to go regardless of what the consequences might be. Certainty is trusting that you are in good hands. Through having certainty, your intuition leads the way.

Mystical experiences and epiphanies boost our certainty in Divinity. Yet those are special treats for our soul compared to the staple of day-to-day validation we need for our spiritual growth. One of the hallmarks of enlightened souls is their choice to validate spirit no matter what the circumstances. The measure of our spiritual awakening is not in *what* happens in our lives but in how we choose to *respond* to everything that happens. If we are to stay awake, we must choose to validate spirit in ourselves and in others; otherwise, we will fall back asleep through our failure to nourish the soul.

Being Spirit

Whenever you express the qualities of spirit in your life, you empower and establish those very qualities in you. I don't know how many mothers I've met who wanted to be spiritual and have their spiritual growth but thought they were too busy taking care of their families to meditate or have spiritual practices. When asked, "What do you do for a living?" most of them answer, "Nothing. I'm just a mother and a housewife."

I've done a lot in my life but I don't think I can do half as well what "just" a mother and housewife does in taking care of a family. Let me ask you: what is *not* spiritual about birthing a child? Name one aspect of taking care of a family—teaching, nursing, nourishing, coaching, advising, healing, and all the thousand other ways of loving its members—that is *not* spiritual?

Jesus taught that there is no greater love than when one lays down his life for the sake of his friends. Most mothers I know lay down part of their lives for their children. The only thing that makes the life of a mother anything short of a complete life of meditation and prayer is her invalidation of it as a spiritual practice and life. In fact, every life is a spiritual life except that one ignores it and invalidates it. When you restore your certainty in spirit in every aspect of your life and cultivate its qualities and express them in your relationships with others, you will validate the truth, the beauty, and the power of spirit inherent in every life.

One of the difficulties in exploring the nature of spirit and choosing what of spirit to cultivate and empower in yourself is that *everything is spirit*. There's nothing that is *not* spirit, from the most solid objects in the material world to the subtlest changes in energy. Spirit is causing it and being it, and all of it is happening within spirit. Everything is God. There is nothing that is not God. So, the exploration and validation of spirit is not about determining what is spirit and what is not. It's about experiencing the essential nature of spirit and being able to discern what spirit is being at any given point in time. A boulder is spirit being a boulder. Its external characteristics are not the intrinsic qualities of spirit; they are spirit giving of itself to be them.

Validation of spirit means experiencing the spirit that is being whatever it is choosing to be. When you are angry, it is spirit being the anger and spirit experiencing you being angry. All of it is spirit. Yet anger is not an essential quality of spirit. Spirit is being anger for the sake of your ego-self. In fact, your ego is spirit being that. The characteristic of your ego is that it is spirit being an island in the ocean of spirit, and it doesn't realize that both itself and the ocean are part of the whole spirit that is Earth. When looked at from the air, the islands of Hawaii appear to be separate but, if the Pacific Ocean were to disappear one day, we would see that the islands are all connected beneath the surface and further, that they are all part of the planet. The more you begin to identify with the truth of the whole of spirit, the more you can become the master of the ego and teach it to surrender itself to the oneness of being.

You find spirit when you experience the energy-consciousness that is being your thoughts, emotions, physical body, and anything and everything that you ever experience. Validating that essential energy-consciousness, you start to center yourself in it. You become more and more your essential being instead of what it is becoming. Instead of identifying yourself as the anger you feel ("I am angry"), you experience the energy-consciousness of anger flowing through you as its witness. Instead of becoming attached to your identity as a doctor or a patient, you experience and express the qualities and abilities of that role when needed.

For example, when doctors are attached to their identities as medical professionals, they cannot flow smoothly into the role of patients when they themselves need medical care. When a mother is attached to her identification as a mother, she ends up mothering her husband when they are away on a vacation. Or when a man is possessed by his job description as a commanding officer, he comes home to take command of his wife and kids instead of relating to them as husband and father.

Exploring the attributes of spirit is largely a reminding process. When you are with others, you must remind yourself that they, too, are spirit, as are you. Once you have that in your awareness, pay attention to the qualities of their energy and consciousness: *He's so bright. She's so creative. It feels so peaceful here.*

When you can "see" that children have so much potential but are not living up to it, you are experiencing more of the essential qualities of spirit while also realizing that the children are not fully manifesting those qualities in the physical. Start to take notice of the difference between who or how people *are* and what or how they are being at this time.

We are always in transition from being (spirit) to becoming (something/someone) to being again. When we are invalidated, we divert our attention, close our mind, and isolate ourselves from spirit. We become our limiting thoughts and feelings instead. Validation, however, inspires us to greater awareness of spirit. It restores us to our essential, spiritual self and reminds us that we are not the divisive perceptions competing in our mind. Our spiritual growth is the wisdom-harvesting journey home, from the world of ignorance and limitations, back to our true nature.

Nourishing the Soul

From our soul perspective, it is our state of being that needs to be addressed first regardless of what we face in the world. All that we can change in the world is the condition in which we exist in relation to it. When we do change where we are with the world, the world then changes relative to our condition. And every condition is a consequence of our relationship to spirit. Our fundamental relationship is with our self and the Divinity that gives us life. And when we look into the depths of our being, we find that we are one. We cradle within our hearts and souls the same Divine Oneness we may call by different names. And we wear different clothes of personality to express our individual and unique relationships to this one sacred and eternal life.

We are all like pregnant mothers carrying an unborn life within the womb of our being. To ensure the health and development of that inner life, we must first take care of our own well-being. For it is only through feeding herself that the mother can nourish and grow the child within her. With what we nourish our soul and by the manner in which we do so, we grow the seed of divine purpose within us into maturity. And that spiritual nourishment is validation.

EIGHT

FROM RESISTANCE TO WILLINGNESS

In the end, resistance is futile; it merely frustrates our fulfillment. The more we resist, the more we divide our power and separate from our soul purpose. If we continue in resistance, we end up in isolation and pain. Only through our willingness can we begin to heal the schisms within us and fulfill our spiritual selves.

At first, it may seem that resistance enables you to stave off your enemies and survive, even win. If you are unable to resist, you may consider yourself weak because we all know that "heroes fight to the death." Furthermore, many of us were taught to resist evil and temptation and we fear that, without resistance, they will swallow us up. After all, aren't we told we get sick because our "resistance is low"? On the surface, it sure looks like resisting is the right thing to do; we're being strong and defending our own interests against evil.

Yet, if you look carefully, you'll find that you never succeed in fighting *against* something; it's always your willingness to do whatever it takes *for* your purpose that brings about its fulfillment. Every time I watched basketball legend Michael Jordan play, I saw him giving his best to fulfill his purpose on that court instead of resisting failure or fearing possible negative outcomes. I remember hearing Michael's secret for his dazzling success after he shot one of his game-flipping last-second baskets. In a post-game interview, he explained that whenever he aimed for the basket, he never worried about whether he was going to make it or not; he just focused on doing everything he knew to take the best possible shot.

Any time you resist what appears to obstruct what you want to be, do, or have, you are courting failure. This is because, in resistance, you hold back from your purpose instead of moving forward, and you also give away your power to the obstacle, whether it's real or perceived. Resistance never *accomplishes* anything but only *impedes*. And your spiritual path is more like a flowing river than a static road. For you to be on your path, you must flow with it; yet, all too often, when we can't see what's around the bend of that river, we become frightened and try to stop our flow. In resistance, the only thing we end up stopping is the inevitable—our fulfillment.

In order to fulfill our soul purpose, we must relinquish the resistance we hold within ourselves and choose willingness instead. Our fulfillment depends on our willingness to look at the truth, to relinquish the restrictive conditions on our love, and to express and act upon that truth with that love. Resistance to discovering the truth about something is called *denial*. Resistance to letting go of the conditions we place on our loving is called *not forgiving*. And resistance to expressing and acting lovingly upon our truth is called *lacking courage*.

Saying that you need to let go of your resistance can be like telling you to *not* think of a pink elephant. Of course, once you put your attention on resistance, you might find yourself in a tug-of-war with it unless you understand what resistance is and where it comes from.

So who or what in you is really resisting?

Resistance and Ego

Resistance begins with possession: it's *mine*. The moment you decide to possess something, you begin to hold on to it. It could be anything: money, a job, a relationship, your image, or your beliefs. When you hold on to what you believe is yours, you begin to resist anything that threatens your continued possession of it. The irony of this is that your possession is illusory. Anything you *can* hold on to has a beginning and an end so, sooner or later, you'll lose it anyway. And anything you *can't* hold on to is eternal and you'll never lose it. From the perspective of fulfilling your soul purpose, anything you can possess is not worth holding on to; in fact, continuing to hold on to it will compromise your fulfillment. So, trying to possess something is an exercise in futility. Of course, relinquishing our possessions is easier said than done. And what makes it so difficult for us to let go is that which has the death grip on our possessions—the ego.

Webster's Dictionary defines the ego as: "The self, especially as contrasted with another self or the world."

Thus, ego is the "I" that distinguishes itself from every "other," whether a person, thing, idea, place, or action. When we observe ourselves or others speak of "I " this or "I" that, it seems so natural and obvious that we know of what or whom we are speaking. Yet do we really?

In truth, the "I" for most people is in enormous confusion and is highly inconsistent. The ego is a master at convincing its self and other egos that it is *the* self and is in control of its life, which is why it panics when confronted with something it can't control. Truth threatens the ego with extinction and the ego keeps trying to cover itself in order to survive.

My experience of the ego in its purest essence is a fundamental, self-identifying intelligence of consciousness. When the human soul was formed as a spark of God, this ego within the soul became a "self-consciousness," separate from the whole of consciousness. When we complete our purpose of shaping this ego with wisdom so that it can integrate with the oneness of being, it becomes whole and knows its self to be the self of the oneness. As Jesus said, "I am in the Father and the Father is in me."

I came to understand the formation of the ego through an extraordinary experience. Early one morning, I was in meditation in the bathroom of a hotel room in which Raphaelle and I were staying. She was still asleep. Once I entered into my meditative state, energy exploded like a thundering launch of a rocket straight up my spine. I found myself both inside my body feeling, as well as outside of it, looking in at the blaze of golden light burning through each of the chakras. Each of the energy centers blossomed into brilliant flowers of light and the volcanic energy erupted through an "opening" at the top of my head. I heard and felt a thunderous roar throughout my entire being. So powerful were the reverberations that my knees buckled and my whole body quaked. To steady myself, I grabbed on to the edge of the sink.

Then, an infinite and eternal spaciousness came over me, limitless peace in an ecstatic sea of energy-consciousness. "I" no longer existed; time, distance, identity, needs to be fulfilled, memory, and comparison all disappeared. Nothing existed, yet all was: limitless energy, consciousness, and being. There was no separate "I" to experience it, much less to describe it. Now, the only way I can describe it is as if "I" had experienced this. (Just giving words to this experience has taken me eight years.)

Since that experience, I have been able to gradually assimilate the profound learning I received from it. First, having been in that space of pure consciousness, energy, and being, in which there was no experience of a separate self-consciousness, I now realize why the original soul-ego in its self-consciousness becomes separated from Unity and doesn't know it. In that expanse of consciousness, there is no time or space and therefore no memory function. Without the ability to "remember" as the spark of consciousness "spins off" in its ecstasy of existence, it "wakes up" to its self without a memory of ever having been part of anything else. From its inception, it begins to explore its self and see everything else as "other."

During this "phase" of the experience, there was eternal consciousness, but I didn't exist as an individual consciousness, which meant that "I" retained no memory of a separate prior existence until "I" returned to my body later. Yet I as spirit had the continuity of consciousness underlying the whole experience from beginning to end, including the awareness that the ego had ceased to exist.

Through this portion of the experience, I realized that, should the human soul merge with the Absolute without completing the building of its immortal body of wisdom, it would be reabsorbed and merely cease to be. We incarnate into a physical form made by nature so that we ourselves can learn to materialize that form in spirit. Without building our immortal body of light with which to return to God, we cannot fulfill our destiny of total freedom. In a sense, we will dissolve back into being an unconscious oneness instead of evolving into a fully conscious creator. To do this, we must have memory; and to build a memory function, we must have time, space, and sense perception. In other words, we have to incarnate into the physical world.

Meanwhile, in the hotel room, my crashing and banging about the bathroom had awakened Raphaelle. As I'd catapulted out of my body, it had collapsed onto the floor, its head crashing against the sink and the door on the way down. Naturally, Raphaelle was concerned about my well-being and called out to check if I was all right. In the consciousness that "I" dissolved into during this part, there were no egos, so when the reverberations of Raphaelle's voice reached this consciousness through my unconscious body, it translated as a kind of a blip in the sea of bliss, a bubble emerging in some cosmic primordial lake, with her voice producing concentric ripples of energy radiating outward. As soon as that blip emerged, a sense began of over "here" in relationship to the blip over "there." The first inkling of a separate ego was forming as consciousness began to polarize.

This was not in any way a clear-cut definition of "you" and "I." It was a general sense of an amorphous congealing of "over there" and "over here." As the intensity of the ripples increased, the polarizing increased. Brilliant and colorful energy waves bounced back and forth between the two gatherings of consciousness within the whole of consciousness. The open spaciousness was closing in or, more accurately, a portion of consciousness was spinning itself out of the open sea by polarizing into a "self" in response to a sense of "other." Then came the blackness. It came at once.

The blackness did not render the wholeness of consciousness unconscious, but rather the turning of the ego consciousness upon its "self" resulted in the separation of its consciousness from the whole. "My" awareness stayed with the whole of consciousness while "it" observed the separating ego-self. The separate "self" consciousness became occupied with the blackness, and the awareness of the limitless spaciousness dissolved. In the original formation of the ego, the awareness of this doesn't continue through the blackout. This is where the ego "awakens" to its self with a sort of amnesia as to its divine heritage and identity. *This polarizing is the first stage of the formation of the separate ego.*

What had been the general sense of "over here" now began to have its "own" experiences. The ego now regarded the ripples in the sea of consciousness as "the other" and separate from its self. Instead of ripples, the ego, now being more contained, began to feel them as larger "waves," as a kind of energy pressure on it. These "waves," of course, were the vibrations from Raphaelle's voice calling to my ego. The ego at this stage of formation "feels," to confirm the reality of its existence. The more it can feel the "other," the more it becomes convinced of its own independent existence. *This is the second stage of ego formation.*

Then, the ego started moving away from the waves, its attention drawn toward a play of lights. Fascinated by the mirage, it acted like a cat mesmerized by the sunlight dancing on the floor, twinkling reflections off a crystal chandelier. The ego did not perceive exact shapes in this play of light but edges were definitely forming. Now, the sense was not only of "other" and "self" but also of a sense of increasing distinctions amongst all the "others." This "other" became more different than that "other." At this point, the ego started to reach out more toward what was attractive to it, withdraw from what it didn't like, and ignore everything else.

Once the ego confirms the reality of its "separate" existence, it desires to explore and relate more intimately to the qualities of "the other." It begins to develop an energy distribution system to determine how to react (what kind of energy to produce) to what it feels. If the energy is attractive, ego pulls on it. When it feels threatened, ego pushes it away. If it feels indifferent, ego ignores it. *This is the third stage in the developing ego.*

The play of lights that caught the ego's attention became a shiny "silvery-ness" against the backdrop of "darker." This mass of energy patterns was attractive to it. At this point, the ego felt incomplete; it didn't have the feeling of control. Up to this stage, its interactions had been simple energy reactions, but it needed more distinct control to establish its sense of security in its ignorance and the world of form.

In general, in order to attain this control, when the ego reaches this stage, it begins to label the seemingly different patterns of energies. Labeling them gives the ego a kind of intellectual control over them. The ego labels things according to its energy reactions of attraction, repulsion, or indifference. If what it feels is attractive, the ego labels it as "desirable." When something repulses the ego, it categorizes that as "undesirable." If it feels neither, it categorizes that under "ignore."

Next, the ego begins to create a sense of order within its ignorance. In this experience, the "shininess" was "interesting," and the ego began searching for associations. This search led the ego back into the memory banks of the now unconscious body-mind. It was trying to associate this new "thing" with something it had already experienced to give it a more identifiable and "controllable" reality. It succeeded in finding a picture that looked just like this thing. The picture itself did not have a concept-label but was associated with another picture that did: the underneath of a bathroom hand basin. The silvery thing was the plumbing. Once the ego associated the thing with the plumbing and got a name for it, a rush of associations followed until the ego had totally categorized this thing as being the underside of a bathroom sink and all the surrounding landscape of the bathroom. Now, the ego had created a whole environment of things to relate to. At that point, the ego kicked into a more logical, reasoning mode for the first time, as well as a solid identification with "I." Before then, there was a sense of "selfness" but not a distinct, solid-feeling "I." (Through the genius of its intrinsic intelligence, the ego names all that it holds on to as "mine" and the holder as "I.") *This is the fourth stage in the "solidification" of the ego and the world of form it relates to.*

Now, it was clearly "I" who was noticing the underside of a bathroom sink. With reasoning kicking in, the ego asked what was wrong with this picture? If "I" am looking at the underside of a sink, where am I? For the first time, there was judgment on its part. As soon as that happened, "I" became aware of "my" body. Once the ego recognized the body, it associated with "my" body and asked, "What am I doing on the floor of this bathroom?"

"I" got up (body and all) and became more oriented. (It is much more suitable for ego survival to be standing in the bathroom than to be sprawled out on the floor.)

Then the energy waves in the background that kept bouncing into "me" became sound vibrations and then, words. The ego recognized them as Raphaelle calling out to "me." Now, the ego recognized that she was calling out with concern, "Michael, what's going on in there? Are you all right?"

By then, Raphaelle had asked me a few times and was walking toward the bathroom. The ego felt the worry in Raphaelle's communication. "Something's wrong" acknowledged that there was a threat to its survival, and that was "not good" for the ego; it has to survive. So, the ego selected "I'm fine" as the response. That was much better for the ego. "I'm fine" is pro-survival. The ego acts only for itself. The body could be dying but the ego will ensure its own survival first.

Up to this phase of our ego development, things were fairly straightforward. Ego felt, reacted, categorized, and evaluated its existence according to its simple reactions: *I'll stay here, it feels good; I'll take that, it's nice; I'll chase that away, it scares me.* But as the ego continued to intellectualize energy into concepts, its associative memory was increasing. It began to categorize the same "things" differently according to its changing experiences of them. (The once "good" fire that warmed it up could easily turn into a "bad" thing that burned it. As this happens repeatedly, the ego becomes claustrophobic in its own fortress that can no longer protect it. Its psychic pain and confusion grow as conflicting thoughts and feelings collide with one another within the ego, akin to a baby desperately seeking the security of its mother's love while feeling that she is out to destroy it. The ego wants out of this mess, but it has carefully barricaded itself in.)

In a panic, the ego accesses its creative imagination and begins to paste a variety of wallpaper on the existing bare and threatening walls.

Much like a child pulling up the covers over his head to make the monsters go away, the ego begins to create images of meaning and value, and projects them onto the futility of the existence in which it's trapped. The ego makes existence a world of its arbitrary, self-serving opinions and judgments. Thus, our ego-self has fully developed and imprisoned itself in the isolated existence of its own fanciful projections. *This is the fifth stage of the ego formation.*

After "I" had convinced myself that everything was just fine with "me," Raphaelle asked about all the banging around in the bathroom. *What banging around?* I thought to myself. That's when I noticed all the blood on the floor of the bathroom. *What's blood doing here?* I wondered. Then it hit me. It was "my" blood. Where was "I" bleeding from? I looked around my body and finally I felt my head. My hand was covered in something warm, sticky, and red. BLOOD. *My* blood.

A rush of association began in my mind. My blood → I'm hurt → that's bad → I could die → I could be crippled → I won't be the same → that's bad → I won't be able to do what I need to do → I'll fail → that's really bad → I don't want to fail → I'm scared → I could die → I'm hurt → I need help → tell Raphaelle.

By then, I had stepped out of the bathroom, my body shaking. I was above my body observing the event. Raphaelle rushed over to inspect my head and she found that I wouldn't need any stitches. I, as spirit, was observing this other part of me, the ego-self, going into doubt. "Maybe 'I' need stitches," it was saying to Raphaelle. Even after seeking help, "I," my ego-self, was still trying to take control.

Our projections themselves have a method to their madness. Underlying this method, of course, is the self-preserving impulse of the ego. In order to escape from its psychic pain of chaos, entrapment, helplessness, isolation, and loneliness, our ego begins to imagine a "better" existence for ourselves. At first, we imagine all that would feel good to be, to do, and to have. We create a virtual paradise in our mind and project it on the screen of our world: *This is a good war because it's helping our people. Because I won the race, I am the best person. You should reward me because I did it all for you. I'm so glad to finally know what is wrong with me.*

But once such treasures are imagined and projected, we swell with pride while jealously guarding them against those who would try to take them away from us. For example, if we make money to cover our pain from past poverty, we hoard our savings. Whenever we collect trophies and credentials to escape the pain of our perceived worthlessness, we proudly display our victories and fend off against failures. We cling fiercely to our dreams lest we awaken to the reality of our isolation, loneliness, and fear. Soon, however, the stress of constantly fighting to maintain our possessions wears us down. We begin to seek the comfort of complacency and unthinking routines: *Don't bother me, I'm just doing my job. I'm tired of fighting. I don't want any more surprises. I just want to be a regular Joe.*

After a time, however, we become painfully bored with such a mundane existence. Our inherent creativity has no room for expression. To ease our pain of boredom, we numb and dumb ourselves into further denial of our being. But anesthesia by nature is temporary. Through the haze of our amnesia, we remember the "good ol' days." We begin to long for the better times of yore. Yet, try as we may, we crash against the barricades that we have erected in our mind to escape our isolation. We cannot truly return to the paradise of our illusory past: *Boy, you should've seen me when I was a star pitcher in high school. Did you know I used to be a beauty queen? At the height of my career, no one could match my sales record. When we were first married, every day was a honeymoon. I used to be a saint in a past life.*

We know we cannot retreat to our past. Nor does the future hold any more strategies for us to escape our fundamental pain. Nothing seems to work anymore. We begin to lose faith in everything we have believed in. An all-pervading doubt sets in and we feel utterly betrayed and disillusioned. We hate ourselves for being in this condition. We can no longer continue this way. For the first time, we truly seek a fundamental change in our existence. However reluctantly at first, we begin to seek a source greater than our separate and imprisoned consciousness. With this, our ego-self begins its long, and at times desperately lonely, ascent to Spirit.

Some spiritual seekers misconstrue the process of emptying out the ego of all of its "holdings" as killing or annihilating the ego. As survival is the first order of business in all of nature so, too, the ego will try to survive first at all costs. If you threaten the ego, you will not succeed in fulfilling your soul purpose. If you starve it indiscriminately, you will not succeed. You, the soul, need your ego's cooperation. The problem is not in *having* an ego—you would not be able to fulfill yourself without it—but in how you *relate* to it on your spiritual path.

Until the ego becomes your friend and ally, it is like a child raised on junk food. You cannot force your ego to eat healthily overnight. The ultimate purpose of your ego is to be your vehicle to your freedom and God. And you need to wean it off a diet of junk food, fast it to purge the toxins, and nourish it with real "soul food." Remember, the ego is the self-identifying intelligence of your consciousness. Until you feed it correctly with wisdom born of experience, it cannot identify with Spirit. The more you learn to act as your spiritual self instead of empowering the fixations of the ego, the more you help empty out the ego and reshape it into your transport to true spiritual freedom.

Resistance to Change

All the resistance you ever encounter, whether in yourself or in another person, is the ego's resistance to change. The difficulty that most of us experience in the process of facing our physical death is nothing more than the challenge of managing the ego-self's resistance to letting go of the protective possessions that keep it real. The often heart-wrenching pain of enduring the death of a loved one is not about the loved one *per se*, as much as it is about encountering the death of our own ego-self in the process. Your ego-self cannot avoid death when someone in whom you have invested your time, energy, love, and awareness dies.

To the degree that your ego-identity depended on that person being physically around, your ego-self will die to that degree.

One of the most difficult of all losses for a human being to bear is the loss of a child. Let's say that a mother loses her child. If her ego-self was 90 percent identified with being that child's mother and 10 percent with being a woman, a daughter, a wife, and PTA chairwoman, she may not make it. With 90 percent of her identity stripped away, she may fall ill and die herself, or spend a long time in a zombie-like existence. If her ego-self was only 10 percent identified with being that child's mother, the initial pain would not be any less perhaps, but she would move on much more readily.

The degree of identification with a role has nothing to do with the degree of love, caring, or competence. In fact, the less ego-identified one is, the more capable one is of giving unconditionally. All the pain of loss and change is the pain the ego endures in its death throes of acceptance and surrender to being. There is no death for spirit, only for the ego. Even what we call our physical death is not truly the death of our physical body, for it is part of nature and merely returns to the earth and elements. The death we experience is the death of the ego identifying with the body. Some souls have transcended their ego's identification with their physical body to the extent that they can die with grace and in peace. When the ego identifies strongly with the mind, then even while the person is living, the ego may experience a deathblow if the mind ceases to function within the ego's comfort zone.

The resurrecting of our spiritual self out of the tyranny of the ego-politic is the journey from denial to willingness. And it is essentially the same as the process of dying, for it is the process of letting go of illusions. The road from denial to willingness is the path we all take repeatedly to our death. With practice and experience, we just get better at it. Sometimes we die a little and, at other times, we die in a big way. Dying is the process of change and growth, of learning and healing. What we call the death of our physical body is only the biggest death in *this* world. For the soul, there are further deaths to experience, which is why we return to our earthly existence to practice dying some more.

Earth is the finest school of higher education and its superintendent is the Grim Reaper! To graduate, you must die with flying colors. (In her book, *Graceful Exits: How Great Beings Die*, Sushila Blackman quoted Swami Muktananda as saying, "If one wants to die peacefully, one must begin helping oneself long before one's time to die has come.")

People practice complaining, gossiping, typing, using their computers, playing the violin, and improving their golf game far more than their dying. Yet only those who practice their dying can hope to master their art, craft, sport, or any other practice in the world. If we do not learn to relinquish our resistance to change and develop our willingness to learn and grow, we cannot fulfill our destiny of freedom.

Whether it is the process of change, of learning and growth, of healing, or of dying, our ego-self first moves through the same basic resistances. Only the intensity varies according to the perceived gravity of the situation. You may hit a plateau in learning to play the piano, or get into a batting slump, or are confronted with a poor prognosis for your health. What is your initial reaction? Consciously or unconsciously, you resist with denial: *The piano isn't working the way it used to. No, I'm fine; I'll get over it. I just need to practice a little harder, that's all. There must be some mistake; I feel healthier than ever.* In denial, you continue to do more of what you've always done, even if it clearly isn't working.

When you can no longer continue to imagine the reality of death away, you move into the resistance of anger, striking out at others. You blame everything and everyone, including yourself. When your tantrums don't give you anything you really want, in your mounting desperation, you begin a garage sale of your possessions: *I'll give you my special treasure if you'll only help me out of this mess.* You may offer a great reward to anyone who could cure you. You may promise to believe in God if He will but give you a miracle. Of course, it never works. You are in your ego-self's resistance and not in a space of the willingness of your spiritual self.

If you resist your condition further, your psychic pain increases. You retreat into an intellectual shell in an attempt to protect yourself from feeling the pain. You think: *I'm special. I'm better than the others (more educated, more refined, more enlightened). Those rules may apply to them, but they don't apply to me.* Nothing is working. You lose faith in everything and everyone. You feel betrayed. You are inundated with doubt: *Maybe I'm not even meant to do this. What was I thinking anyway? I don't have what it takes. This is hopeless and everyone is stupid for thinking they could help me.*

Finally, when nothing seems to work, you abandon all hope, all solutions, all negotiations, and all rationalizations. You can't fight any longer; there is no meaning to life and nothing matters anymore. You resign to defeat: *Just take me out. I don't care; let me die. Let's get it over with quickly.* You close your eyes and wait for the blow.

In that moment, you move from resignation to acceptance, from resistance to surrendering to the inevitable. *Anything is better than where I am.* You turn within from your outer ego-self consciousness toward your spiritual self-consciousness. Instead of resisting and building up illusions against your fears, you choose willingly to experience *what is.* You realize that most of the pain was your fear and resistance to what might be instead of what is. Your ego mind empties out its resistance. It is now open to new awareness. You begin to observe the workings of your mind, and understanding pours in. Past beliefs about your identity become visible and begin to dissolve. You start experiencing a greater awareness of who you are. This is the beginning of change, an awakening to spirit, true learning, and healing. You are no longer being the ego rearranging the furniture and putting new wallpaper over the old paint. You have stepped into a new and larger house—that of your spiritual self.

Your awareness is the pendulum that swings to and fro between the outer and inner worlds. And your attention is what directs it to the vantage point from which you experience life. Sometimes we perch ourselves higher up on our spiritual swing and perceive our world and life from a more expansive awareness. At other times, we experience life from the low point of our swing and create a narrow view of the world and our relationship to it. The process of awakening ourselves is the process of choosing more and more the vantage point of Spirit, centering our awareness in our true nature and extricating our consciousness and energy from the myopic perceptions and isolation of our ego-self.

Willingness

It is said that God loves a cheerful giver. And where there is willingness, there is a way. Our ability to respond freely as a spiritual being to anyone or anything in the world is born out of our willingness. It is our willingness that directs power. When we choose to be willing, power moves to our being. When we are in resistance, we give our power away to the very object of our resistance. It is not God who kicks us out of His grace; it is *we* who drop out of the oneness, abundance, and flow of Life when we resist anything. In resistance and reluctance, we begrudge the divine gifts that are our birthright.

Early in life, as we start to identify with and give our power to the ego-self, we learn to resist. Notice how willing small children are to explore, play, love, and laugh. If they don't learn to make space for their spiritual self, that willingness will give way to much resistance. Until we reach our early teens, the reasoning self of our soul has not fully developed. The associative, feeling self of our soul dominates the navigation of our life until then. It comes as no surprise then, that overnight, with the onset of teenhood, we "figure it all out." *Wait just a minute*, we declare. *I've been duped all this time! I've been wagging my tail for biscuits and licking your face even if you kicked me. Well, I'm not going to do that anymore!*

During the time when the feeling aspect was mainly in charge in the body, each time you were in pain-survival and felt that your parents or caretakers were not there to tend to your needs, the experience was filed in your associative mind as a kind of abandonment. "You're on your own. If you don't take care of yourself, you'll die."

Since the reasoning self was not yet fully in operation, the feeling self looks for associations for help. In computer terms, it was "garbage in, garbage out." *Last time I got sick, I got attention and love, and had my needs met, so I'll get sick again.* Or, *Last time I broke something valuable, I finally got noticed.* Again, this is not a conscious reasoning strategy. It is a subconscious, associative process. So the child doesn't sit there figuring out intellectually how to break something. It's just a subconscious "accident" waiting to happen.

Furthermore, on this associative level, all caretakers are put in the same file: parents, babysitters, relatives, police, doctors, or God. Unless there is a separate file on any of them with substantially different and more positive evidence to the contrary, if your file has an abundance of abandonment verdicts against your parents, it establishes that no one is there to take care of you. *God is never around when you need Him.*

When we feel abandoned, we curl up in fear. We retreat into a shell of resistance to brace ourselves against the threats of the world, feeling helpless. If you were identifying with the ego, you would feel the resistance as *you* protecting yourself against *them.* Again, when we resist anything, we surrender the awesome power of our being to the very thing we are resisting. And as spirit, we become what we resist. If you keep hating and resisting a particular person, eventually you will become just like what you hate most about him. In this manner, the once idealistic cop may end up more corrupt than the criminals he catches; the righteous minister may end up committing many sins; the rebellious hippie ends up going corporate; and the atheist becomes a believer.

The feeling self either associates with the spiritual self or "other." If it associates with other, it looks for things, people, and situations outside itself for its validation and reality. It depends on the outer world and is disempowered. If it associates with the inner self, it depends on a higher aspect of the soul for leadership. It empowers the inner self. Once the feeling self attains a degree of unity, turning inward to spirit, it accepts the guidance of the reasoning self. It becomes willing.

When you are in resistance, the reasoning aspect and the feeling aspect of your soul split up. The feeling self goes off on its own while the reasoning self becomes aloof. It begins to justify and rationalize the actions and feelings of the lower self as separate from itself. "I didn't mean to do it, it just happened. I couldn't help myself," "I *meant* to do it. I know it's not right, but I just felt like doing it," or "I had to. There was no other way."

Willingness begins to build the bridge between these two parts of the soul in the body. The heart and the mind must work together. Until the feeling self begins to get out of resistance, the reasoning self cannot work with it. Until then, the body runs on feelings, untempered by reason or intuitive knowing. Once there is a feeling of willingness, the reasoning self can influence and guide the actions of the feeling body. They begin to work more and more together.

When you like something, you become willing to be with it. As oneness gets stronger, resistance gets weaker. When you are willing, you are giving to oneness. To develop willingness, at first you don't have to be willing about anything in particular. You just have to choose to be willing. If you examine your reluctance, it is specific. You are not reluctant about everything, but just about certain things. You may be reluctant to forgive the person who was mean to you or took something away from you. For the moment, that's all right. But just because you're reluctant to forgive *that* particular person, you may not be reluctant to forgive someone else or reluctant to spend time with your best friend. In fact, you might just be perfectly willing to do that. You may be quite willing to go see a movie or read a good book, watch TV or call your girlfriend. You may be willing to go for a swim or a vacation. You may be reluctant to go to work but willing to go for a leisurely walk. Willingness is intrinsic to spirit but whether or not you feel it in the body is a consequence of your state of mind. The conscious mind may be willing, but the subconscious may be reluctant. And the subconscious is the doorway to the body and its reactionary emotions. This is where you need to use your intuitive mind.

When you discover you have resistance to something, step back from that resistance. Redirect your attention away from what you are resisting and put it on something for which you have willingness. Is there something else that you are willing to do, be, or have that can help you toward your goal? Ask your spiritual self intuitively what you would like, what would be more beneficial. Defuse the amount of energy you are putting into the resistance first. If you don't add more fuel to the fire, it will naturally get smaller.

For example, you may be resisting talking to someone about a disagreement, but you may be willing to write about it to yourself or a friend. When you choose to do that, you're not running away from what you need to do. You're still moving in the right direction but are taking your energy out of resisting and putting it into willingness. Willingness always paves the way for responsibility. By the time you pour your heart out on paper, you'll find that not only did you give yourself the space to express what was in you, but you began to separate what is truth and what was just a bunch of reactions inside of you. Then, you start to gain more understanding of the situation as well as where you are with it. It's even better than counting to ten.

Willingness is an energy-feeling of openness, of receptivity to movement. Resistance, on the other hand, is an energy-feeling of shutting out, of denying change. To transform your resistance into willingness, you must change your energy space. When you concentrate your attention on the object of your resistance, you will generate more resistance energy. When you put your attention on willingness for anything, you start to create within yourself an open, more receptive energy space. Even if you merely stop for a moment in your hectic day to savor the fragrance of a rose, your outlook changes and you feel more open. Remember that when you validate *any* aspect of spirit, your state of being changes for the better. If you make a way for it, you will find the willingness.

Know that, when you choose willingness, resistance is always of the ego-self. Be willing to look beyond the ego-self at the true spirit that you are. When dealing with someone else's ego resistance, be aware of it and how your ego-self is reacting to it, but also look beyond at that person's true spirit. All you need is one lamp to light up the whole room. In case the other person forgot to turn on his or hers, turn yours on so both of you can move more toward the spirit within. When you put more resistance toward someone's ego-self, you give it more power; if you turn your awareness toward her spiritual self and say "hello" to it, she will start to heal. (The exercises in the Your Spiritual Toolkit section later in the book offer more direct ways of stepping out of your ego resistance.)

A Zen master once said, "If you want enlightenment as much as a drowning person wants air, you would have it instantly." This seemingly simple statement contains the secret to our awakening from the resistance of our ego-self into the willingness of our spiritual self. When we are drowning, we are certain of only one thing: that we need to breathe if we are to live. If a wake-up call summons us, it means that we are in the midst of drowning, whether in the middle of the ocean, in an abusive relationship, in self-pity, in despair, or in denial of some aspect of our true being. And our spiritual growth always begins at the threshold of death, for it is the soul's journey through dying into eternal life. Not one human soul receives immunity from this challenge. Yet hidden at first beyond the wall of our illusory projections await the loving arms of Spirit, always reaching out toward you in support.

We are never alone in our challenging journey back to wholeness. We are always loved and cared for by Spirit. Yet how does this support of Spirit feel? Imagine the taste of freedom after escaping the horrors of a cruel and unjust imprisonment. Imagine also that your family and friends are still incarcerated. Wouldn't you want to do everything in your power to set them all free? God's love is like that, only greater, for that love is boundless. Spirit continually summons us to liberate ourselves from the prison of our illusions. And when one aspect of Spirit is freed, it sends for the others still behind bars, whether the imprisoned are members of humanity or aspects within one individual soul. The light always seeks out and fills the darkness. And we repeat this cycle of awakening until we are truly whole and free.

NINE

GROWING NEUTRALITY

With willingness, you chose spiritual growth over the ego's resistance to change. Now, with neutrality, you can disengage from the gears of resistance such as judgment and expectation, competition and effort, and the turmoil of the emotions that drive them. The longer you remain in their clutches, the more you turn your back on your soul. Choosing to be neutral, on the other hand, opens the windows to your inner divinity and purpose.

A sanctuary for the soul, neutrality already exists within you. When you first find it, it may seem like a mere whisper in a thunderstorm. It's easy to miss it in the cacophony of expectations and demands pulling on you. Yet, no matter how intense it may get, each of us has an oasis of neutrality always within reach. Nothing can destroy that. In fact, you can probably recall a time when you were caught in a maelstrom of terror, rage, or depression, yet there was that sliver of awareness somewhere in the midst of it silently observing it all. It was that detached awareness of "This isn't who I am. What am I doing this for?"

That eye in the center of the hurricane was the neutrality of spirit that never engaged in the madness of the ego. And you can always seek refuge in it no matter how bad the situation seems.

But amidst an emotional torrent, it's difficult to find a dry spot, so we must cultivate our neutrality and grow it daily. From a mere whisper, with daily practice we need to grow it into a profound silence that cannot be missed. Then, when you do find yourself in a deluge, you'll be able to swim to safety.

Growing our neutrality means reclaiming it. Neutrality is the natural state of our being, but what did we do with it? We gave it away. Every time we invested our energy in reaction, we gave away some of our inherent neutrality. That's how neutrality became so small within us. By choosing to stop fueling judgments, expectations, competition, and effort, and your emotional reactions that run them, you start growing your neutrality back.

Stop Projecting

In the last chapter, we outlined the stages of ego formation, and we reclaim our neutrality in the reverse order of that. Energetically, the ego forms as layers of defensive protection around its pain of isolation, much like the layers of nacre that the oyster secretes around the pain-causing grit to create the beautiful pearl. The bigger the pain, the more layers of protection and the "bigger" the ego. Like the beautiful pearl, the ego's pain is in the center and the luster is on the outside. So when we encounter the ego from the outside, we are hit with "I'm the best," "I'm the most beautiful," "I'm the most important," or "I'm the baddest and the meanest" on the one hand and "I'm the most hopeless," "I'm the worst person in the world" on the other. On the surface of the ego-pearl, we find the illusory luster of comparison, competition, and effort.

The last step in the ego's formation was it projecting its values on the world in order to secure the illusion of its own reality and worth. When we live as our ego, we project expectation, judgment, and blame onto others. We are in competition and effort. So the first step in growing our neutrality is to reverse that impulse of projecting out. We must bring the focus of our attention away from others as "cause" and back into our inner being and purpose.

Now, projecting blame onto others can mean blaming "yourself," as well. When you are thinking, *It's all my stupid fault. How could I have done such a horrible thing? I'm so bad,* then you have split "yourself" up into two: the "you" that is blaming and the "you" that is the target of your blame. There is no difference in this dynamic as you are blaming "someone else." You're still projecting your blame "out there" to your image of "I-me-myself." Instead of your image of "someone else" doing it to you, it's your image of "I-me-myself" doing it to you.

Some of the most common challenges to spiritual growth and fulfillment are the myriad variations of "the stupid jerk who cut me off on the freeway." "What an asshole!" you curse as you glare at the rear of his speeding car. A parade of torturous things you could do to him marches across your mind. You feel quite justified. "After all, the jerk could've killed me," you protest. Well, perhaps.

Unless you're a double-A-type personality, this particular scenario might not irk your ire, but what if that "jerk" is your husband who cuts you off from pursuing your spiritual interests, your wife who cuts you off from your career dreams, your parents who cut you out of their will, a boss who cuts you from the payroll, or a friend who cuts you off, period? Over and over, I hear people struggling, saying, "I'm doing everything I can to save my marriage / fix my business / harmonize my family, or something equally important to them, *but someone else won't cooperate.* They keep saying, "If only (the other person) would (do, be, or have something to fulfill my expectations), then I would be happy. Is that too much to ask?"

It's not about how much you ask for; it's about whom you're asking. By keeping your focus on the other person (even if it's the "bad-you"), you invest more of your energy into the very thing that's not giving you what you want. You need to bring the focus of your questions back to yourself and your purpose. What do *you* want to fulfill in *yourself* in this situation? What is it in *you* that insists that the other person (or the "bad-you") has to change? What threatens *you* about where the other person is? What are you afraid will happen (or not happen) to you if the other person doesn't conform to your expectation-need?

Even before you get any answers to your questions, you'll find that just by asking questions that bring your focus back on you, you will reclaim much more of your power from the other person and the situation. In this way, you disengage from the ego's insistence on projecting onto someone else. But just because you disengage from the ego's projection doesn't mean that the ego is going to stop trying to project. You must let that be. Don't feed it, or you'll fall back into its pull. Keep bringing your attention back to yourself. Ask questions that give you back your power.

If you find yourself "stuck in a rut," you are under the spell of the ego's projection. The same pattern keeps happening. A pattern begins when we desire something and choose to pursue its fulfillment; we begin a cycle of action, the consequences of which keep returning to us again and again until its resolution. This cycle can only be resolved when you are fulfilled. Resolution ultimately means your return to love. You must be satisfied with where you are. Fulfillment comes when you can love yourself with respect to what happened in that cycle of action.

You may have started that cycle because you wanted to get married and the marriage didn't turn out as you expected, but can you still love yourself? Or the cycle was one of you wanting to fulfill your dream of being on TV, but you were only on for two minutes. Can you love yourself now, or are you going to withhold your love until you star in a prime-time show?

As long as you are projecting blame or fulfillment-expectation on someone or something else, you cannot ever complete the cycle within yourself and are stuck. And you bind yourself to that person and/or situation, giving over control to it, until you take that power back to your inner being. The less you love some aspect of yourself, the more you will depend on others to fulfill your need for love, and the more you will project your needs on them. You'll be stuck in that rut until you return to loving yourself.

Effort and Competition

When you're struggling with a person or situation, ask yourself, *How hard am I working against the problem? How much effort am I in?* The more effort you're in, the more you're caught in the ego's web of illusions. In spirit, there is no effort. But the outer surface of every layer of the ego-pearl is hardened with effort and competition. So, for the next step in growing our neutrality, we need to step out of the layers of effort and competition.

You begin to produce effort when you get into competition against invalidation. And invalidation is any energy that says, "You can't," "You won't," "You aren't," or "You don't." We've all run up against "You're never going to make it," "You don't have what it takes," "You'll never get there," or "You can't be serious." The list goes on. To get back on track with spirit and your soul purpose, you must get out of effort. And getting out of effort means *getting out of competition.*

In the sports arena and in a fun game, competition serves its purpose. There is, however, no place for competition in your spiritual development. Competition in life invalidates spirit. It divides you against yourself.

Whether you decide that you are better than others or that they are better than you, it comes from the same place: you cannot be who you are, where you are, what you are, or how you are. When you're in competition, someone else's expectations and judgments define who you are and how you can be. If you compare yourself to anyone else and get into competition, where that person is no longer matters, for the truth is, you are only in competition with yourself. If you have to be as good as, better than, or even worse than the other person, you've forfeited your right to be precisely where you are as yourself. Competition ultimately involves no one else but you.

Competition is the stepchild of self-invalidation. "You are not enough as you are. You're not good enough, not intelligent enough, not fast enough, not attractive enough, not rich enough." When you're in competition with anyone, you can't be present and you can't fully incarnate, so you can't fulfill your soul purpose. In competition, you can get better and better in something, but you don't grow spiritually. Only when you can be true to yourself can you grow and fulfill your destiny.

Competition in sports, school, or business may *seem* to make you a better, stronger, and more capable person. It isn't, however, the competing that accomplishes this. If you are reaching deeper within yourself with compassion, patience, perseverance, and forgiveness as you work toward the goal or victory, then you will learn and grow. And *that* makes you more capable. In the sports arena, those who end up in competition *against* the opponents ultimately lose in life, even if they win the game. The field of competition provided by sports, academics, and other life opportunities allows you to learn to transcend the snare and invalidation of competition and find unity with purpose. That's the *team spirit.*

Being in competition says: "I'm not a very good singer so I'm not going to sing, even though I like singing." Or, "I'm not going to let anyone tell me I'm not a great singer because I know I'm better than everyone else."

Not being in competition says: "I love to sing. I want to share this love of singing with the world. I'll practice and study singing so I can develop this part of myself I love." Or, "I'll sing in the shower and fulfill my love of singing in whatever way I can."

Being in competition says: "He's such a great healer because he's given so many amazing healings to people. I'm not much of a healer since I've never healed anyone, even though I love to see people being happy and healthy more than anything else." Or, "All those people who claim to be healers are frauds, and people who go to them are just gullible. I know better." Or, "I'm a better healer than you are because I've healed more people than you have."

Not being in competition says: "I love to see people happy and well. I want to find out what I can do to bring more of this out of myself. Perhaps I can develop my healing abilities."

In competition, you go against yourself. It begins from the judgment that you are not enough.

Expectation and Judgment

Next, beneath the layers of effort and competition in the ego-pearl, you will find layers of expectation and judgment. We create expectations to avoid the condemnation and pain of judgment. And we try to escape the pain of unfulfilled expectations and unworthiness by incarcerating ourselves in judgment. Judgment is what you blame your pain on; expectation is what you hope will relieve it. Judgments hold you in the past and expectations keep you in the future. One way or another, we try to avoid pain by erecting barriers of expectations and judgments against it. And we hold the false assumption that, since we are feeling the pain now, the pain must be here and now. Thus we seek refuge in the past and future. However, neither in the past nor in the future can you fulfill your purpose, for your soul lives *only* in the eternal present.

We create judgment and expectation to escape from the pain of unworthiness. We want an assurance that something besides us—even just a reason why—is the problem, and that *we* are still okay. When we're disconnected from our soul purpose, we become so afraid that our life has no meaning in and of itself that we create judgments to secure the illusion that we are worthy. We tell ourselves, "I did a good job, so I'm a good person," "I did everything right, so no one can say I'm a failure," or "I was nice to everyone, so no one would think I'm selfish." We don't want to be a "nobody."

Purpose gives meaning, and therefore value, to our existence. So when we isolate ourselves from our purpose, we fall into a profound loneliness, bereft of meaning and worth. In reality, however, our worth isn't predicated on *what* we do, *how much* we do, or *how well* we do. Although our society seems to measure one's worth according to one's accomplishments, no one lacks worth or meaning. No human being has any more or any less value than another. Each one of us has 100 percent worth, for our worth is intrinsic to our being. Your inherent worth as a human being never changes, regardless of the amount or quality of your accomplishments. What makes your worth apparent in the world is in how you treat it. Those who see great meaning in their lives can change the whole community with a smile or a simple helping hand, while years of hard labor by someone in self-invalidation don't seem to do as much. It isn't in accomplishing something of greatness that you gain your worth; it's in appreciating your true worth that imbues everything you do with great value.

What happens to the world-class athlete who becomes a paraplegic or the concert pianist who loses use of her hands? If what they *did* defined their purpose, their lives would become devoid of meaning. And often they do . . . at least for a while. Yet, sooner or later (maybe even in a subsequent lifetime), each one of us restores a deeper connection back to our purpose and discovers that life not only goes on but also becomes more meaningful.

To step out of judgment and expectation toward neutrality, find the meaning in what you're doing right now. You don't have to know the whole purpose of your life, just the meaning of what you are doing *right now*. For example, you may be judging yourself that you aren't doing anything productive. You may be expecting yourself to be doing a lot more. But what *are* you doing right now? You might discover that you're just sitting and thinking. What's the purpose of sitting and thinking? We often sit to relax, to rest from activity. Thinking is a creative process. How can we do something more if we don't first rest, pull ourselves out of other activities, and do some creative thinking to look at the possibilities of what we can do next?

Every moment, life provides us with our next step. But if we're wrapped up in expectations of what we *should* be doing, where we *should* be by now, as well as the judgments of how bad we are for not fulfilling those expectations, then we can't discover the purpose, meaning, and value of what we are doing and where we are right now. Just as water naturally flows downstream, we naturally gravitate toward what we need to do next, but our expectations and judgments get in our way of doing that.

Anytime you find yourself in a "should" or "shouldn't" situation or any variation of them ("supposed to," "ought to," etc.), you are caught in an expectation and out of touch with the present reality. Take a breath and relax. Ask yourself, "What is the purpose, meaning, or value of where I am and what I am doing right now?" Step out of the expectations and return to the present. *That's* where you'll find meaning—never in the past or future.

When I speak of being in judgment, I don't mean the detached discernment of things but the attachment to an arbitrary value and opinion about someone or something. It's not in the words you say but in where you are with them. One person can say, "He's retarded" as a statement of fact in terms of the person's mental development and love that person unconditionally. That's not being in judgment. But another person can say the same thing maliciously, holding a person in condemnation. That is what I call being in judgment. Judgment always involves comparison, often with one's own self.

Being able to practice discernment and communicate the truth as you see it are important to your spiritual growth. In our society's obsession with political correctness, however, we're sometimes criticized for being "judgmental" when, in fact, we might have been making a neutral observation. The difference between judgment and discernment is that, in judgment, we are attached to it. In discernment, there is no assigning a value to the observation: "He is a criminal in that he committed a crime." In judgment, we are invested in being right: "He's a convicted criminal and therefore a terrible person. That's all there is to it."

In judgment, we withhold our love. It doesn't matter who or what we judge; we hold back our love. Love comes from wholeness and the oneness of being; judgment splits us up. Even if we are approving that someone is "really good," as compared to disapproving if he were "really bad," we split ourselves between loving the good and hating the bad. We equally reject the "bad" part within us as we approve the "good" part.

We may fool ourselves into believing that we are fundamentally different from the person we are judging but, in truth, we can never recognize in another what we don't have in ourselves. If I'm bothered that someone is a "klutz" or an "ugly duckling," then I must have had the experience of being one myself and must still be upset about it. Had I forgiven myself about it already, I wouldn't have any negative reactions about someone being clumsy or homely. By the same token, if I admire greatness in another person, I must have that same greatness and admiration within myself as well. Either way, it always takes one to know one.

It is to our great fortune that we can recognize things in each other. Our relationships provide unlimited opportunities to pull the logs from our own eyes as we notice the slivers in others'. We act as mirrors for one another's judgments and, if used correctly, we can relinquish our judgments in favor of our freedom.

When you find yourself judging others harshly, remember that your upset is not about them. It's about you not being able to forgive and love yourself because you're holding that judgment inside you. If in the past you were humiliated for being "stupid," then you might create judgments against stupidity in order to cover your invalidation and loss of love for having been "stupid" yourself. You end up blaming "stupid" for your pain. Those who fit that same judgment of "stupid" threaten to reopen you to the pain within you, so you chase them away by judging *them*. Let it be all right that someone once judged you, for it's really that person's problem to solve, not yours. Those who create the judgments must live with them and endure their consequences, not those who are the target of judgment. "Do not judge," teaches the Bible, "lest you be judged."

We fear letting go of our judgments because we don't know what would happen to us if we did. Intuitively, however, we suspect that if we let the judgment go, we will have to face what we have not been able to forgive and love in ourselves. As long as we hold fast to our judgments, we cannot discover the lies for which we abandoned our love.

If you find loving yourself difficult, look at what you can't love about you. Often before surgeons make a final diagnosis of a serious condition, they perform an exploratory surgery to take a deeper look at underlying conditions. Such an exploration might reveal to you that what you can't love about yourself is not the real you. The apparent ugliness, stupidity, failure, or lack of some quality or ability is a judgment based on someone else's unfulfilled expectation, fear, and invalidated self-image. As you begin to love the aspect of yourself buried under that judgment, you will dissolve the invalidation and resurrect that part of you.

Judgment is based in fear born of an unwillingness to love and forgive. In order to protect our own investments, we create a mental image of making something worthy or not. Judgments are picture barriers we put up against what threatens us. We use the barriers to try to keep the bad things away from us and hold on to the good things. Judgments feed the illusion that these are absolute values. "Of course this is a good thing," we convince ourselves. But in reality, what is good for you may be deadly to me.

In spirit, truth is absolute but, in the various cultures of the world, truth takes a multitude of forms and is therefore a relative, local ordinance. In the world, we must relate everything to our soul purpose and whether it rings true within us or not. No "things" in the world are intrinsically good or bad but just *are*. In relation to your purpose, a thing can be fulfilling or not, and sometimes the thing that everyone condemns can be the very thing that propels you to your enlightenment. Perhaps a natural health practitioner might adamantly oppose synthetic medical treatment, yet the person whose life it saved may be forever grateful for it. A die-hard allopathic doctor may denounce psychic healing but, for those who have benefited from it, medication may be a far cry from real healing. We must learn to abandon judgment if we are to find our own paths.

In Egypt, there is a beautiful mural on an ancient temple wall that depicts the journey of the soul of a man recently departed from the earthly plane. In the first scene, the jackal-headed god of the netherworld, Anubis, leads him down the Hall of Ma'at to the scale of truth upon which the life of the soul would be evaluated. Anubis then carefully balances the large instrument. Upon one side of the scale sits a single white feather, Ma'at's feather of truth. On the other side, Anubis places the heart of the new arrival. If the man's heart were pure in the life he had just completed, it would prove to be as light as the feather and the scale would balance. If instead it were laden with judgments and lies, the scale would immediately tip. The soul with a pure heart would ascend to the heavens while the soul with a heart divided (heavy with karma) would return to the earth for another opportunity to learn to make it whole again.

Emotional Reactions

Stripping away the layers of effort and competition, and expectations and judgments, we begin to find the underlying emotional turbulence of the ego personality. Once again, the more we can disengage our awareness from reactive emotions and reclaim our neutrality, the better we can realign ourselves to our soul energies, awareness, and purpose.

Within the soul are a spiritual self, a reasoning self, and a feeling self. The spiritual self communicates with light, the reasoning self with inner landscapes of picture-words, and the feeling self with emotions. The light of the spiritual self shines down through the inner landscapes created by the reasoning self and is felt by the feeling self as emotion. If the reasoning self creates the correct landscape of fulfillment aligned with the spiritual self, the feeling self feels fulfilled and conveys the emotion of fulfillment—happiness, enthusiasm, joy, etc.—back to the reasoning self, which then acknowledges this and sends the fulfilled light or wisdom back to the spiritual self. The cycle of communication is complete, and the reasoning self will be more inclined in the future to discover other circumstances that bring the joy of spiritual expression.

However, if the reasoning self creates a landscape of division and isolation, then the feeling self will express an emotion of lack such as unhappiness, anger, grief, or fear, and will send that emotion back to the reasoning self. In turn, the reasoning self interprets the emotional pain and creates the landscape that it reasons will bring fulfillment, and the unfulfilled energy cycle, or karma, is sent back to the spiritual self. The spiritual self then gives its light to the landscape that the reasoning self made to give itself the experience it needs for fulfillment. This goes on until the cycle is completed. The bulk of it is predicated upon the kind of inner landscape the reasoning self creates. Without neutrality on its part, the reasoning self will keep overcompensating and the cycle will not be completed. Once in neutral and disengaged from the emotional reactions of the feeling self, however, the reasoning self can objectively assess what is needed for the soul's fulfillment. This, however, cannot be done by intellect alone. Having certainty in the spiritual self and the use of intuition play a much larger role in the ultimate fulfillment of the soul.

Neutrality starts with disengaging and letting be that which has already happened or is happening. Don't try to hold on, fight off, run away, or ignore. Just be aware and okay with your inner self that, "What's happening is what's happening."

We are afraid of letting things be because we think that if we don't do something about it now, then it's going to go on forever. Even in critical emergencies where every second counts, first finding neutrality makes the difference between life and death. With practice, getting to neutral becomes easier, even in the worst of situations. It only takes a moment to get neutral, and then you can correctly assess the situation and plan a course of action. You'll find that the more neutral you can become, the slower time goes. In fact, sometimes time stops altogether and you can see your whole life flash before your eyes.

At the emotional level, the ego-pearl reacts to everything by either being *for* or *against* it or by *ignoring* it. To disengage from that, be aware of that energetic impulse to take one of those three stances. That impulse is not you, but merely the reaction already in motion. Neutrality, on the other hand, is never for or against anything. It is detached awareness. And awareness, by its very nature, does not ignore. When ego asks, "Whose side are you on?" spirit's answer is always, "There are no sides, but only oneness of being."

So, to choose spirit and to fulfill your soul purpose, you must choose wholeness, which includes the movement of polarities, not attached to one side or another. When you really get down to that level of the ego, you'll find that the whole universe is all energies with positive, negative, and neutral charges interacting with each other and that you are in the center of it, experiencing it all without engaging in any of it.

Being Neutral

Being neutral doesn't mean you don't feel anything. Far from it, neutrality is your essential state of *being*, and only through that state can you feel and express your true inner purpose. Without being neutral, you cannot experience real happiness and joy. When you're bound by the effects of your outer life and your emotional reactions to them, all you can hope to feel are poor surrogates for love—the thrills and spills of infatuation and obsession. Neutrality puts you in touch with God and the feelings of Divinity, i.e., acceptance, laughter, compassion, forgiveness, serenity, and freedom.

Becoming neutral is actually ridiculously simple, which is why most people have such difficulty with it. We always expect it to be hard because we first encounter the effort-competition layer of the ego-pearl. As with everything to do with spirit, to be neutral, all you need do is to just *know you are*, and so you are. Have your certainty and don't play "Prove it" with yourself.

What makes being neutral challenging is not doing it but managing its consequences—those layers of effort and competition, judgment and expectation, and the related emotions that will begin to surface. Most of us underestimate the power of spirit within us, but one small step for spirit brings about a giant leap in our life. So, when you decide to be neutral in spirit, the reactions already happening within you subconsciously start surfacing into your awareness in the body. Old pain, emotions, unresolved memories, and other people's energies tucked away within you begin bubbling up. And often they don't feel good. This is where you practice being neutral some more. Then, the old pain passes and you will be in a higher state of being of more awareness and energy. And remember, nothing happens that you can't handle. Have more certainty in yourself.

Everything in this book so far will help you to practice growing your neutrality. Grounding yourself and centering your awareness behind your eyes are two of the first tools to use, followed by validating spirit and being willing to change your relationship to whatever reactions you encounter. The Spiritual Toolkit section at the end of this book offers additional exercises to help you find and grow your neutrality.

TEN

PURPOSE IS THE ASKING: RESPONDING TO LIFE

We pave our road to freedom by how we respond to life in each moment. We cannot always control what happens in our lives, but we are never without the choice of how we respond to it. Do we let ourselves unconsciously *react* to everything, or do we express our divine nature by creatively *responding* to our experience? How do we use our ability to respond?

A New Understanding of Responsibility

To grow spiritually and fulfill our soul purpose, we must examine our true responsibility. Simply put, responsibility means "the ability to respond." As spiritual beings incarnated in physical form, we have the ability to respond creatively to life in this world. That ability comes from our awareness, free will, and imagination, and is meant to lead us to our true freedom.

In spirit, there is no responsibility. There is nothing but *being*—being in the oneness of spirit we just *are*. We have nothing to which we *can* respond. Only when we incarnate into a world of polarity do we develop the consciousness of form, space, and time. Without that consciousness, there is no memory and, therefore, no awareness of consequence or cause and effect.

When we first began to inhabit what we created into form, we had a type of spiritual amnesia since our memory function did not exist prior to that. Once we started retaining a memory of our experiences, however, our recollection began with our first experience of duality, not our true existence in unity. Thus we continue to remember that we have always been a separate, individual being without a connection to the whole of existence. *That* is the real "original sin"—our first assumption of being a "separate" entity, based on our first memory. It was our "fall" from the grace of oneness.

The fruit of the tree of knowledge is our memory. When we *believe* what our memory tells us instead of experiencing the truth of spirit, we have "eaten" the fruit. For eons of "time" as we know it, we accumulated memories of everything we touched with our consciousness or what we call experiences. Essentially, all our memories are illusions since they are each a static imprint of a fragment of an ever-changing process. We often look at a picture of a runner and talk about it as "that exciting race." That picture wasn't the race but captured only a fleeting moment of the whole race. And even a film of the whole "race" takes that particular event out of the context of the whole of existence.

It wasn't until the creation of the human body that we were able to incarnate into a form that could accommodate "free will"—an ability that required the full reasoning capacity of consciousness to deduce its own existence. Then, we could choose how we wished to respond to our experiences instead of being limited to instinctual reactions controlled by all our memories. We were given the greatest gift of our liberation from imprisonment in form. We could then begin our exploration of truth to discover both the causes of our unhappiness and the sources of our true fulfillment. As we sought, the door began to open to a larger reality, one beyond the limits of our memories.

In our body, we have the freedom to make choices about what to give, whom to give to, how to give, or even whether to give at all. By the way we choose to respond to the ever-changing conditions of existence, we shape our spiritual path. *That* is our responsibility.

Traditionally, we speak of responsibility as accountability, reliability, duty, or obligation. There is nothing inherently wrong with those definitions. Having the ability to respond freely and creatively means that we are the *cause* of the consequences that arise out of our responses. We are accountable. We are reliable in that we have the ability to respond and are responding all the time. And it is our duty to respond—we cannot do otherwise. Even if we choose not to respond, that, too, is a response. However, in most cases, when we speak of responsibility, its meaning becomes skewed.

Whenever we are in resistance, fear, competition, and judgment, and we say, "That person is responsible for what happened," we want him to be held "accountable" for the effects of his actions on us. We want him to pay for it; we want to assign blame; we want justice; we want him to make us feel better; we want him to make it all right for us again; we want him to make our suffering go away—and we want him to do it in the way we want it. In our disappointment, hurt, anger, or grief, we forget to whom each one of us is accountable. We forget our true inner Source. We then refuse to trust that person anymore. He hurt us badly so he is no longer a reliable person to whom we can give our trust. We brand him irresponsible. He didn't fulfill our expectation to carry out his duty of not hurting us.

But when we are hurt, who is really accountable? Can someone or something outside ourselves hurt us? When we become the effect of someone else's actions, who, in the final analysis, is truly accountable? Of course, we can say, "But *you* hit me and I have the scars both physically and emotionally to prove it."

Then he could say, "But *you* slighted me *first!*"

To which we might reply, "But I never *hit* you."

And he will produce a laundry list he's kept over the years of all the failures in his life because we didn't make him happy at home, and he paid for our home with hard work because he loved us. It sounds like two little kids fighting and running over to Mommy to rule who's responsible, doesn't it? Yet, fundamentally, all our karmic entanglements that can go on for lifetimes boil down to sounding like this. And if you think it sounds bad between two people, how about leaders of countries doing some form of this with the power of millions of people screaming about who did what to whom? It can be frightening, but the only cure for this is seeking the truth of responsibility.

We have responsibility, in that we must choose how to respond in relationship to everything in our life. But we cannot be responsible for how *others* choose to do the same. We cannot make *others* respond in a certain way, yet we try all the time. We try to force people to feel the way we want them to feel. We even give up our own freedom to become how others want us to be, so that they will be the way we need them to be. The more we give up our ability to respond freely and creatively, and the more we abandon our accountability to our inner divinity, the more we expect others to be responsible for us.

Responsibility cannot be a rigid set of rules to control how you live. If you make it so, you restrict your ability to respond. If you follow other people's "rules of responsibility," you will never be able to creatively fulfill your purpose. As a teacher, a minister, a counselor, a healer, a writer, and an administrator, I have held positions of responsibility most of my life. Yet I would never have succeeded in them had I been "responsible" in the way most others expected of me. Through my failures, I learned this every time I did try to be "responsible" according to everyone else. For example, when people hear that I am a healer and they haven't learned to look within themselves for their own truth, they approach me as they have always related to their doctors, saying, "You're going to cure me."

Of course, if I buy into that, they will hold me "responsible" if I don't "cure" them. I remember a government official who cut short our discussion when he discovered I was a minister because, he said, "You're not acting responsibly for a minister." What did that mean? I didn't *look* "pious" enough? I wasn't talking in hushed tones with "reverence"? I talked too openly about any subject (sex, money, power, psychic abilities, etc.)?

When I am being accountable to God's love that resides within me, I often get into trouble with others. But if I'm not being true (responsible) to the God of my own heart, then I *always* get into even bigger trouble! So, I'd rather get into trouble sometimes with ignorant, powerless people than be in trouble for sure with the Omnipotent. Even if you're in fear, you still have that choice!

I was a nurse in the days when men were generally not nurses. I trained in a Catholic hospital administered by a sister superior. During my training period, the sister would often call me into her office to punish me for my failures to carry out my responsibilities. What were they? A student was expected to do certain jobs but not others; a nurse's duty was to do this but not that. I seemed to regularly not do what I *was* responsible for and do what I was *not* responsible for doing.

When I was assigned to the cardiac intensive care unit, I reported for my assignment, and immediately the physician in charge and the nurse were called away, and I was left with no staff supervision. Within seconds, a patient went into cardiac arrest. With absolutely no one else to do anything, I called "code blue" and started CPR. The crash team arrived immediately and the doctor took over. I assisted him in the emergency procedures and the woman recovered.

Half an hour later, I was summoned to the sister superior's office. "Who do you think you are?" she screamed at me. "Don't you know your only responsibility as a student nurse is to follow staff orders?" This inquisition continued for ten minutes until the doctor who headed the crash team came to give his report to the sister. "Hey, Michael," he said, "I want to thank you for saving not only the poor woman's life but also the hospital from a hefty lawsuit."

The sister sputtered in mid-sentence and glared at the doctor for interrupting her tirade. When the doctor realized that I was "on the carpet," he passionately explained to the sister, "The real violation here was that the staff of the cardiac unit was all absent and, had it not been for Michael's quick response, not only would the hospital have unnecessarily lost a patient's life but would have been charged with gross negligence and sued to the hilt."

Every single time I was hauled into the sister's office for reprimands, someone in authority came to my defense. The sister had the right to reprimand me because technically, on each occasion, I was violating the *letter* of my responsibility. But I was always vindicated because I was carrying out the *spirit* of it. My suffering was a few minutes of being chewed out, but my fulfillment continues.

Once, when I led a spiritual group to receive healings from faith healers in the Philippines, one of the travelers started to convulse and pass out while waiting his turn in the reception area. I ran over to him and "karate chopped" him across the side of his neck. Immediately he regained consciousness and was fine. Everyone else stared at me in disbelief. Here was a spiritual healer hitting a poor convulsing tourist! Several felt that I had not acted "responsibly" as a spiritual leader. Yet what no one else realized was that this man had left his body very quickly due to the energy generated by the faith-healing session. He had started to go into a past-life death scene and another entity was taking over his body at the same time. He had to be brought back into his body immediately. Hitting him on the side of his neck the way I did threatened his body's instinctive survival response and his soul broke through his distractions and came back. I had administered "spiritual shock therapy." Had he gone further into that scenario, he would have suffered a full seizure and might have ended up with a lot more problems. In cases such as this, I follow my intuition instead of a set of prescribed rules of responsibility. The consequence that I have to live with, I leave up to God.

Well, you might say, "You're different. You're clairvoyant." However, when you think about it, we all have the ability to respond intuitively in our own way. Dr. Norman Shealy talks about the fact that all the successful doctors he knows use their medical training first but their final decision to diagnose this or that condition, or prescribe this treatment over that treatment, always relies on their intuition. No matter what equations, formulas, and theories you work with, in the final analysis, your choice is always checking in with your intuitive truth. It's just that when you doubt it or invalidate it, it doesn't come through as effectively.

The examples from my life I offer here aren't meant to encourage rebellion or going against tradition or established protocols. It would be advisable to keep to the speed limit when you're driving but, if you have to speed up to get out of the way of a runaway truck, you wouldn't call that irresponsible. No matter who says what, justice is intrinsic to spirit and will be served. But it may not be in the way you expect or want it to be. We are each accountable, not to each other, but to the Divine Oneness within each of us. And the only judgment that Oneness makes is love. Love is always *for*-giving.

Love always gives us another chance to learn, heal, and grow to our fulfillment. Yet, often, we become afraid to extend to each other—or even to ourselves—that same opportunity. We demand *our* brand of immediate justice; we want the responsible party to *pay*. What are we afraid of? We fear that if we should forgive, or if we fail to make another person *responsible* in the way we can control, we would be hurt again. All we really want is to stop suffering, and we believe that assigning blame will do that. In fact, we are so afraid that we try to make people responsible *before* they have a chance to hurt us. We often fill our children with so many rules of responsible behavior that, at the first sign of independence, they go in the opposite direction just to try to find the truth of their own ability to respond.

Even some of the "best" and most conscientious parents have been ignorant of their children's true spiritual nature and needs. They give their children a good education, a healthy lifestyle, and as much love as they know, but are they communicating with the spirit of their children? Are they validating who the real spiritual beings are in those little bodies? Are the parents aware that the souls of those children are the ones who have the intelligence and power to respond to life? Or do they try to mold the bodies and minds of their children to their own expectations, to limit their power so they won't expose their own pain, or to cover their own fear of being failures as parents?

As parents and teachers, our true responsibility to ourselves in relationship with our children is to teach the spirit of the children in the ways of the body and mind so that, as souls, they can learn to respond spiritually in the world to fulfill their purpose in life. It is not our responsibility to make them fit *our* expectations to cover *our* fears.

Most of us were raised programmed with the responsibilities of our parents, relatives, teachers, and ministers. We found that the more "responsible" we became according to others' expectations, the more they relied on us for everything and the more restricted we became in our mobility. We became so "responsible" that, today, we are forever tied to our desks, our phones, or our housework, and find we have ceased to live our true spiritual purpose. Our "life" has become one of checking off our mental "to do" lists. We begin to live for the sake of fulfilling our assumed responsibilities and obligations to everyone else in our world, rather than for fulfilling our purpose in life.

Responding to Reactions

In order to fulfill our soul purpose, we need to take charge of our ability to respond. We can choose to express our spirituality or succumb to the machinations of the ego and our bodily reactions. Responding consciously puts us in touch with our spiritual self, whereas unconsciously reacting makes us slaves to the ego and the body. Here, *neutrality* is the key to our success. Once we are neutral to our emotional reactions to things—what people do, how they are, what happens—we can decide how to respond to them. As spirit, we have that choice; the body however can't choose and can only follow our lead.

Reactions happen automatically without our conscious intervention. By the time you become aware of a reaction, it's already in full swing, but don't try to suppress it or stop it. Disengaging from the reaction doesn't automatically make the emotion disappear. It just means you can observe the reaction instead of becoming it or stuffing it. You can just let it flow on its own without trying to stop it or add to it in any way. Just let the images, thoughts, emotions, and sensations flow past the screen of your awareness. If you don't engage and lend your power to the emotion, it remains just an energy cycle and nothing physical has to happen. It's like putting your car in neutral; the engine is running, but the wheels don't get any power. You don't have to cut off the engine to stop the car.

Once you are in neutral, you have a limitless choice of how to respond to the situation that got your reactions churning. Anger may be coursing through your veins or sadness may be taking the wind out of your lungs but, since you're not engaged in it, you can ask yourself, "How do I wish to respond?"

What kind of response would help you toward your soul purpose? Sometimes just shrugging it off and moving on would best serve your purpose. At other times, that would be a waste of a golden opportunity to learn something that can benefit your purpose if you were to stick with it. But before you jump into what to *do*, you must find out how to *be*. What kind of energy space would you like to respond from as a spiritual being? Anger? Boredom? Seriousness? Enjoyment? Enthusiasm? Kindness? To respond, you need to ask, "How can I use this opportunity to grow, to fulfill more of my true self instead?" The ego may insist on blame, revenge, or escape, but choose what response would best serve your spiritual purpose.

A woman I met a few years ago healed her lifelong dysfunctional relationship with her father and transformed her whole life by responding with much more consciousness of spirit. She had not communicated with her father for over fifteen years due to the scars of intense physical and psychic abuse that she'd endured from him in later childhood. She had undergone years of therapy and had even become a professional therapist herself. After practicing therapy for a few years, however, she couldn't reconcile counseling others in family matters when she couldn't face her own father. So she finally decided to invite him to come and see her, and he agreed. However, as the appointed weekend arrived, her dread and anger became intolerable. She asked me how to manage facing her father without running away again or trying to kill him.

I first taught her about finding her neutrality. She was already mostly there. She was neutral enough to decide to see her father again, but she didn't know how to be neutral to all the emotional reactions that churned up as she even thought about being in the same room with him. I only needed to remind her, "You are not your reactions, and if you can just let them be without adding more resistance and energy to them, then they will run themselves out."

Next, I explained, "You have been taking responsibility for your father's spiritual problems for years. Instead, you need to choose a new way of responding to them. What is your father's main spiritual problem that you have not been able to solve? Most of the abusive man you grew up with was not your father. The soul whom you chose as your father is a kind and loving soul. You knew him in your earliest years as that gentle man. Yet, as you grew a little older, he increasingly became a violent stranger to you. The soul who is your father would leave his body and allow another vengeful being to enter into it and abuse you. That other entity blamed your father in another lifetime for the loss of *his* child, so he was trying to destroy your father's relationship with *his* daughter.

"Your father wasn't able to forgive himself and took 'responsibility' for the accidental death of the other man's daughter. The more your father loved you in this lifetime, the more the other being erupted in anger and vengeance. Instead of taking charge of his own ability to respond, your father tried to escape the rage of the other being and would leave his own body. While he was out of his body, he didn't even remember what had happened so, when he returned, he encountered your hurt, shame, and anger but didn't know what had transpired. When accused, he would vehemently defend himself and deny that he would do such a thing. Yet, somehow he felt that he was involved in bringing harm to his daughter, so he started to distance himself more and more from you to prevent further harm from befalling you. So you grew up with memories of abuse, defiant denials, and what you experienced as an aloof, uncaring father."

"That makes so much sense," she said. "I always knew that my father was a gentle, loving man, but he would suddenly become a violent stranger. His face, his eyes . . . they would become someone I didn't know."

I went on to tell her, "When you see him, hold the intention of speaking to the spiritual being that's your *real* father. When we communicate as spirit to the other person as the spirit he is, healing can begin. And do not take responsibility for the other being who used to come into his body; that's your father's problem to solve. At the same time, you must tell your father spiritually that you want to have a relationship with *him* and not the other being."

She told me later, "I spent the entire weekend with my father. I kept intending that everything I said was going to him as the soul no matter where he was. I also spoke to him mentally, not verbalizing, those things he may not understand right away. On our first day together, things were quite tense and, the couple of times he started to open up a little, I could not only sense the other being but could almost see him trying to get into my father's head. His eyes and voice would start to change completely. Each time I noticed that, however, I mentally communicated to my father's soul that it was he whom I wanted to talk with, not this other being. Then, his countenance would change back and he would visibly relax.

"On the second day, I got the courage to actually tell him what you had told me about him. He listened to me with undivided attention for the first time I can recall since I was a little child. Then, he started crying and saying that he could not have described more accurately what has happened to him for most of his life. He told me that he never thought anyone would ever believe or understand him if he had told such a seemingly outrageous story, and he begged my forgiveness. Since then, we have become great friends."

The last I heard from her was that they were enjoying the kind of father-daughter relationship she'd always dreamt of. With her communication and understanding, her father was able to forgive himself, be senior to the other being, and learn to be more present in his body. As she changed her response to her father's problems from blame and trying to solve it to how she wanted to fulfill her soul, she began healing her whole relationship with him.

If you, as a spiritual being, allow another soul to use your body to express destruction, that being isn't responsible—you are! It is *you* who gives that soul the opportunity and the body to do what it does.

Without your power, agreement, and body, that being could not do what it does in the world. Many go to prison, even death row, with no recollection of their crime. Though many of the souls serving time are not the ones who were in the body committing the crime, they are the ones who bear the responsibility of the crimes because it was through their neglect that they allowed the destruction. If you get drunk and leave a loaded gun where a four-year-old can get it, and that child shoots someone, it wasn't your responsibility to control the child; your responsibility was to keep a lethal weapon out of the hands of an ignorant child. In the same way, your body-mind can be a lethal weapon in the possession of a diseased soul who otherwise would not be able to incarnate because of their ill condition of consciousness. Your karma is that you made the potentially lethal weapon of your body-mind available to an "underage" soul.

Responding requires that you own being spirit and communicate *as* spirit *to* spirit. We need to relinquish our attachment to what happened on the outside and look more deeply into the spiritual cause of the material effects. In the case of this woman, she intuitively knew that the man she had a problem with was not her father—he just happened to use the same body. But until I validated her, she couldn't respond to that truth. What kind of energy space do we need to be in so that we can respond more in alignment with our inner divinity?

Humor, Laughter, and Amusement

Once you find some neutrality, the fun begins. Detached from reactions, you can tap into your creativity and imagination. You can choose to enjoy life. And with your laughter, you take your first step toward your spiritual fulfillment. Your soul stagnates in boredom and apathy or fear and anger, and there's no growth. But, with a little humor, amusement, and laughter, you begin to embody your spiritual self.

Enjoying your life is easy when you're having fun. The challenge is enjoying being part of it when the going gets tough. Of course, it doesn't mean that you have to enjoy tragedies. It's knowing that you can choose to be happy with yourself no matter how miserable you feel or how terrible the circumstances that helps you connect with your soul energy. It means learning to love yourself when you're feeling angry, grief-stricken, or like a failure. It means finding the humor in the cosmic joke, which is *believing that truth, love, and your fulfillment are not within you and that something could take them away.*

Laughter isn't only the best medicine, but also the first line of healing. Being amused doesn't mean laughing things off, being sarcastic, or denying what's happening. It's appreciating the humor and playfulness of Life. Someone once said that angels could fly because they take themselves so lightly. And what do we say to someone who gets submerged in seriousness? We tell him, "Lighten up." Amusement and laughter are the wings that lift our energy so that we can ride life's joyous thermals like hawks soaring on a summer's day.

Humor saved the day once when a friend had stomped his foot onto a metal stake. We were out in the boonies and the paramedics wouldn't be there for a while, so I had to decide how to deal with the profuse bleeding and the 1½ inches of metal embedded in his foot. Normally, I would have staunched the bleeding and left the stake in his foot because removing it could have set off further uncontrollable bleeding. In his case, however, the stake had gone through his sneakers and I couldn't stop the bleeding without removing his shoe and hence the stake. But in excruciating pain, he wouldn't let anyone touch his foot (and he was six-foot-seven). As I gave him spiritual healing, I explained to him that I had been a nurse before and I knew what I was doing. I made it look like I was assessing the situation carefully. Then, I looked at him solemnly and told him, "You're going to be fine. I found no sign of brain damage."

In spite of all the pain, he started laughing and replied, "The brain damage has already been done. That's why I did such a stupid thing as stomping on the metal stake to try to shove it into the hard ground."

The laughter broke through his judgment and anger against himself for having been "such an idiot." Then, I was able to remove the stake and shoe and successfully stop the bleeding. He later told me, "After all the joking and laughing, the pain diminished by eighty percent!

The physical pain was only twenty percent. The unbearable part was my self-punishment for making such a dumb mistake and injuring myself."

Often we think that feelings just come to us (from heaven, perhaps?). That would be like writers waiting for an inspiration to hit them like a thunderbolt before they started to write. Every accomplished writer I have known or heard about has said the same thing: "When I start writing, the writing starts. If I wait for it to come to me, I don't write much."

The same is true with your spiritual feelings. When you start *being* happy with yourself, you start *feeling* happy. If you wait for the feeling of happiness to descend on you while you sit in sadness, anger, or boredom, you will just stew in more of what you have. You must meet life, not wait for it to find you in the closet. God never leaves you but, in order to hear God, you must first say, "Hello."

Most of us are inundated with everyone else's energies. We carry in our space thoughts, emotions, beliefs, responsibilities, judgments, problems, and other energy baggage that belong to other people. Until we lose some of this excess psychic weight, we're going to be feeling all the garbage. And garbage stinks. If we want to smell the roses, we must first plant some.

Laughter is one of my favorites roses to plant. I know with certainty that I would never have made it this far without being able to find laughter when there's nothing funny. Seriously. Laughter is one of life's sweet elixirs—the laughs shared with friends; the toasts of camaraderie; the sparkling laughter of children; songbirds in the park; the side-splitting, eye-tearing hilarity when we finally acknowledge ourselves in our own comedy of errors. But laughter is also our trustworthy ally on our often too-solemn trek of spiritual growth. Laughter helps break us out of the gravitational pull of our reactions and helps catapult us to the next level of our being.

With amusement, we discover the divine comedy of life. How can we hope to heal from our suffering if we can't have a little karmic relief? Our eyes oft clouded with unshed tears, we need a little laughter to wash them clear. And when was the last time you laughed so hard that tears flooded your cheeks? If you laugh long and hard enough, your sides start to cramp and your muscles ache. This is because laughter heals the tears and emotional pain you've held within you.

For this reason, most people can't sustain laughter over a prolonged period of time. Too much heartache begins to surface with laughter. So we stop laughing and get back to our serious selves and the business of living the way responsible people "should." Sadly, I once read that the typical person laughs—really laughs—for only thirty-seven minutes in a lifetime. So why does laughter threaten so many people? "You're not taking me seriously," someone may complain. Or, "Wipe that smile off your face or I'll do it for you."

Trying to "control" a child who is in total amusement is nearly impossible, for they're having too much fun. So adults, controlled by pain and fear, often resort to inflicting pain on children to get them out of their happiness so that it's possible to subordinate the little ones to the adults' will. Who of us has not had at least some experience of that? Even as adults, we often encounter those who insist on putting us in our place when we're having too much amusement. Laughter to those in great emotional pain is like suddenly opening the curtains to the bright morning sun for those with a hangover. The ego always feels threatened if it doesn't secure its illusion of having control over everything, including other human beings who possess free will. It thinks, *If I don't control them, what are they going to do to me? If I can't control them, they may not do what I need them to do.*

Parents, relatives, doctors, teachers, preachers, babysitters, and others who take responsibility for us inundate us, whether intentionally or not, early in our lives with their beliefs and emotions. Often, as spiritual beings, in childhood we are not in command of our new bodies enough to fully respond to them, so we generally end up taking a lot of their energy into us. As we mature physically, emotionally, and mentally, all that we took on earlier in life begins to re-emerge. This is a large part of why we have so much rebellion when we reach our teens; we're trying to reclaim the spiritual space that we gave up earlier. Unfortunately, most of us didn't learn to manage our reactions and respond creatively as souls by that point. And besides, being in resistance, we wanted to be taken *seriously* by others, to be accepted as members of whatever tribe we found ourselves in.

By the time we reach adulthood, we've had enormous practice in reacting in apathy, boredom, anger, jealousy, pride, seriousness, and a host of other forms of resistance that are approved by the culture we live in. And practice does make perfect. We become so good at it as we do things over and over until we perfect them. Then we do it more to refine our skill.

Responding is definitely an ability you have. One way or another, you are practicing every single day, all day long. If you've practiced for years to be unconscious, on autopilot, and just become whatever reactions kick off in your mind and body, then you're going to be an expert in that way. So, like a person who learned for years the "wrong" way to play the piano, as you learn a more effective way, you're going to have to unlearn your old habits as well as develop the new. It's not going to happen after just one lesson.

Practicing being in amusement in response to whatever happens takes awareness. First you must notice that you're in a routine you've practiced thousands of times before, and step back from it. Then choose instead to be in good humor about all the reactions that are going on within you about what is happening around you. You might think to yourself, *Wow! This anger is great! What an amazing energy. Isn't it wonderful? Go, baby, go!* Meanwhile, you're getting into more amusement and enjoying yourself as you discover how you used to be buried and controlled by all this rather than just playing with it. Remember, first, it's not about what's going on out there with the other person; it's about you having your soul purpose and fulfillment in life. And it begins with a little humor. Smile! You're on *Cosmic Camera!*

One of the greatest thieves of your natural humor and laughter are secrets. We pretend we're able to hide things, to keep things to ourselves, and no one will ever know. How silly. We're all on *Cosmic Camera* 24/7. If you don't realize that now, you'll get quite a surprise after you die. You'll get to experience your life from the view of that all-seeing, all-knowing "camera." Not a thought or feeling is missed. Whoops! There goes a nasty thought you just had.

Trying to hide things takes an enormous amount of our energy. Sure, we could hide many things from many people, but not from everyone, and *never* from the Cosmic Camera. We have a choice; we can build walls and more walls to keep others from finding out, or realize that everything is already known, that there's nothing to hide, and just be amused at the cosmic joke. Personally, when I see people's deep dark secrets, I'm not interested. I feel that secrets are only exciting to those who keep them. At least for me, other people's secrets are about as interesting as their summer vacation slides.

I once spent a whole year—365 days—practicing every day to respond more in amusement to life. Although I always had plenty of humor and could laugh pretty easily, I discovered it wasn't enough. When I was just starting to teach, one day during my meditation, I asked God what I needed to develop more in myself. "More amusement," I heard distinctly. *Okay*, I thought to myself, *I'll practice every day for the next month to have more amusement.*

Naturally, whenever you decide to practice something, you're going to encounter much of its counterpart. For instance, when you set out to develop patience, you get caught at every red light, traffic jam, and the longest line in the supermarket. When you're learning to be more loving, you often encounter people and situations you just want to teleport to another universe.

So, you can imagine what I went through in that month. A lot of the time, it just wasn't funny at all. Not a day would go by without me having some aggravating assault on my senses and sensibilities. But, by month's end, I was quite amused that I did a pretty decent job of it. I could see that responding in amusement to difficult and unpleasant situations was beginning to come much more easily and that I could laugh at myself more readily. So, it came as a surprise when my next monthly meditation came with a repeat assignment: I needed to develop still more amusement.

Okay, I thought. *At least it's a fun practice, so I'll sign up for another month.* Then, I got the same assignment for the third month! And again and again for twelve consecutive months. Maybe God was out of town and left me a recording. Well, I stuck it out. In fact, I mustered up some amusement and was able to catch up on some good humor.

On the last day of the twelfth month of developing more amusement, a particularly difficult morning at the local bank provided my graduation. At the time, I was overseeing seven different accounts for the organization I directed, and it seemed that all of them had discrepancies. Four separate times that morning, the bank asked me to come in to help straighten them out. Later, that afternoon, with everything worked out, I realized that I needed to take care of my personal account at the same bank.

Shaking my head and laughing, I went into the bank for the fifth time. Of course, I had to wait for the next available teller. While waiting, I "amused" myself by inspecting the FBI's Ten Most Wanted poster on the counter. I looked at the auras of the wanted bank robbers to see if there was any common denominator among them. While deeply absorbed in this, commotion erupted behind me. But, having lived in notorious Berkeley (a.k.a. *Bezerk*eley), California, for many years, sudden shouting, screaming, and other public displays of outrage had ceased to faze me. I didn't even turn around when deathly silence blanketed the room. Now *that's* strange, I thought, and I finally did turn around, only to discover that I was the only one left in the bank who wasn't facedown, spread-eagled on the floor . . . that is, besides the two gun-wielding bank robbers and the manager with a gun in his back.

I was standing smack dab between the two gunmen. The first decision I made was to not move unless ordered to do so. Then, I grounded and centered myself more and pulled my aura in closer. I took stock of what I had and decided they could have them all—clothes, wallet, everything. When I let go of all my "possessions," the humor in the situation struck me. Here I was in the midst of an armed bank robbery, sandwiched between two gunmen, one of them holding everyone on the floor at gunpoint, except me. He stood less than four feet directly in front of me and, every time he ordered someone on the floor to shut up, he swept his gun across my face to point at another person. In my amusement, I hoped he wouldn't sneeze while doing that. Then I realized that they never ordered me to lie down because they couldn't see me. I was not in their universe.

The two robbers were in fear and anger. Everyone in the place was in fear, except me, who was neutral and in complete amusement. To them, I didn't exist. As when you boil water and it turns into steam and becomes invisible, the power of amusement, laughter, and happiness rendered me invisible. Compared to the dense vibrations of fear, anger, and hostility, amusement was so much higher that, to those immersed in the lower vibrations, I had disappeared. Not once throughout the ordeal did either gunman notice me. And the moment I communicated to God that one of them was going to get violent, his partner shouted to him, "We've been here too long. We gotta get out of here now!" With that, he just turned and ran out of the bank, the other close behind.

After studying the surveillance tapes, the FBI detained me for over three hours because they couldn't figure out how I was "hanging out" with the gunmen while everyone else was on the floor. And the next morning, I was on the front page of five newspapers, shown calmly standing between the two gun-wielding bank robbers. I realized then that I had passed my final exam in amusement. Since then, I never got that assignment again.

Amusement is your inner laughter. It's about laughing with yourself in whatever condition you find yourself. It comes out of knowing that you got yourself into that situation in the first place, and the certainty that even this shall pass. No matter how bad things get, know that God is smiling at you: let's see how you're going to deal with this one.

Cultivating Compassion

Neutrality cuts us free from the tethers of reaction, and *amusement* gives us wings to glide upon God's smile. Now all we need is the compass that always points our way home. That third ingredient of awareness that helps us navigate through our life's journey to fulfillment is *compassion.* By having neutrality, amusement, and compassion, we lay a powerful foundation from which we can respond to the many challenges of our spiritual growth.

Compassion is love's own touch, the salve that heals the rift in the heart bleeding with fear and torn with judgment. Compassion restores the Oneness in all. Compassion toward others allows them to return to Oneness. You become as a magnetic compass, faithfully pointing always in the same direction.

Compassion heals the will that has been violated and makes it whole and free. Compassion says: "I know you're divided, in pain, and suffering, but I'm here with you in Oneness. You're afraid of where you are, but I am here with you and not afraid of where you are. There is nothing that you can be, do, or have that can keep me from loving you, for I am part of you. I do not hold the judgments you may have against yourself. I grant you the freedom to hold yourself to them or to free yourself of them. Either way, I respect and honor you, for you are part of my self."

Compassion isn't something we can possess. It isn't something some of us have and others do not. It's planted in each of our souls but, like a delicate plant, if we don't take care of the garden, it cannot grow. Daily, we must cultivate our awareness of the oneness of our Divine Being to grow our compassion.

Compassion is your soul's response to suffering. It's not so much what you do about suffering; it's about where you are with it. None of us deserves to suffer, yet we all do. We don't ask for suffering, but we each suffer sometime or another. I know of no one who lives a whole life without some suffering. Suffering is not what we ask for but the consequence of all our desires in conflict. It is the psychic pollution that results from an incorrect relationship with our inner divinity and soul purpose.

Once I was listening to a man complain about how he never gets any help. "I never get what I ask for," he said.

I pointed out to him, "Over many years, more than anything, you wanted to be left alone. You wanted to do things your way and were always asking, 'Why can't everyone just leave me alone?'"

He was surprised by how true that was and realized that he asked to be left alone when he was getting help and he asked for help when he was left alone. No, he never asked for suffering, but since he had never recognized how much he was getting what he asked for, he suffered regularly.

Compassion gives us the space to complete the cycles of our asking and receiving. Instead of insisting that we get what we want, how we want it, and when and where, by being compassionate we allow our whole process of receiving to develop in its own way and time, just as we must with a growing plant . . . or a human being. When we ask to be more neutral, the various judgments and expectations within us will surface. With compassion, we can let the old energies leave, and with acceptance and kindness, we can welcome in the new. When we ask for love, we discover how much jealousy, vengeance, and hate we carry within our heart, and realize all the things we do not love about ourselves. Naturally, we must clear that space before we can receive the love we asked for. Compassion provides the sanctuary in which we can complete our cycle of experiencing all the consequences of our asking and of our decisions.

If we live together in the same house, the crack in the wall is neither yours nor mine. Yet the house belongs to both of us, and if we fail to repair that crack, our house will eventually fall. Neither of us would then have a place to live. If we live in a large apartment complex and the sewer system isn't working, it's neither yours nor mine. Yet, once again, if we fail to have it repaired, we will lose our home. The same goes for our culture, our race, our humanity, and our universe. Who is suffering matters not. As with the crack in the wall, suffering belongs to no one, but we must all repair the damages or the whole house cannot stand.

When you overflow with compassion, you become the fountain, and the thirsty will come to drink of it. And God's inexhaustible well makes compassion available to all of us. Be the fountain for God's healing waters and make it more accessible to all. Respond with compassion to all that you encounter in yourself, in others, and in the world, and you will walk in the footsteps of Divinity.

ELEVEN

YOU ARE THE ANSWER—PART I: BUILDING THE TEMPLE OF THE SOUL

. . . just as one might suppose
a living figure to be in the hard alpine stone,
so to bring it out,
it gradually grows, as the stone falls away;
in the same way some good works,
worthy of the trembling soul
lie hidden beneath the lid of our own bodies,
underneath our crude, rough skin.

—Michelangelo (from Rupert Hodson's
Michelangelo: Sculptor)

With truth as our chisel, we sculpt the temple of our soul. And from the quarry that is our life, we must chip away the illusions of a solid and fixed world, to gradually let our "living figure" grow "as the stone falls away." Perhaps what made Michelangelo such an extraordinary sculptor was that he persisted in looking beyond the appearance of the cold, hard, and unmoving marble block to see divine purpose breathing within it. And rather than imposing his personal creative will upon the piece as most artists are wont to do, he dedicated his life to liberating the ever-flowing radiance and beauty of God's love, whether in celebration of our glorious achievements or as it embraced the most tragic of human suffering.

When I behold Michelangelo's *David, Dying Slave,* or *Pietà,* I see Divinity shining through its various human disguises. Under his passionate care and profound vision, all the solidity, rigidity, density, and immobility of stone could not contain and limit the divine splendor. For our part, we can choose to let our life remain simply a block of stone—our infinite, eternal, and immortal spirit encased in the seeming limitations of our material existence—or, like Michelangelo, we can choose to resurrect Divinity from our illusions of a limited and mortal life.

To provide a sanctuary for the soul amidst the clatter and clamor of the world, we might build a temple, a place of worship, which reminds us that, despite the ever-changing conditions we face in the world, all is still God, and that we must stay awake, must not forget. A temple serves to ground heaven on this earth. And around it, we can form a community to help build humanity into a true house of Divinity. We must make our body such a temple of the soul.

Divine grace births for us a physical body, created from the elements through our parents. Our incarnation into that body is an adventure more exciting and fulfilling than any story ever imagined. Our purpose is to discover and resurrect from this physical elemental body our true immortal body of light and become a complete human being—God's only begotten.

The Secret Formula

In its symbol for the planet Mercury, esoteric astrology gives us the secret formula for becoming the complete human being. Mercury is the planet ruled by the messenger to the gods and its symbol shows the moon perched on the sun resting on the foundation of the earth. The cross represents the earth with its four directions. It is our physical body grounded in the earth. Supported by it sits the radiant sun represented by the circle. This is our life-giving heart, which when full of love and undivided by judgment, overflows with oneness. The moon, represented as a crescent, like an empty bowl, rests atop the sun. If we can empty our mind of fear's chattering resistance, we inherit the cosmic consciousness of Divinity. When we live by this secret formula, like Mercury, we bridge heaven and earth. And so out from "beneath the lid of our own bodies, underneath our crude rough skin," we gradually emerge into the living figure of a complete and radiant human being.

The Three Aspects of the Soul

We do not "have" a soul. We *are* the soul that incarnates into the human body-mind. And we do so as three aspects of our soul-self, each functioning independently as its own "self"—the feeling self, the reasoning self, and the transcendent, or higher, self. During much of our incarnation, however, the three selves may not align in unity of communication and purpose, as represented in the symbol for the complete human being. Often the feeling self and the reasoning self quibble as do children while a benevolent parent, the transcendent self, looks on patiently, a god waiting to be asked to help.

You may have experienced this inner quarreling at times as feeling the tug of your heartstrings while your head reasons against it. Or, once your head offers you the only logical solution to a problem, your heart pleads its emotional case. Worse yet, have you ever had a sense of God's will while your head ran around in circles and your heart simply went AWOL? You know your heart can't think and your head can't feel, so how do you get them to cooperate in sync with Divinity?

When Jesus declared what was the first of the two greatest commandments, He gave the ultimate instruction in how to align and integrate all three selves: "You are to love the Lord your God with all your heart and all your soul and all your mind" (Matthew 22:37). In this, your "heart" is the feeling self, your "soul" is the higher self, and your "mind" is the reasoning self. To fulfill your purpose in the Oneness of Divinity, you must realize the unique experience of oneness in each of these selves.

The feeling self takes care of your memory. And preserving memory makes use of the sensate and imprinting capability of soul energy. This self "feels" the experience as vibrations and retains an "imprint" of it. In order to retain it as memory, it associates the energy impression with other imprints. The feeling self then acts as a clerk who files and cross-indexes all the imprints of experience by association. Similar vibration patterns are catalogued together. It also retrieves the memories by association. Thus, when you smell a particular perfume, you may "remember" a loved one who wore it. Or you may feel dread in a new environment if it is similar to one where you were traumatized or around a person resembling someone who hurt you. Your feeling self continuously oversees your subconscious memory transactions.

Not all the selves incarnate simultaneously. The feeling self, for example, enters the body at about age four and serves as your main directing consciousness in the body until around age seven. It normally takes residence in a soft, cavelike energy space at the top back portion of the heart.

The reasoning self oversees your analytical functions. This part analyzes sensory, memory, and intuitive data to formulate conclusions. It acts as the executive director in your "corporation," following directives from above and receiving data from below. This aspect enters the body at about age seven and becomes fully functional and the major directing force of your body-mind at around age fourteen. The seat of the reasoning self is the pineal gland in the brain.

The higher self normally remains outside the physical boundaries of the body, about three feet above the head, residing within an energy center (chakra) there. This transcendent aspect of the soul is the "spark of God" and functions as the "North Star" for the soul's journey of incarnation. It is also like the CEO and oversees the life and purpose of the corporation. The higher self has your "blueprint" for directing your destiny as well as retaining your complete incarnational record.

These three selves can work independently of each other but, when certain conditions are met, they work in unison. When your feeling self experiences unity between body and spirit, it surrenders its control to your reasoning self and acts under its direction. When young children, still mostly directed by the feeling self, feel unity with a parent, they will trust and willingly follow that parent's decisions and guidance. If, however, the feeling self experiences a break in the unity of body and spirit, it takes its own control and will not follow reason. On an associative level, it can actually operate even on an irrational formula such as "I have to destroy myself in order to survive."

Unless it feels the oneness again, it can continue to distance itself further and further from the reasoning self in order to "survive." If, for example, you try to *reason* with a teenager who, after experiencing a split in unity between spirit and body, is operating as the feeling self, you are unlikely to succeed. Only if you can foster the *feeling* of oneness will you bring about cooperation and rational communication.

Once there is unity of body and spirit, and your reasoning self assumes the role of directing consciousness, whenever you have certainty, your reasoning self will relinquish its control of your body-mind to your higher self. You will then function on a higher intuitive level. In this way, you begin to embody more of your spiritual awareness and energy.

Your certainty in Divinity brings about intuition, and intuition brings about the *experience* of God. The founder of the Sufi Order in the West, Hazrat Inayat Khan, quoted from the teachings of the *Gayan*, "When you make God a reality, God will make you the truth." The more you distill your karmic experiences into divine wisdom, the more you will align your three selves into a harmonious spiritual body of truth. Out of the apparent solidity of your elemental body, as you chisel away divisive and limiting beliefs, invalidation, and suppressed emotional energies, you will unveil the true temple of the soul through which Divinity manifests Itself.

Building Our Temple

The greatest sculptor cannot create a masterpiece without the stone from which to carve it. Likewise, we cannot shape our awareness and energy into a radiant immortal body without an elemental body. For it is only through our body-mind that we, as spiritual beings, can gain our experience of time, space, and manifesting form, and experience objective reality in the full spectrum of creation.

The body into which we incarnate is made up of the elements of the earth and the karmic patterns of our past actions, sentiments, and thoughts. The body, which we shape through our conscious response to all that we encounter in life, must transcend the karmic cycles of cause and effect, and be able to accommodate the infinity, eternity, and immortality of spirit. If we pollute our awareness with ignorance, indifference, resistance, attachment, and powerlessness, we would not be able to express the omniscience, omnipresence, and omnipotence of Divinity. Life must be able to flow through our body unimpeded. We must truly let our light shine.

You are the answer to the promptings of life's purpose. What kind of answer are you now? What do you see when you look at who you have become? What kind of answer would you like to be? What do you like about yourself and what do you wish to change? You *are* your work-in-progress. Just as sculptors must hold a vision of the masterpiece and at the same time as acknowledge how the sculpture looks at present, we must appreciate our potential as well as our current reality. Both are necessary. Artists who have no vision of the destiny of the stone merely chip away at it with no purpose. If they cannot accept their work-in-progress because it isn't perfect enough, then they cannot proceed with it. Your life is one of being and becoming . . . until at last you are.

TWELVE

YOU ARE THE ANSWER—PART II: MASTERING YOUR MEMORIES

Spirit is limitless. We are not inherently restricted. All limitations—the conditions of our existence—are learned and memorized. They are not intrinsically real. All our suffering is remembered. Our memories hold everything that restricts our total freedom to be our divine spiritual self. The true purpose for remembering is to forget what we are not, so that we may become who we are. Memories are not our masters; we do not have to be beholden to them. This is the choice we have, and it is the secret to our freedom.

Anatomy of Memory

Memory is what we remember. It is information preserved over time that can be recalled. Memory consists of:

1) the actual "data" or energy pattern of experience;

2) the "charge" or polarity of experience (attractive, repulsive, or neutral);

3) the labeling of experience;

4) associations of elements within the experience with other memories (filing and cross-matching);

5) the space (energy field) in which the data is preserved;

6) the search and retrieval engine.

Our memories begin with the polarization of our consciousness and our interaction with the forces of attraction, repulsion, and neutrality. Until we establish neutrality within our self, attractive forces attract us, repulsive forces repel us, and we remain indifferent to the neutrality of the oneness of spirit. Pulled and pushed by these forces, we attach labels to each change of polarity in our continuous experience. Once we attach a label to a segment of our experience, it becomes preserved as a "holographic multisensory" picture. Only when we attach something such as a label or another picture to the original experience can we preserve it in memory over time.

Each individual "memory" is preserved in time by association with some other information not part of the actual experience. For example, let's say you're dancing. The original experience is a flow of movements accompanied by various sensations. Unless you associate that particular sequence of movements under the label of "dancing," you wouldn't be able to say later that you had been dancing. You would not have remembered "dancing" as a separate activity from the rest of your life. So, your experience became associated with the label: "dancing." If you thoroughly enjoyed the experience, you may further associate the experience with the label: "enjoyable," which in turn is associated with many other activities. If instead you fell down, broke your leg, and were embarrassed by it, dancing may be categorized as "painful and humiliating." You may even create a judgment to add to that, such as "dreadful." So when you remember your experiences, at first most of them are fraught with associations. Some memories are so buried in associations that you may not be able to easily recall the original experience itself.

Any time we alter the essential "data" of the original experience by associating something else with it, we preserve that memory as a separate "picture" in time. If we don't alter our experience of the original event, no memory persists and we just have the experience in our being as wisdom. This is why we can't remember a "truth." When we have that shining moment of realization, an epiphany, we might try to hold on to it, but it passes by like the proverbial flash bulb going off over our heads. "I got it!" you might exclaim, only to find yourself unable to explain exactly what it was to your friends. But if you examine your being, you'll find that the experience of truth changed you fundamentally even if you can't "remember" what it was. "Facts" can be remembered, but truth can only be experienced, moment-by-moment.

When we fully digest and assimilate our experience, it turns into wisdom, which becomes part of our being instead of remaining a separate memory unit in a file. For instance, as beginners learning to play a new sport or a musical instrument, we "remember" to hold our hands this way and our posture that way to do what we need to do. It's awkward and slow since we need to remind ourselves how to do everything. We keep shuttling back to our memories. After enough practice, the process becomes "second nature." We no longer need to "remember" each time we attempt it; we just "know" what to do. We no longer have to think to make ourselves do it; our actions effortlessly flow from our being. We have distilled our experience into wisdom instead of accessing individual memories—our being *is* the doing.

A separate survival memory "file" begins in our associative mind during moments of our unconsciousness caused by a division of our consciousness. During our physical incarnation, this happens when we experience trauma. When we sustain physical trauma, such as a blow or cut of sufficient force, it can interrupt the vital flow of energy throughout the body. This flow of energy is our life force flowing through the body just beneath the skin, and is our connection to our body. Our initial experience of pain is actually a kind of short-circuit in the body, much like blowing an electrical fuse.

Once our connecting flow is interrupted, we leave the body. Our light goes out temporarily and our consciousness is separated from the body consciousness. If the trauma was intense enough, however, we may be "out cold" or may even become so completely disconnected from the body that we die. With the exception of our death, when we return to the body, the light goes back on and consciousness is present once again.

If we fail to replace the "blown fuse" upon our return into the body, however, the mind bypasses that circuit, and the various components that made up that traumatic experience become held as unconscious survival memory. This self-preservation aspect of the mind is strictly associative, automatic, and has no intellectual reasoning capacity. Its only "logic" is associating one frequency with another. Whenever there is a match (as when a tuning fork vibrates in sync with a guitar string), the associative mind puts them together in the same organizing file in memory.

During our out-of-the-body unconsciousness (even partially), the reasoning self turns down and the associative mind "remembers" everything that happens. If and when we return, all of that information then becomes associated under the "survival" file. After all, we made it, didn't we? Unfortunately, that means all that happened while we were "out" translates into what made it possible for us to survive. If we are threatened again, the memory held in unconsciousness gets restimulated and dictates that, if we are to survive again, we need to reenact the elements of what happened previously when we were traumatized.

Here's an illustration of that: during a healing session with a woman who wanted to have healthier relationships with men, I uncovered an incident in her early childhood in which her father beat her. The initial pain of being struck by her father knocked her spiritually out of her body, and while she was out, he continued his physical and verbal assault. So the abuse became part of her unconscious survival information. When she was first out in the world, she was in fear and doubt over her ability to survive on her own. This kicked in her survival memory and she unconsciously gravitated toward an abusive man with whom she went into a relationship. Whenever her survival was threatened—whether it was concerning finances, her job, or her relationship—her partner would begin to abuse her physically and verbally. And every time she was so traumatized, she left her body and collected more "data" of abuse to "solve" her survival needs. Consciously, she hated this cycle of abuse, yet she could not seem to step out of the vicious pattern. Every time she tried to leave, her memories dictated that she "needed" the abusive relationship in order to survive. Only when she began to validate her spiritual self, choose truth, and consciously practice being present in her body did she emancipate herself from her unconscious memories. Having developed seniority over her subconscious memories, today she is a spiritually aware person involved in healthy relationships and on her path of fulfillment.

The "blown fuse" is the location where we hold in our memory the physical pain of the original trauma. It is held in the actual physical location of the trauma in the body as well as stored as an unconscious survival memory in the associative mind. Replacing the fuse means de-energizing the mental picture that holds the original trauma pain, reclaiming that energy back to our spiritual self, and letting the life force once again flow through that circuit in the body. By taking charge of our spiritual awareness, we can free ourselves not only from the cycles of abuse, addiction, and any other patterns of self-destruction, but also from the limitations of our physical body.

Many years ago, a young woman came to me for healing. She was blind, but her desire for healing was not about her blindness. It was about her emotional problems in her romantic relationships. When I looked at her clairvoyantly to find out what was affecting her, I found one of her "blown fuses." I saw the memory picture of her as a small child walking into her parents' bedroom while they were making love. The severe reaction from her parents threatened her, and all their fear, shame, guilt, and anger, as well as their mental commands of "don't look," "don't see what we're doing," and "go away," became imprinted on that image of a romantic/sexual relationship. As a result of the forbidden sight, over the next several years, her vision deteriorated until she finally lost her sight altogether and, whenever she became romantically involved, she would re-experience all those past emotions of her parents.

The instant I extracted the emotionally charged picture, she broke down sobbing. When she wiped the tears out of her eyes, she stared past me at the wall. Half laughing and half crying, she turned to me and exclaimed, "I can read the words on that poster!" Then, she proceeded to examine each face in the room. Her vision returned to her for the first time in over seven years.

Not all healing works this easily, however. At times, the initial unconscious survival memory has been buried under so many other associations that getting to it may be more a process of peeling the layers away over time. In this one woman's case, she hadn't built up that much on the particular trauma that started her blindness. Much of this owed to her tremendous acceptance of herself and the conditions of her life.

Often, the sooner you can get to the pain incident, the easier it is to reverse it. One time I mistook a hot steam pipe for a handrail. As I lost my footing next to it, I grabbed the pipe. My hand instantly sizzled, the skin literally steaming off my hand. As my body went into a mild shock, I found myself floating above it. Once I realized what had happened, I returned into my body and felt the excruciating pain in my hand for the first time. I grounded myself and tuned in to the pain picture that had formed in my unconscious survival memory. Once I mentally dissolved the picture and called back the energy from it into my being, the skin on my hand healed right before my own eyes, as if someone had turned the movie on reverse. The blistered, ashen-white skin of my hand rapidly returned to its normal smoothness and healthy pink color. All the pain was gone and no trace of the severe burn remained.

In other instances, I have nice scars to show for injuries for which I didn't get to the trauma pictures completely. In most cases, I had other priorities and neglected to do the necessary exploration. Often, only after peeling off layers of pictures and energies over the years do I finally arrive at the original pain I incurred. In many cases, until I discover the survival memory picture, I don't even recall having had such an experience.

One of the keys to healing, of turning karma into wisdom and fulfilling your soul purpose, is to reclaim your power from your memories. The more energy you invest in your memories, the more power they will have over you. In order to build your temple of the soul, you must choose truth over memory. Then, your subconscious memories cease to be your slave master.

It's Only a Picture

At first, it may be hard to believe, but most of what you think you're experiencing as "reality" are merely memory pictures. And the majority of those pictures aren't even yours. At first, the associative mind works subconsciously since it controls much of your awareness. The more energy you reclaim from the pictures held there, the more conscious you will become of the inner workings of your mind.

Your associative mind is constantly working beneath your regular consciousness. It's always shooting out pictures from past experiences to try to keep you alive and "together." The intentions are good but, unfortunately, the pictures have little to do with the present objective reality. They are just associations from the past that happen to "match" some of the energy patterns of what's going on now. It's like the high-tech TV sportscaster calling up on the computer screen all a player's statistics as he enters the batter's box. Those statistics are old history and the sportscaster telling us what happened the last time this batter went up against this same pitcher has nothing in reality to do with their current encounter. But the athlete's performance may be greatly influenced by the emotions and expectations brought up by recalling those past experiences.

We all have that high-tech booth right in our own body-mind. Our computer is constantly telling us how we goofed up the last ten times we did what we're now about to do, or how great we did it the last time so we have to do better now. All that is nothing but old news and everyone else's judgments and expectations that we kept in our memory. Why? We thought they were important at the time. How often have we done things to please our parents, partners, teachers, friends, or bosses?

How important have we made their opinions about us? We hang on to a lot of that until we become more aware and start to choose what to keep in our memory files.

By choosing truth each time we encounter these hidden pictures in our mind, we take back our power from them. Instead of allowing our past memories and others' opinions about them to control our destiny, we begin to choose which way to go to fulfill our purpose. One way or another we must fulfill our purpose, but we have total freedom in how we choose to go about it.

When you get stuck, always remind yourself that what you're stuck on is "only a picture." If you're beating yourself up because you failed in something, those feelings of grief, anger, and frustration as well as the thoughts that go with them are all contained in little pictures in your associative mind. The intensity of those emotions and thoughts that you experience is the amount of your power you put into them. You must decide to step back from the pictures and realize that, as totally real and unchangeable as they may seem to you now, they are nothing more than pictures. It is comparable to the way a slide projector magnifies the slides to become larger than life on the screen. What you see on that screen may have happened before, but it isn't happening now. It would be silly to get all worked up and try to do something about a slide show of what happened when you were three years old, wouldn't it? Yet that's what most people do, day in and day out.

Here's a recent example involving a couple that I observed clairvoyantly. The wife was complaining to her husband that she didn't want to feel the way she was feeling. Since resistance feeds more energy to what is being resisted, her negative feelings grew. The husband in turn matched her resistance. He became frustrated that his wife, being self-absorbed in her own discomfort, wasn't tending to his needs so he started trying to "fix" her.

What was happening beneath the surface? I saw restimulated within her subconscious mind a picture of her as a four-year-old. In the picture, she felt rejected and that she couldn't do anything right. She wanted to be comforted and was sending her feeling of inadequacy and rejection to her mother. That same picture included her mother resisting those feelings because she didn't want to feel them either. The judgment that got superimposed on her daughter's picture was that something was wrong with her since there was no reason for her to feel the way she did.

Meanwhile, with the couple in the present, the wife was channeling her energy through this picture package and her husband was becoming the terminal for it. She was subconsciously sending to him all those feelings just as she did to her mother. This in turn reactivated in the husband's subconscious a memory picture of him as an infant on a high chair.

In it, he has soiled his diaper and, being quite uncomfortable, wants to be cleaned up. His crying upsets his napping father, at home from work on his one day off a week. The father, in anger and resistance, feels that it's the mother's job to take care of the baby, especially on his day off. He yells at the mother to "shut the baby up." She reacts in total resistance and indignation. She feels he's the one who's closest to the baby, so why doesn't he take care of his son for a change? She silently complains, *When do I ever get to rest? Why do I always have to do everything? What's wrong with my husband?* Yet she also feels guilty about letting her baby cry, and she can't tell her husband since she is afraid of him. So she gets up in a huff to tend to the baby.

Now, back to the husband in the present example. In this picture of him as an infant, there are three distinct viewpoints:

1) Himself as an infant depending on someone to take away his discomfort.

2) His father resisting the judgment that taking care of the baby is his responsibility.

3) His mother's guilt toward him and her resistance toward his father.

So, in the present example, the husband is shuttling from one viewpoint to another, all of which contain resistance. How this plays out for him now with respect to his wife is that he resists her complaining (his father toward the baby crying), resists the wife expecting him to do something about it (his mother toward the father), yet having to do it (his mother toward taking care of the baby), and resists that no one (his wife at this time) is taking care of his needs (him as a baby).

Now, as involved as that may seem, this is the simplified version of the actual mechanics that took place in a reactionary interaction between two people. What I described was just one clustering of pictures in each person. Most people simply move from one picture cluster to another throughout the day, every day, and consider that living. Yet, as you consciously reclaim your power from these memory pictures, you begin to transfer your energy from the associative (subconscious) mind to your conscious mind, and you start to more fully respond to the joyous celebration that is life.

When we forget that we are merely dealing with pictures, we get stuck. We have such power and ability to make these pictures "come alive" that we end up believing in them more than we do in ourselves. It's akin to being so absorbed in a movie that we start trying to control or change what happens next in it. Of course, we all know that we can't change what the movie characters say or do, yet, when it comes to the pictures in our memory, we constantly fight against them and try to change them. But we cannot change the pictures in our subconscious memory. If you took a picture of an elephant, you can't change it into a mouse. The picture you took originally is always going to stay that way.

Why we often remember things differently is not that the original picture changed but, because we put so many other pictures on top of it, we no longer remember the actual original picture. It's the classic "fish story" in which the fish you caught gets bigger each time you tell the story. But examining the original picture of the fish you caught would surely bring it back to size.

If the original picture contains painful feelings, no matter how many times you recall that picture, it will still contain the same pain. The difference will be in the intensity. The intensity depends on how much of your energy you put into that picture. When we forget that we're dealing with a picture, we experience the same feelings, resistances, thoughts, and everything else that was in that picture. If we don't like what we feel and think, we're going to try to change it or "fix" it. Since we can't change or fix a picture to be any different than it is, we end up putting more and more energy into it. It then begins to exert more influence and control over us. Once we realize that we're only fighting a set of pictures, we can consciously decide to release our hold on these pictures and let them go. When we reclaim our energy from the pictures, they no longer control our experience or actions.

When you pull out your old photo album and see that picture of yourself as a kid in elementary school with buckteeth and wire-rim glasses, do you try to change it? Even if it were possible, what good would it do now? You aren't that kid anymore. You might laugh and say, "Oh, look at that ugly duckling!" But you know it has nothing to do with you now. You can enjoy it for what it was and then let it go. Appreciate what you learned from that experience.

The same goes for your memory pictures—they will always be the snapshots as they were taken. You grow and change, but the pictures stay the same. Every time you become aware that you're looking at your life, relationship, or whatever you're currently involved in, through the filter of past pictures or even other people's pictures, know with certainty that you don't have to solve, fix, or change them, so just decide to let them go. Don't try to change the picture; just shift your relationship to it. Decide that you're no longer beholden to it. Know that when you're stuck, all you're feeling and thinking are the contents of that picture. Decide you can "un-become" it. If you're thinking, *I hate this, I hate this*, that's what's in the picture. If you're thinking, *I don't want to feel this way*, that, too, is part of the picture you need to step out of. If you're feeling guilty, sad, or angry, they are all parts of the picture, and not some separate truth that is happening. They're all just reruns! Been there, done that before. It's time to get off the treadmill.

If you can't seem to get directly to the whole picture right away, by mentally repeating the word or thought that keeps coming up in your mind, with detachment, you will de-energize that part of the picture. You might find words, phrases, or sentences going round and round in your head, such as "What's wrong with me?" "I'm so tired," "I can't keep this up," "How could I have done this?" "What a jerk he is," or thousands of other possibilities. When you mentally repeat them, don't project them to yourself or anyone else. Don't make it an affirmation but, in neutrality and with a touch of amusement, just mentally repeat them in order to shake all the energy out of the words. In other words, don't mean it. Just repeat them and detach from their meaning or value. And if you find a little humor in them, you might just start laughing. When you are repeating, "How stupid can I be?" smile, because you know it's not true. Even if it is true, so what? All conditions change. Nothing can ever stay the same.

Remember, they are just words, and words are just energy. Relieve them of the power you had previously given to them and you will free yourself of the power of those words. (Originally this was the purpose of "confession.") With detached repetition, the "charge" and the amendments to the original picture begin to fall off. In this way, you peel off layers of illusion from the truth of your experience.

THIRTEEN

YOU ARE THE ANSWER—PART III: CHOOSING TRUTH AT EVERY CROSSROADS

Life is full of tough choices, ain't it?

—Ursula, the Witch, in *The Little Mermaid*

The crossroads in your life are always places of choice. Although an external life situation may challenge you to make a choice, the process of deciding is always internal. Often you may try to make the "right" choice. Yet truth is not in *what* you choose, but in you. You are the answer and your choice is your expression of that truth. Choosing truth means that your decision will be based not on some external circumstance, expectation, judgment, or other fixed belief but on your relationship with your inner Source. What is important is not whether this is the "right" or the "best" choice, but how you make the choice and what you do with the choice you make. That is what shapes you, builds the temple of the soul, and fulfills your purpose.

Truth sets you free. It is the *only* choice for your freedom. Real choice isn't about right or wrong, good or bad, for or against. It's about whether something is true to the Oneness within. Does it ring true to your divine purpose?

Facts don't constitute truth. You can be factual but not tell the truth. Facts are created. They are established by agreement through memory. They are, by nature, of the past. Truth can only be known here and now.

Touching truth is so wonderful that you want to hold on to it. Yet you find it is impossible to do so. You can never hold on to truth because the moment you do, you have changed it and are no longer in the present with it. What you will be holding instead is a subjective memory of how you experienced the truth and what you thought and felt about it. You've put your own window-dressing on the truth. No one can hold on to truth. Truth not only sets you free; it *is* free. So, each time you choose truth, you liberate a part of your divinity.

Fulfilling your purpose is a process of choosing truth at every crossroads. Do I take the path to the left or to the right? Do I give or do I receive? Shall I stay or shall I leave? Do I say yes or no? To choose truth requires you to surrender the judgments you hold within you. Are you willing to discover what is real and what is merely a projection of someone's belief about it?

Dichotomies

The entire universe we live in is created through polar opposites in constant interaction. Energy flows through the dichotomies: positive/negative, male/female, spirit/material. When you create a judgment against something, you are denying one pole of the dichotomy. Examples might be "I have to be right," "it isn't good enough," or "this is the only way it will work." And since your energy needs both the positive and negative poles for it to flow, judgment short-circuits it. The more judgments you hold on to, the less the universal energy can flow through you. Then, you become isolated from the wholeness of the universe. You fall from its grace.

When you're attached to something, you fall out of the flow of this energy of oneness. If you try to hold on, you slip away from truth. For truth is attached to nothing and nothing is attached to truth. Truth is. It stands alone.

We always have a choice in everything. "I didn't have a choice" is never true. We choose to be a certain way. We choose to do what we do. Even if someone has a gun to your head or is holding your loved one hostage, what you do is still your choice. You may choose to do exactly as your captor tells you or resist, but it's still your choice.

The real choice is always between truth and what appears to be. The person threatening you may say, "If you don't do as I say, I will do something you wouldn't want." That's what he's saying but it's not the truth. He may be totally prepared to back up that threat, but the threat itself is not the truth. It's still only what he's *saying*. It's outside you. Truth is always within. It is never outside your being.

The amazing thing is that when you are willing to choose truth, anything can happen. A few years ago, Patty, a friend of mine, did not seem to have much of a choice physically. The car she was driving was suddenly squashed like a bug up against the front of a semi-truck. The big rig had changed lanes right into the side of her subcompact and snatched it up like some monstrous vacuum cleaner sucking up fuzz off a carpet. She was immobile, having no control, barreling down the freeway in a crumpled heap of metal pressed up against the grill of the behemoth. Incredibly, the truck driver saw nothing, heard nothing, felt nothing.

Although Patty could do nothing physically, she decided she wasn't powerless spiritually. First, she grounded herself energetically. Then, she chose to let go of trying to control the physical events or their outcomes. She chose truth over fear of what could be, should be, or had to be. She chose the truth that no matter what the outcome—even her physical death—she would be all right. As soon as she made that decision, in spite of all the chaos around her, she found herself completely at peace.

According to horrified eyewitnesses, the big rig dragged Patty and her car more than a mile before they could finally get the trucker's attention. And when he finally stopped, in shock and disbelief, he helped Patty out of what was left of her car and she walked away without a scratch.

Truth transcends cause and effect. Miracles happen. What is true right here, right now? With truth, there is never a standard answer. The situation may appear identical to another situation, but the truth may dictate a different decision.

Getting Stuck in a Dichotomy

How much of your energy, awareness, and being have been held hostage to a choice such as, "Shall I go or shall I stay?" This could be about a job, a marriage, a residence, school, or anything. How often do we become prisoners to a pair of opposite choices?

What happens, at first, when you ask yourself this kind of question? When you look at one side of the choice, you are barraged with considerations and emotions going against it. You find all the reasons why you shouldn't or can't have that choice. Then you look at the alternative and the same thing happens. You get all the reasons and feelings why you shouldn't or you can't. One way or the other, it's wrong, bad, or not good enough.

You get stuck in the middle. What do you base your decision on? What's the right choice? Which choice is better? Which will make you happier? Which is the lesser of two evils? As long as you're stuck, you can't fulfill your purpose.

When this happens, you're giving up your power to the choices. You must free yourself in relationship to the choices. Give power to your inner being that's always in touch with God. There is no standard "right" or "better" choice. Remember, the truth is in *you*, not in the choices. You can consult others for information and opinions, but use them only to find and validate your own intuitive knowing.

If you're attached to either end of the dichotomy, you will not be able to choose truth. A battery needs both positive and negative terminals in order for electricity to flow between them. Similarly, when you are free to have each side of the dichotomy in your choice, your energy flows between them. When you're attached to, or cannot allow yourself to have, one side or the other, the two ends short-circuit. You become stuck.

Initially, in making a choice, you might think that it's the choice you make that's going to make a difference in whether you can or cannot have what you want. In truth, it is the opposite. When you can have (are free to receive) the outcome you desire, you'll make the right choice. You create everything in spirit within you first. Then, you can manifest it into your life and the physical world.

Having Your Freedom of Choice

Let's consider the dichotomy: I stay / I leave. When you consider staying, you get an avalanche of thoughts, feelings, and images that say no. If it concerns a job, the considerations that come up might be: "I won't ever have enough money," "I'll have to suffer with this boss," "I can't get into a better position," "I'll be miserable."

On the other hand, when you look at leaving, you may become aware of the fear of not making it on your own. Thoughts may surface: "What if it's no better in the next job?" "What if I don't get a better job?" "What if I don't get a job at all?" "What if I lose my benefits?"

Mountains of these pictures are stashed in your subconscious memory. They're all lies. They may have happened to you or someone else at one time, but it's not true here and now. If you feed those pictures enough energy, history will repeat itself. However, you can change history.

Know that, as you meditate on each side of the dichotomy in a choice, all the confusion, emotions, and thoughts that surface in your mind are only pictures. And they're not even yours! Choose neutrality and disengage from them. Release them and take back your energy and seniority. Then, you will find, as Patty did, that whatever the outcome, you'll be all right, and fulfillment and happiness are within you. Now you're free to make your decision. Remember, if you're not free to leave, you won't truly stay. If you can't have staying, you won't fully leave. If you can't be happy with yourself about dying, you won't truly be happy with yourself about living. You must be complete with both sides.

Once you free yourself from the attachments on each side of the dichotomy, you will discover that truth always says: "both and," "now and always," and "one and the many." It's the ego and its fear that insists, "either/or," "now or never," and "one or the many." You will also find that once you are free of the power of "either/or," you are not limited to a choice within its dictate. What you can have will be limited only by your imagination.

Mystics throughout the ages have called the body "the temple of the soul," for it houses the soul and it is through this body that we can know our Creator. When a soul is born into the world, infinity, eternity, and immortality incarnate into space, time, and mortality. Limitlessness encounters limitations. Omniscience meets ignorance and illusion. Omnipotence feels powerless in making things obey its every command. And the soul faces the supreme challenge in its journey through eternity: "What if a man gain the whole world and lose his own soul?"

The journey never ends, but there is a turning point, a kind of graduation from limitation and mortality to freedom and immortality. Through the crucible that is our life, each time we choose truth, we distill wisdom, drop-by-drop. And in doing so, we resurrect our divinity from the illusory cross of materiality, and we fulfill our soul purpose.

FOURTEEN

LOVE IS THE QUESTION: ANSWERING TO THE GREATER MIRACLE

Is it a miracle if you walk away unharmed from an accident that should have caused you serious injury, if not death? What if a thug lunges at you with a knife but suddenly changes his mind and lets you go? Is that a miracle? Would you consider it miraculous if money or other objects materialize right in the palm of your hand? How about if angels and other celestial beings show up in your living room to talk with you? Or what if you shake a man's hand and his cancerous tumor disappears? Is that a true miracle? But is it any less extraordinary when a woman decides not to kill herself because you offered her a little compassion and understanding?

I have experienced all of these things and countless other examples of what many might consider miraculous—or even impossible—happenings. In fact, I have had so many extraordinary occurrences that, at one point in my life, I found myself taking them for granted and becoming indifferent to them.

I was giving healing to and teaching hundreds of people, and every day miracles abounded. Some even called me a "miracle maker" and many came to me *demanding* that I produce miracles for them. In the same way that some people go to work day after day to flip burgers, I found myself going to work every day to flip miracles. There was something definitely wrong with this picture. I realized there was nothing wrong with *what* I was doing, only in *how* I was going about it. It was then that I woke myself up to a greater miracle.

I had felt the same feeling many years before when I woke up to the fact that I was smoking three packs of cigarettes a day. *What are you doing to yourself?* I asked in horror. In my ignorance, I had been taking for granted this beautiful life I was given, complete with a healthy body, intelligence, talents, and abilities. I may have excelled in school, but I'd lost sight of part of my purpose for living. For whom was I smoking anyway? Certainly it wasn't serving me any good purpose other than masking my pain of not being true to myself. I was compromising my soul purpose in favor of being acceptable to and respected by others. And I had been willing to endanger my very life to do that.

My smoking was merely an external reflection of a deeper inner conflict: that how I was living did not truly reflect who I was and how I felt about life. I felt I had so much love to offer, but there seemed to be no one available to give it to. I was lonely. Often we attempt to assuage such pains and fears with external salves such as smoking, drinking, taking drugs, chasing thrills, seeking relationships with the "perfect" person, or collecting heroic accomplishments. Whatever painkiller we use, we become as addicts needing more and more of it. Quickly, we become immune to the dosage because whatever relief, high, or happiness we feel is not true fulfillment but merely temporary escape. When we fail to appreciate what we already have, we become disconnected from the purpose and meaning of our life, and experience this disconnection as the pain of isolation and loneliness.

The moment I awoke to what I was doing to myself, I threw away my cigarettes, never touched one again, and have never missed the habit. And shortly after I quit smoking, I changed my whole life; I changed residence and began to develop my healing abilities. With a renewed faith in myself, I was able to take the leap.

A dozen years later, I found myself at a similar crossroads. This time my salve of choice was not cigarettes but indifference to the many miracles with which life blessed me. This was an even bigger wake-up call for me, for, although cigarettes can kill the body, indifference kills the heart. What was I doing to myself this time? I needed to re-examine my relationship with miracles and the indispensable role they play in the fulfillment of our soul purpose.

By definition, a miracle belongs to the extraordinary. Yet who defines what is beyond the commonplace? To a passionate biologist, an amoeba may be one of nature's greatest wonders. An artist contemplating an exquisite rose may say that it is truly a gift from God. Most mothers would agree that having a baby is the greatest miracle of all. And to those who have overcome the tyranny of a life-threatening disease, being alive may be, by far, the most extraordinary miracle.

Yet, as children, didn't we used to jump out of bed in the morning, eager to welcome whatever surprises the new day would bring? We had no use for alarm clocks to wake us up to our obligations and responsibilities. Wide-eyed and innocent, life itself was the miracle. And the next miracle awaited on every tree, under every rock, and in every stream, and we were willing recipients to each of them and to life itself. Because of this, Jesus pointed out the little ones and said, "Of such is the kingdom of God."

When we entered this world, we brought within us the sensitive and loving nature of Divinity. But often we fell prey to the invalidation of unkind thoughts and violent tempers of others. To survive in a world dominated by those who have forgotten their spiritual heritage, we learned to deny our own. We learned that we were not enough. We had to be smarter, stronger, prettier, faster, better. We had to be anything except who we were already. We learned to compare ourselves with others and compete for acceptance, approval, and love. Our desire to be worthy of that love collided with our dread of failing to earn it. In time, we would not find miracles waiting under every rock and around every corner. We had succumbed to the "reality" of those who, through indifference, had fallen asleep at the wheel of life. Now, instead of miracles being extraordinary because life itself was extraordinary, they were extraordinary only because we rarely noticed them anymore. Besides, they usually didn't happen to us.

Most of us rarely notice our heartbeats, although they are essential to our life. In the same way, miracles born of God's love pulse through life without interruption, yet generally remain unseen and often ignored. But, on occasion, we glimpse the magnitude of divine love as it rises above the horizon of our everyday consciousness, a dazzling sun spilling over the mountain range. When the inner workings of Divinity flicker into our awareness, we tout them as miracles, happenings separate from the familiarity of our ordinary existence. Yet, to God, it's just another day. And in fact, *every* day is a symphony of miracles inviting us to dance in its celebration.

The root of the word "miracle" means "wonderful." And when something fills us with wonder, we often call it a miracle. But it's our *perception* that makes us decide what is wonderful, is it not? Some days, you might feel as if life couldn't get any better. Life is absolutely wonderful. Then, on other days, it's the pits. How can life be a miracle one day but not the next? And while you're having the worst day of your life, your next-door neighbor might be having his best. Can something be a miracle for one person but not for another? Is a miracle only so in the eyes and hearts of the beholder?

On the surface, when a miracle does occur, it may appear that it opens your heart and mind. You begin to see the undeniable signature of the love and creative intelligence that weave the very fabric of your life. Yet, if you were to examine it more closely, you may discover that when you open your heart and mind to Divinity, it is precisely *then* that you experience the true miracle. For miracles do not speak to you in the language of your mind but of your soul. Your intellect may not be able to explain them, but you *can* intuit their reality.

Some miracles shake us to our core. Others operate quietly in the corners of our lives. At times, a miracle fills our life at our most desperate hour of need. At other times, they flow through us in our celebration of life. But always, a miracle reminds us that we're not alone. We are not separate and isolated creatures of the flesh, but one unto the divinity of spirit from which we emerged into our individuality. It reminds us time and again that, whenever we choose to return to the wholeness that is life, the miracle has always been there. We need only to receive and experience it.

We don't "do" miracles, as if each one were a separate stage act. Life itself is the miracle and, to the extent that we're open to it, we can have the miracle in so many ways. What we label as separate miracles are but glimpses into the miraculous nature of life itself. What we may call a miracle is divine grace made manifest. And so overwhelming is its power that most of us seem able to have it only in small doses. When we feel undeserving of God's love, we begin to shut our heart and turn a blind eye to its miraculous expressions. On the other hand, when we decide that we are worthy of that love, we begin to relate to life more lovingly and honestly. Then, we can celebrate all the miraculous creations in our lives.

After realizing this, the miraculous in my life became less flashy but more profound and permanent. For example, instead of dramatic "instant cures" of physical symptoms, the healings I gave people brought about more fundamental changes in their being and their lives. Then I began to understand the question that my teacher asked me early in my training: "Which is the greater miracle: that I cure your illness or teach you how to heal your whole self?"

Over the years, I have been privileged to be part of so many wondrous healings. I have also taught many people to heal themselves and others. Which is the greater miracle? To me, the greater part of all healing is learning, and the greater part of all learning is getting to know yourself. So, in the final analysis, whether I "give" you a healing, you learn to heal yourself, or it's God that does the healing, it is *you* who had to learn something more about yourself, change, and grow. A thunderbolt didn't come down from the sky and make it happen. You *learned* to *have* the miracle. You changed your relationship with your inner Source, with the God of your own heart.

You may feel that miracles come from somewhere outside of you, that they just happen to you, or not. If you feel that way, you'll believe that you have no control over them happening. Then, you may give up on your dreams and your fulfillment of purpose. You may feel that there's a greater chance of being struck by lightning than to have the kind of miracles you'll need to realize your destiny. And you *will* need *many* miracles to fulfill your soul purpose since it's never been done before and you are the first person ever to fulfill *your* purpose.

Miracles, however, don't just happen to you. You can't be a helpless victim and expect miracles to save you. Miracles are God's answers to your every need, dream, and prayer. And you must be there to catch them. God may be the one who provides the miracle, but *you* must create the space within you to receive it. Only *you* can pray to make yourself who you are. Through you, the Divine Artist weaves your life into the most extraordinary tapestry. Each breath we take and each choice we make provide the threads that are interwoven into the masterpiece of relationship we call life. So we must choose carefully how we wish to respond to all of life's varied offerings and design this unique and beautiful tapestry of our dreams.

Of course, you might say all miracles come from God. But where does God reside if not within each of us? Remember, we all began as God-seeds. And God-seeds must grow into God-trees that eternally produce all the fruits of Divinity. This is the fulfilling of your soul purpose and this is the greater miracle. For without miracles, we cannot hope to accomplish the miraculous. You must be able to pull those miracles out of a hat. And that hat is you.

When you stray from your spiritual purpose, you will sooner or later find yourself facing a desperate situation. You will be terrified and will need help. The terror you feel is from you abandoning your true nature of oneness and love. The help you must seek is your choice to return to that wholeness. When your life is on the line, you need to dig more deeply within yourself than you have ever dared. Then you may rediscover that courage that, in our ordinary world of busyness and complacency, we often fail to muster up.

Having courage doesn't mean that you experience no fear. Being courageous means choosing to love in the face of fear, choosing truth in the face of invalidation. Every time you make that choice, fear ceases to be the unbeatable evil monster. It returns to its rightful place as your devoted courier delivering the much-needed message: "You've forgotten who you are and must return to your purpose."

Only in a loving heart can we hope to forge our courage. And each time we choose to love, we gain the necessary courage to surrender the next layer of fear and resistance. We place more of our trust in an unseen Divinity deep within our own being and with that faith we can ask for miracles that transcend the ordinary boundaries of cause and effect, and have the willingness to run with them when they are given. If we choose to love when confronted with fear, and we choose truth when faced with invalidation, we will develop the faith needed for the miracles to fulfill our soul purpose. For it is faith that tends the garden in which miracles bloom.

At a wedding in which I officiated, I met Harold, an elderly man of great faith who suffered from a cancer of the prostate. When he'd first heard that the minister who was to officiate at his young friend's wedding was also a spiritual healer, he'd said to the bride, "That is the man I must meet, and I must shake his hand. I know then that everything will be all right."

The wedding was held the day before Harold was scheduled to undergo surgery to remove his prostate. At the reception, he finally gathered the courage to approach me. When we shook hands, something extraordinary happened. We both felt a tremendous surge of power and light. Harold was certain he was healed.

The next morning at the hospital, much to the consternation of the surgeon, Harold stood by his conviction that his cancer was no more. The doctor reluctantly re-administered some tests. Test after test showed no indication of Harold having any cancer. Needless to say, the surgery was canceled.

No person, however, creates a miracle by himself. A miracle is like a symphony and it takes an entire orchestra to play it. In this particular healing miracle, I was the fortunate one selected to play the final phrase of a long and complex symphony. For months, Harold had been consulting with doctors, praying with family and friends, and looking deeply into his own heart and soul for answers, guidance, and healing. That often-frightening journey led him to an invitation to a friend's wedding and to that momentous sunrise when we shook hands.

As dramatic as a sunrise can be, it is still only a moment in the circle that the sun makes in our world from day to night to day. And so it is when the miracle shows us its beautiful radiance. Like the sun, it has always been there but, until it rises above the horizon of our consciousness, we do not recognize it. When it does, however, we realize that it is our *faith* that restores us to the Oneness of Spirit, and it is this oneness that heals all things. As Jesus proclaimed time and again, "Your faith has healed you."

Faith leads us to the certainty that needs no material evidence or proof of logic. It blossoms from an inner experience of Divinity. Then, we *know*. Yet we are often reluctant to abandon our need for a preemptive proof to appease our fears. Many of us only seek the miracle of divine intervention when all other avenues fail and our situation appears hopeless. But what purpose would it serve to choose God only as a last resort? Both Krishna and Jesus teach us to always seek *first* the One within that gives us everything, and everything will be given to us. And what is a miracle but having a need or prayer fulfilled? It would seem senseless to carry our buckets seeking water everywhere but where the faucet is. We must re-examine our priorities. We must seek our spiritual faucet first.

Whenever we choose the Source of Life, the open divine invitation becomes a divine intervention that transcends the known laws of cause and effect. And grace intercedes. The simple truth of life is that God wants us to have all that is life and for us to fulfill all that is life. Love is the question that life continuously answers. And the greater miracle is life giving to life: the inner fulfilling the outer and the outer fulfilling the inner; the feminine and the masculine fulfilling each other, and the spirit and body fulfilling each other. And galaxies joyously dance in abundance around the hub of creation. All that we need to enter into that Sacred Dance with the miracle that is Life is to ask to participate . . . and graciously receive the hand that is offered.

FIFTEEN

LIFE: THE SACRED DANCE

Anyone who has ever loved can tell you that the dance of love is not all sweetness and light. At times you soar on its heavenly wings, but then come the crashing heartbreaks. Love breaks your heart, again and again, until there is nothing left to break. Yet love destroys not; she heals. Love returns you to the oneness that is your inner Source and purpose. It isn't your heart that you feel breaking; what you feel instead, tearing away from your heart at love's beckoning, are the walls of resistance you had built around it over the years in vain protection. And when love gently taps at your heart's inner door, the walls come tumbling down, exposing those long-forgotten times of isolation and loneliness. With love's own grace, you begin to pardon from your heart's faithful hold the abandonment and neglect, once too hurtful to manage.

If you cling to your losses and disappointments, and lose hope of ever fulfilling your dreams, you turn away from your purpose. You shut the door to your heart. And when you carry too much heartache, it's easy to become needy. You end up turning your giving heart into an indigent beggar. You implore life to ease the pain of your separation and loneliness. Yet you demand control of how and when life is to do that. Instead of participating in the miracle that is your life, you cower from love's calling.

"For where your treasure is," Christ said, "there your heart will be also" (Matthew 6:21). Your heart only desires to fulfill *your* dreams. It never wants anything for itself but seeks only to fulfill you. When you fill it with expectations, demands, judgments, criticisms, and blame, you deny your heart its purpose and its power to give to you. If, however, you are willing to knock on your heart's door with love, it will open *you* to the grand ballroom of life wherein awaits the Sacred Dance.

We are not meant to live in isolation and loneliness. When we look around us, we see that nothing in nature lacks a partner. Planets whirl around the sun. Within our cells, virtuosos play to the batons of their nuclear conductors. And electrons spin around their proton partners, dervishes whirling in ecstatic dance. They are God dancing throughout the universe, inviting partners. "Come dance with Me," He sings, and entire galaxies waltz to the divine metronome of His heartbeat.

The oneness of life needs the twoness of polarity through which it can dance: positive and negative, light and dark, spirit and body, heaven and earth, male and female, good and bad, right and wrong. Life offers *both/and*; only fear limits us to *either/or*. Look and discover that everything in life contains the seed of its opposite. And it is out of the darkness of our utter loneliness that we embark upon our journey into the light of realizing God.

We experience life in relationship. Even a person is not a singularity but a symphony of relationships: of flesh and spirit, of breath and blood, of heart and mind, of denial and acceptance, of celebration and sorrow. And a couple is, in reality, two cultures abandoning their political borders to fulfill a common purpose. We are a single orchestra composed of a multitude of relationships playing one magnificent cosmic symphony.

God invites us to join in and enter this relationship, this Sacred Dance with Life. This divine invitation *is* the call of our purpose. And no division can withstand the awesome power of the oneness of divine purpose. Against this call of oneness to return to love, resistance is futile. The sooner we can surrender the walls we have built around our heart, the more quickly our light can disperse the shadows they cast upon our life.

Yet we often misinterpret our own calling. Our soul purpose beckons us to participate in and share our abundance with all of life. Instead of realizing this, we often believe that we lack the objects of our desire and attempt to seek them *from* life. In truth, the more intense our desire *for* something, the more we have it within us to give. It is impossible for any of us to imagine wanting something that we don't already experience within us. It's like asking yourself, "Tell me something you know nothing about." Just because you don't see it or feel it in your physical possession, don't be tempted into believing that it isn't already within you.

When you feel a lack of joy in your life, it is in reality the joy in your soul wanting expression. It may seem that you have little or no joy to share, but that is only an illusion born of years of burying that joy. What you truly crave is the chance to share your joy with life.

The same is true for anything else you may be hoping or praying for. If you intensely desire more love in your life, it is because of the unexpressed abundance of love within you. If freedom is what you seek from life, first look within you, and you will discover that the freedom you so love is pleading to be let loose in life. When you know things could be so much better in life, it is because that better life is already within you, waiting for you to birth it. Life never deprives you of what you so desire. For the life within you yearns to join the life around you.

What you experience as scarcity comes not from you or from life, but from you not giving yourself the permission and opportunity to share your abundance with the rest of life. And if you allow yourself to fear losing what little you believe you have, you become arrogant, jealous, and demanding in your possessiveness. You turn yourself into a taker from the giver that nature made you to be, you withhold from life and from your own purpose, and so you fall out of the grace of love dancing into life.

How do we return to our natural givingness and enter into the flow of grace? What do we already have that we need to share? And with whom do we share it? The answers are quite simple for each of us. Here is the recipe for humanity to reach divinity:

Life says: "I was hungry and you gave me something to eat; I was thirsty and you gave me something to drink; I was a foreigner and you offered me hospitality; I was naked and you clothed me; I was ill and you visited me; I was in prison and you came to see me." And "Whatever you did for the most inconspicuous members of my family, you did for me as well." (Excerpts from Matthew 25:35–45.)

We often look at what we *don't* have to share with others: "If I had enough money, I would feed the hungry," "If I knew what to say, I would talk to a stranger," "If I had the time, I would visit the sick in hospitals," or "If I knew how, I would help a prison inmate." Instead, we must examine what we *do* have. And we must be imaginative in expanding our opportunities for sharing. People hunger and thirst in many ways. We must not only feed our physical bodies but must nourish our hearts, minds, and souls as well.

You may not have enough actual food to feed everyone in the world, but you certainly have some form of nourishment to share with each person you meet. You may be much more capable of nourishing another's soul hunger than cooking up a bowl of soup, or you may be able to do both. You may be naturally inclined to tend to the emotional needs of others rather than explain everything to the fulfillment of their intellect. Even if you cannot readily provide physical shelter to others, you may have ample emotional shelter of your trust and reassurance to offer them. You can cover a naked person with the shirt off your back or you can give much-needed support to one who has just experienced humiliation and is feeling totally exposed. You may be able to bring hope to a prison inmate or you may have the tools to help liberate people who are stuck in the prison of their habits, relationships, or jobs. When you don't have money to share, you might have the time. Every day, life within each of us experiences some form of hunger, thirst, alienation, exposure, illness, or incarceration. Surely, we can each find one way or another to share our abundance with life.

Life also lives in every form you can imagine. Whatever you share with "the most inconspicuous members" of life's family you share with life itself. Some of us are brain surgeons and heal life in people's brains. Others are manicurists and heal life in the fingertips. Still others are architects and builders and provide shelters for life. Although love may break our heart in so many ways while we each learn to surrender the conditions we place upon it, love also provides each of us for the other as answers along our path. If each of us extends a hand when one of us falls, we may all yet fulfill our destiny. For love's own destiny is freedom: the freedom to be, to give, and to receive.

This is the secret of entering the Sacred Dance with Life: ask to share all that you have within you willingly with life, now, rather than waiting and wondering how life might be able to fulfill you. And no matter how little you may think you have within you, share it with others. You may discover that the tiny seed, when given a chance to see the light of day, grows into a magnificent fruit-bearing tree. Learn this well: life gives to life. In order to move with its oneness of purpose, you too must give to life in all of its diversity.

Do not withhold what is within you, complain of your lack, or criticize others for not providing for it. Instead, realize that the very thing you feel you lack, or that you perceive the world lacks, is exactly what you are here to share with life. Therefore, whatever it is you desire, it is only in the giving of it that you will find your fulfillment in it.

Remember also that you are made from your asking. Be conscious of what you ask, how you ask, whom you ask, as well as the state from which you ask. This is the secret of prayer. Your asking always brings the answer. So, when you ask from your fears, the answers at best only cover your fears. When you ask for things, the best you can hope for are for things. But when you ask to fulfill, the answer fills you with life. So ask for permission to give, for the opportunities through which to give, and for the courage to give that which you desire most in life.

Here is an example of asking to fulfill written by Francis of Assisi, a master of prayer:

Lord, make me an instrument of thy peace.
Where there is hatred, let me sow love;
Where there is injury, pardon;
Where there is doubt, faith;

Where there is despair, hope;
Where there is darkness, light;
And where there is sadness, joy.

O divine Master,
Grant that I may not so much seek
To be consoled as to console,
To be understood as to understand,
To be loved as to love;
For it is in giving that we receive;
It is in pardoning that we are pardoned;
It is in dying to self that we are born to eternal life.

The Stages of Entering the Dance

In the beginning of our journey, life appears fraught with threats and obstacles as we peer through the lens of fear and survival. Then, as we empower ourselves through neutralizing those threats and overcoming those obstacles, we begin to see life as a series of challenges. Instead of merely surviving, we begin to strive. Through our ambition and effort, we gain more out of life and begin to have a sense of comfort. We relax from our striving and begin to reflect on the deeper meaning of life. With a renewal of spiritual purpose, we enjoy a taste of life's true abundance. We begin to thrive. Finally, we come to realize that when we shift from thriving in our own interests to serving the oneness of our Divine Being, life's needs become our needs, and life provides all that it needs *through us*. This is the secret of sharing in its abundance. We are truly the minds and hearts, and the hands and feet, through which God dances with life.

From this new vantage point, we see that life doesn't punish or throw down the gauntlet to taunt us; rather, life in all of its abundance and splendor blesses us with limitless opportunities for growth and fulfillment. Each moment, life invites us with a cornucopia of opportunities, both inner and outer. And we have the power of choice within us. We shape our life and our self not by what happens to us in our life or by what or how much we know, but by the choices we make and the actions we take.

What may appear to be a problem to one person may be a challenge to another, and to yet another it may offer a great opportunity. What some may experience as a curse, others consider a miracle. One of us might respond lovingly to a particular person while another turns away in disgust. Each of us responds differently in every situation. In this way, we forge the unique paths that we each travel to the same destination.

Like a basketball player constantly practicing one kind of shot until he can consistently make the basket, we keep giving ourselves the opportunities to refine our responses to the same situation, the same kind of person, or the same type of energy. Did you ever notice that you keep running into the same type of person in your relationships or into the same kind of work situations until you learn to manage your responses correctly? Once you learn your lesson and are no longer in resistance, that type of person or situation seems to magically fade out of your life except in passing.

Life gives us every opportunity to learn and grow. With each recurrence, we learn to refine how we respond to that type of person, thing, situation, idea, or energy. We get to practice as much as we need. The sooner we get it, the less we have to do it. And every invalidation, failure, and hurt is an opportunity for learning, healing, and growth. Every time we are invalidated, we may feel pain, sadness, anger, and hopelessness. We can choose to sit in our depression, lash out in resistance and anger at others, or forgive and discover our freedom and our divinity.

Forgiveness: Dancing with Grace

Forgiveness is love giving us yet another chance to learn, to heal, and to fulfill our purpose. Like a compassionate mother, forgiveness kisses us despite our mud-and-tear-streaked faces and gently cleanses our scraped knees and wounded feelings. For as we enter into the Sacred Dance with Life, we often trip and fall like a struggling toddler. Without the grace of forgiveness, we would never learn to walk, much less dance effortlessly with life's radiance, transcendence, and majesty.

Our spiritual development is not so much about falling as it is about getting back up each time. Forgiveness gives us the strength and courage to do that. It is the towrope on the beginners' ski slope that pulls us back up to the top of the hill. It is the barre in the dance studio that we hold on to until we find our spiritual legs and achieve coordination and balance. With forgiveness, we learn that the world may not have changed so much, but that we have changed our relationship with it. It reminds us gently, but in no uncertain terms, that we are in the world, but not of it. Forgiveness guides us not to react unconsciously to life's passing comments but to respond consciously to the essence of its communication. Rather than throwing our tantrums of fearful judgments and expectations at the world, we must learn to look inward and discover the invincible source of our being.

As we forgive others, so we are forgiven. When we hate others for what they have done, we hold ourselves hostage with our hatred. It makes us the prisoners of hatred, serving sentences of isolation and deprivation. When we forgive others for what they have done, we are forgiving ourselves for their actions. In forgiving ourselves for their actions, we free ourselves from our self-made prisons and can walk openly in the light of day. Whenever we withhold our giving from anyone's self, we divide what is whole and cast its pieces into darkness. In forgiving, the separate becomes whole.

The healing of all relationships begins with forgiveness. The object of your relationship doesn't matter. It can be with a person, a thing, an idea, an organization, your body, your mind, God, or yourself. No matter what kind of relationship it is you are having, without forgiveness, it will produce suffering in place of fulfillment.

It's obvious that a relationship full of hatred needs forgiveness to begin to heal, but what about a happy relationship? In any relationship, there are certain restrictions and limitations. When you become aware of such a limitation in a relationship, forgiving yourself for that limitation brings about your freedom from it.

When you are beholden to a limitation, restriction, or control, before you can become free of the obstacle and move ahead, you must forgive yourself of it. Forgiving begins with your willingness to give to spirit regardless of what condition it's in. Just as we are taught not to judge a book by its cover, we must learn not to withhold from spirit because of the form that it occupies. When you give to the essence of life, all divisions dissolve and anything becomes possible; the miracle is made the reality.

Lonely is the soul who cannot forgive. For when you hold something against another, you hold it against yourself and isolate yourself. When you are angry with someone, you withhold that which is of value to you, the positive qualities of being, from that person. What happens when you do this? As long as you are withholding that which is beautiful, valuable, and wonderful from the other person, you cannot give it to yourself either. Try it and see what happens.

On the other hand, if you become happy with yourself when you are angry with another, the anger disappears. If you insist on being angry with someone, you cannot experience happiness with yourself at the same time. When you hate the government, you withhold from it what is of value to you. When you do so, since you are holding back on it, you cannot give the same to yourself either.

Once a man asked me to see why, in spite of all his abilities and hard work, he couldn't seem to make a decent living since his divorce. One of the main factors that I found in him was that he was refusing to forgive his ex-wife. When they divorced, he subconsciously decided that if he were to make much more than a subsistence income, he would have to give her alimony. What he withheld from her, he could not give to himself. When I explained that to him, he protested, "She doesn't deserve a cent! I'd rather be a pauper than give her anything."

Later, he married a fairly well-to-do woman and within a short time, they started to struggle financially.

On the other hand, a woman came to see me about a back injury she'd sustained in an automobile accident. In her situation, I saw that she hadn't forgiven the person who had caused the accident and she wanted him to pay. But she had formulated subconsciously that if she healed before the trial, she would not be able to convince a jury that she was injured and that the defendant should pay handsomely for her pain and suffering. As soon as I communicated what I saw in her, she decided that her health and peace of mind were much more important to her than punishing him. She chose to forgive him and decided that however he proceeded in his life was between him and God, just as her life was between her and God. Immediately, her back, as well as her life, began to heal *and* she won a substantial but fair out-of-court settlement. Whoever or whatever you punish, you are in reality punishing yourself. Whoever or whatever you forgive, you forgive yourself and you transcend the limitations held by the other.

Forgiving means that you are *for* giving instead of *against* giving. Forgiveness doesn't demand that you condone what others do with their lives or how they use it against you; you only need to give willingly to the life within them, which is the same one life within you. Each time you forgive, you heal the spirit trapped within the action and the person.

Often we resist forgiving for fear that, in forgiving, the hurtful experience may be repeated. In truth, however, it is only in forgiving that we cull the wisdom from our experience and, once the lesson is learned, we need not repeat it. Forgiveness grows out of the wisdom of the heart and forgiveness *is* the heart of wisdom. Love for-*ever*-gives.

Dancing to the Music

Music moves you. It compels you to dance. You can't impose a dance onto the music. The music *chooses* the dance. When it invites you with its song, you get up from whatever mirage you may be sitting in and begin to dance to its pulse, its rhythm. And to the lead of its melody, you follow in sweet harmony.

If you listen carefully, if you stay awake, you can hear the music that is life itself singing. At first, ever so faintly in our inner ear, we hear the echoes of life's haunting melody. And when we follow its soulful invitation, it leads us always to life's deeper purpose.

I know it was that music that chose the dance I was to enter that fateful night in Los Angeles. It lured me out of the hotel elevator, out of my oh-so-sweet dream of falling into bed and the comfort and peace of sleep after a demanding day of teaching and healing. Instead of heading up to my hotel room for the night, I was compelled to visit the gift shop. I rationalized that I might want a magazine to read and perhaps a bottle of water. But just as I stepped up to the magazine rack in the shop, a young Chinese man flagged me down as if he were hailing a cab. He turned out to be Harry, the store owner, and he asked if I was the spiritual healer who gave the seminar in the hotel that day and, if so, could he ask me a couple of questions?

Once I said yes, he locked the shop up, turned over the "closed" sign, grabbed three plastic crates, and brought out from the back a beautiful young Chinese woman whom he introduced as his girlfriend, Carol. Harry motioned me to sit down on one of the crates. I was now a prisoner in a hotel gift shop and no one knew my whereabouts. I took a deep breath and surrendered my plans for a full night's sleep.

"A couple of questions" grew into a mini-seminar on spiritual healing and the soul's evolution. My two "interrogators" were delightful in their enthusiasm for learning. But, after an hour and a half of lecturing, I felt that it had been enough talk; now it was time for a little action. I gave Harry a healing during which I saw his deceased mother in spirit, laughing and cheering him on in life. When I described her and what she was saying to him, his surprise was eclipsed by Carol's jubilation. "That's exactly what I've been seeing and what I've been trying to tell Harry!" she screamed. "But he won't believe me."

At that point, I thought that my job was done. I figured that this was the reason I had to come to the gift shop. But no, I then saw the spirit of his departed brother. When I communicated this to Harry, he was visibly shaken. For years, he'd blamed himself for his younger brother's childhood death since he'd been with him on a bike ride when his brother had fallen into a concrete culvert and died from his injuries. The grief and anguish poured out of Harry. So *this* was what I had to get to, I thought to myself. But wait! There's more.

As I watched Harry's miraculous transformation, I realized I couldn't leave without giving Carol some healing as well. When I asked her if she would like a healing, she jumped into the "hot seat" without hesitation. As I looked into her spiritually, I saw the pain of her relationship with her mother. I jokingly called her Cinderella. After all, wasn't her mother much like Cinderella's stepmother in how she was treating her? She clapped her hands and laughed gleefully in agreement. Then, when I mentioned that her mother didn't approve of her marrying Harry, Carol became forlorn and frail. "No," she said, "I want more than anything to marry Harry, but she refuses to give her consent."

I understood that both Carol and Harry came from very traditional Chinese families. Marriage without parental consent was out of the question. "Your mother is afraid," I explained to Carol. "She's afraid, not for you, but for herself. She depends on you since your father's passed away. She is also angry that he left her on her own. She has not yet forgiven him or settled into living with herself. She's been wandering and you are her anchor. She's afraid of losing you."

I also addressed an incomplete karmic cycle between them. Carol had been a slave of her mother's in a previous lifetime. As such, her mother felt that she had the right to control and own Carol. Carol's lesson was to reclaim the power that she gave up to her mother. Her mother needed to learn to give Carol back her freedom and to respect her individuality and her life. Then, I helped Carol spiritually complete the karma.

It was one thirty in the morning and we'd been at it for almost four hours! I knew I had to get some rest. Both Carol and Harry were glowing and I was happy for them. Harry asked me what kind of magazines I liked and grabbed a handful of them along with bottles of water and juices. "On the house!" he said.

Then, the inner music of life grew louder. Carol pulled me aside in the hallway while Harry fumbled with the lock to close up. She looked straight into my eyes and simply said, "Thank you for saving my life tonight."

I knew she meant it, but I felt I'd done no such thing. She continued, "You see, when you walked into the store tonight, I don't think you knew that I was behind the counter, crying. I had just talked to Harry about our life and about my mother's decision to not let me marry him. I told him everything I wanted him to know because I knew this was the last time I was ever going to see him. Then I was going to go home and kill myself. You changed all that tonight. Now, for the first time in a long time, I feel like myself. I feel happy about who I am. I also know that I'm not crazy, that I haven't been imagining things. I feel I can forgive my mother and work things out with her. I feel I have my life back. For this, I am thanking you."

I stood dumbfounded and speechless. This bright, beautiful, and exuberant woman had been prepared to end her young life because no one ever told her a few simple truths and gave her validation for who she was. Words fail to describe the gratitude I felt to God for guiding me to Harry and Carol to share in the magic of this healing. In exchange for a couple hours of sleep, a wonderful life was spared. And we are all the better for it. Today, Carol and Harry are happily married. I am so glad that I had the sense to rise out of my myopic self-interest and choose, instead, to dance to the music of life.

I count that evening with Carol and Harry as one of those golden moments that make the hard work, trials, and tribulations in life all worthwhile. Those are the times when, if asked if I'd do it all over again, I would immediately answer with a resounding yes!

What do you find when you examine your life deeply for the times of your greatest fulfillment? You may be surprised. Those moments of fulfillment may not be about you. As exciting as they may have been at the time, those moments may not be about you receiving a gold medal or a scholastic award or being honored at a business banquet for your achievements. They are more likely to be you experiencing the joy of learning that your baby is healthy, of seeing your daughter kick a drug habit, of honoring your parents' fiftieth anniversary, of hearing of the peaceful passing of an old friend who has suffered greatly. They are the quiet moments in which you share in the happiness of those who have fought their personal demons and emerged victoriously. They may be you one day discovering that your children have grown into wonderful adults after all the blood, sweat, and tears. They would most likely include that indescribable feeling of an overflowing heart as you hand a diploma to a confident, shining graduate who, a mere couple of years before, came to you as a scared and confused student. So many of these moments in our lives give us a glimpse of the Sacred Dance.

Yet many people I meet believe they must find some particularly heroic form of service in order to fulfill their life purpose. While some may, the idea that our purpose is a job is only an illusion, a subtle form of invalidation that can cause unnecessary confusion and doubt. Our life purpose is not a thing, a function, or an identity. It is the grace with which we relate to our life. Living with this awareness through all the ordinary and extraordinary encounters of life is the fulfillment of that purpose. This is our Sacred Dance with Life.

And when we dance with our beloved, we place her in the center of our awareness. Our life revolves around her as the planets around the sun. She becomes the breath and purpose of our existence and we respond to her every move. We exult in her beauty and melt in her smile. When we are truly in love, nothing matters anymore but our beloved. We are prepared to die for her and thus we come face to face with truth; and all the illusions we so carefully preserved in our fear evaporate in its fire. We only desire to fulfill her every need. Thus in love, we come to discover our true purpose.

When love gives birth to purpose, it commands two things of each of her children: freedom and friendship. When you love your children with all of your heart, you want them to be free to live life to the fullest. You want them never to be lonely. You want their lives to be full of love of family and friends. Such are the commandments of love. Thus, from within its oneness, love gives birth to all the diversity of forms and consciousness so that we may be free to be and to love one another.

Entering the Sacred Dance, we begin to live in the world in cooperation instead of competition; in willingness in lieu of resistance; and with certainty in Divinity in place of doubt and distrust. As we respond to the

Source within all things, we begin to enter the one continuous stream of life coursing through the multifarious and interweaving tributaries of creation. So when our beloved, the Divine Purpose of Life, asks, we give of ourselves fully, step-by-step, day-by-day, letting the music choose our dance. It is then that we realize: we *are* the answer.

PUTTING IT INTO PRACTICE

If the Beloved is everywhere,
The lover is a veil,
But when living itself
Becomes the friend,
Lovers disappear.

—Rumi
(from *The Illuminated Rumi*
by Coleman Barks)

Guidelines for Entering the Sacred Dance

In order to enter the Sacred Dance with Life, we must start giving to life's purpose instead of continually seeking from life. The truth of what we desire most *from* life is that we have it most to *offer to* life. Yet, through repeated invalidations in our lives, we have forgotten our purpose and have come to misinterpret our desire as a *lack* of what we have the most to share. And it is only in the giving of something that you will find your true fulfillment in it.

Here are a few guidelines to help you practice in your daily life some of the essential steps in entering the Sacred Dance with Life. Please practice them in addition to the material in the rest of the book.

Entering the Sacred Dance requires you to move from needing and wanting to having and sharing:

1) Examine your wants and eliminate those that are not yours.

2) Clarify what you want and why you want it. What purpose will you fulfill in having it?

3) Change from wanting it to having it.

4) Know your worth.

5) Trust in your inner spiritual self and the One that gives you everything.

6) Be enthusiastic and willing to meet whatever comes up in the course of receiving.

7) Once you have it, share it with Life.

1) Examine your wants and eliminate those that aren't yours.

Have you ever thought you really wanted something, bought it, and then realized you didn't even know why you bought it? It wasn't even your desire that you acted on. Your first step is to examine in meditation intuitively whether what you think or feel you want is really your own desire. Review chapter 3 (Making Space for Spirit). Use the practice in "Meditation to Ask a Question and Intuit an Answer" (Your

Spiritual Toolkit, section B) to find out whether the desire is yours or not. Then use the meditation tools in "Creating and De-energizing Mental Pictures" (Your Spiritual Toolkit, section D) to de-energize and let go of the desires that are not yours.

2) Clarify what you want and why you want it. What purpose will you fulfill in having it?

Once you know what you want, examine in meditation if having it is going to help you in some way to realize one of your dreams, or is it what you *think* you *need* in order to get something else you want?

Example A: Let's say you want money. Is it the money that's important to you, or do you only want money because that's the only way you can see to getting what you truly want? Perhaps, you need a new car to help you get around. So, you don't really want the money but a new car. The next step, then, is for you to decide to *have* a new car, not keep on wanting money. Does it matter to you if you buy it, it's given to you, or you win it in a sweepstakes (as long as it's the kind you'd like)?

Many people try to create this way: *I need a new car. I must have more money to get it. To have more money, I must earn it by having a better-paying job. To get a better-paying job, I need to go back to school. To go back to school, I need more money. To get more money, I need a better-paying job. To get a better-paying job, I need to not only go back to school but also get a new car. To get a new car . . .* I think you get the picture.

To clarify your want, find out what your real purpose is for having what you want. By wanting this, are you covering your fear? Do you think by having it that you can avoid what you don't want? Or will having what you want help you give more to life?

Example B: You feel intensely that you want someone to love. Meditate on what purpose it will fulfill if you had someone to love. You might discover, for instance, that you have a lot of love to give. Perhaps, you desire to take care of someone and share your kindness with him. So, then, the truth of what you want is not necessarily *someone* to love but to be able to share your abundance of love with life, with people, with nature. As you start to share that, little by little, with everyone you meet, in the course of it, you will attract into your life someone to love in that special way.

Example C: You may desire a close partnership with someone, whether a friendship, marriage, or a creative teammate. When you meditate on what purpose that may fulfill, you may find that you know how wonderful a partnership with someone can be. If you can imagine such a thing, you have within you what it takes to realize it. You may discover that you have a lot of wisdom about what is needed for a great partnership. Your true desire is to bring that wisdom out in a way you can share with others. It may lead you to be a teacher of it. Share your wisdom little by little. As you do, you'll attract many partners of all kinds.

3) Change from wanting it to having it.

Once you've clarified what it is you want, change your attitude from *wanting* it to *having* it. The energy of wanting is like hunger; there is an emptiness that longs for fulfillment. Wanting is nature's way of creating the energy we need to take action in fulfilling our needs. The more you want something, the more creative energy you generate within you. If you don't take the next step, however, you end up just producing more and more energy that has nowhere else to go but into the *wanting* itself. It's a vicious cycle. You want more and more and more, and wanting gets so powerful that it begins to control you. In reality, all you need from *wanting* is enough energy to bring the want to your attention so you can examine it and, if it's yours, clarify it.

Changing your attitude from wanting something to having it is simple. You just have to decide that it's already within you, in spirit. Yet many people have difficulty going from wanting something to having it because they believe that, if it's not actually in their physical possession, they don't have it. Actually, the opposite is true. It isn't until you *know* that you *have* it within you that you can produce it in your physical life. It isn't out there somewhere in the world for you to go get. It's inside your own being and it only needs to be brought out of you into the world and into your life. Deciding that you already *have it* is making a commitment to yourself that you are willing to make your dream real. Also, be truly grateful that you have it, for your appreciation and gratitude open you up and make you the beneficiary of life's abundance.

4) Know your worth.

As you decide that you already have what you want within you, know that you are deserving of it. Both the fear of not deserving it and the fear of the consequences of getting it keep many people from making the simple yet powerful decision that they already *have* something within themselves. If you believe that you have to *earn* something before you are worthy of it, you are living under an enormous illusion. *Everything* you have was given to you. Earning something only means you were able to prove to yourself that you're deserving of what you were given. You might judge that you worked "hard enough," "long enough," or "well enough" to be worth it.

For starters, however, you never *earned* your life. It was a gift. If you live it, it's free. If you refuse to live it, it'll cost you plenty in pain and suffering. If you don't feel your own true worth, you'll feel that you have to earn every little speck of goodness in life. You'll believe there are no free lunches in life. The truth is, not only every lunch, but also breakfast and dinner, are free—just for the asking.

Society tends to measure our worth by what we do, as well as by how much and how well we do it. Yet, in truth, our worth never depends on our accomplishments or lack of them. It's not in accomplishing something of greatness that you gain your worth. It is in appreciating your true worth that everything you do becomes of great value. When you truly value your life, every smile, every handshake, every word you speak carries the truth and power of your worth.

When we do not know our worth, everything we do carries our ignorance and reflects the very destruction of that worth. It isn't that when we commit a crime we become worthless denizens in this world. It's that when we forget our true worth, we reflect our ignorance of our worth in the crimes we commit. In ignorance, we isolate ourselves from the purpose for which we came into being.

Practice the "Creating and De-energizing Mental Pictures" exercise and the "Working with Dichotomies" exercise (Your Spiritual Tookit, section D) to de-energize and release the invalidation of your worth (mental pictures) that come up in your mind when you choose to *have* something.

5) Trust in your inner spiritual self and the One that gives you everything.

In order to start manifesting in the world what you know you have within you in spirit, you must practice trusting your inner Source. So often we lose trust in our own selves and abandon trust in God because we misinterpret the dance of asking and receiving. Why is it that if we always get what we ask for, there is so much suffering? No one really asks for suffering. Yet none of us has escaped the experience of suffering.

I have heard people say in frustration and despair, "I asked God for love, but I got hatred and anger instead," "I asked for healing, but I got sicker," "My husband was a peacemaker, but a warmonger killed him," and, thus, "How can you say God is loving and just?"

Unless you are without any pain, limitations, or unawareness, when you ask for something or decide to have something, some of the very opposite will surface from within you. In fact, the reason you are asking for something in your life is because you don't yet experience it fully in your life. Something is limiting your full experience of that. Those restrictions are pain and fear, along with all their permutations of invalidation, control, guilt, judgment, and so on. When you ask God for something, He gives you the opportunity you need to start emancipating yourself from the shackles that keep you from having all that you seek.

For example, if you were to ask for more patience, all that makes you frustrated and impatient will begin to surface out of the depths of your subconscious mind. When you ask for more love, any vengeance and lack of forgiveness born of anger and hatred will emerge into your consciousness.

The more dedicated the peacemaker, the more violent the opposition he will face. The moment you ask for better health, any hidden illness gets revealed to you. Otherwise, how can you become healthier? I have known many people who became sick shortly after they committed themselves to a healthier diet and lifestyle. This is the detoxifying process. If there are hidden toxins, they will come out and, in a misguided attempt to regain their former "health," some people revert to their unhealthy lifestyle out of fear.

If you were to ask to become a doctor, but refused to go to medical school, in our society at this time it would be quite difficult for God to help you fulfill your dream. You'll keep on receiving opportunities to work out your fear and resistance to medical school. If you didn't know your prayers were being answered in this way, you may end up blaming God for your miseries.

This is why the simplest act of asking and turning to the One that gives everything often becomes a thing to be feared and distrusted. Whatever fears you formerly empowered will surface when you choose to have what they limit in you. Once again, practice the "Creating and De-energizing Mental Pictures" meditation to de-energize and release the fear-containing pictures.

6) Be enthusiastic and willing to meet whatever comes up in the course of receiving.

God bestows the abundance of His will on the willing. Do not be afraid of God's will, for it flows out of the well of unconditional love. It gives to you all that you ever need. Fear of God's will comes only as a misunderstanding of the process of the healing that results from your asking. Know that the toxins that surface in your life after you communicate with God are what you need to let go of so that you can have the space to receive what you asked for. God isn't ignoring your plea or punishing you. He is helping you become an empty cup so He can fill you up with all that you truly desire.

Just because the boat starts heaving in the stormy sea, do not lose sight of your heading. Be even more enthusiastic and willing because you know you're getting closer to your destination. Don't become the negativity that you're releasing. Be willing to let it all go and be grateful instead as you celebrate the space you're making for the miracle.

The Sacred Dance is the flow of divine grace. It is Oneness joyously dancing between polarities: the choreography from here to there, male to female, dark to light. For this flow to happen, there must be both an acceptance of the conditions of the here and now, as well as the ability to clearly have the goal, dream, or destination as a reality, here and now. Some people refuse to accept the reality of the condition in which they exist in favor of a better dream. Others resign to the reality of their current condition and fail to even consider an alternative. However, it is only when you can fully accept your present condition as well as have the certainty and clarity of vision of your dream, goal, or destination that you can enter into the flow of the Sacred Dance and grow. Without that space created between your acceptance of present conditions and your vision of what truth can be, you do not manifest your destiny.

To develop this space, practice the "Working with Dichotomies" exercise using this pair of dichotomies: I can totally have being the way I am / I can totally have being the way I know I can be. (Other examples: I can totally have what I am / I can totally have what I know I can be; I can totally have my body the way it is / I can totally have my body the way I know it can be; I can totally have the relationship I'm in the way it is / I can totally have the relationship I'm in the way I know it can be.)

7) Once you have it, share it with Life.

Remember that whatever it is you long for most, you have it within you in abundance. When you change your attitude from wanting it to having it, be grateful and decide to make it real in the world, little by little, by sharing it with life. First, the sharing is energetic; then, it becomes manifest. Here are a couple of examples:

Example A: Let's say that an inconsiderate, aggressive driver is tailgating your car in the slow lane. You want him to be considerate and back off. That is exactly what you have within you to give—you know what would work; he's ignorant. Choose to be neutral, get into a little amusement, and have some compassion. In an energetic sense, he has a spiritual vitamin deficiency. Just using your intuitive knowing sense, ask what color and quality of energy he most needs right now to fill that deficiency. Perhaps you may get a certain kind of green (yellow, orange, blue, whatever). Imagine making up a small ball of this green energy and gently offering it up to him (just let it go like a helium balloon with that intent). Give it a few moments and see what happens. In my experience, four out of five times that I do this, the driver behind me either falls back to a safer distance or finds a way to pass me. Do this intuitively, but with your eyes open and on the road!

Example B: You're at a restaurant and the waiter is rude, throwing his personal frustrations at you when he's supposed to be serving you. You want friendly and courteous service and to enjoy your meal. Once again, those are the very things you have within you; how else would you know what they are? Find your neutrality, humor, and a little compassion, and ask your intuition what energy color-quality he most needs to fill his deficiency now. When you get the energy color-quality, imagine making it into a small ball and let it go with your intention that you can have him be well. See what happens. I had an amazing experience in a situation like this when I was in charge of a group of twenty people at a luncheon. The waiter was so hostile that he was literally throwing the plates down on the table in front of us and snarling at everyone. A few people were considering leaving or complaining to the manager. I asked them to give me one moment and did this practice. The waiter then went back into the kitchen and when he returned to our table less than a minute later, he came straight to me with a smile and in the nicest way said, "How may I serve you today?" We all received excellent service from him for the rest of our luncheon.

A Story

Once I was in a quandary because I was physically away from my sons, yet they were in an important transition in their lives where I felt they needed my presence. After reviewing all the logical options, none was satisfactory to me. I then asked myself, "Is it more important for my sons that I physically be there to guide them? Or is it more important for them to get the best support and guidance available?"

Granted, there are times when no one can replace a father, whether he can give the best guidance or not. Yet I intuitively realized that this was clearly not one of those times. I discovered that it was my arrogance getting in the way of what was most important to them for this situation. My desire came from my love for my sons, but what I thought I needed to do to express that love came from my fears—those of not being able to prove my love for them by being the one to guide them, and of not being a good enough father. Arrogance has a habit of making itself most important.

I realized that in this particular transition, the boys needed the guidance and support of a man. It had to be a man who had some special wisdom to share with boys opening the doors to their life as men. I also realized that, in this case, it would be best if that man were someone besides me who also cared about them and that they could respect. With that realization, I decided that *I* could have the boys having a loving, spiritual man appear in their lives to give them the validation and guidance they needed at this time. Then, I gave this to the center of the universe, into God's hands.

Within a few days, the first of such men came into their lives. He was a Native American and the spiritual doctor of his tribe. There would be several adventures, but the first was my sons being invited to two of the most sacred healing places of his people. No matter how I could have rearranged my schedules or canceled my trips, I would not have been able to give them this experience myself. Yet, when the time came for this adventure, magically, I ended up in the right place at the right time to accompany them on this sacred journey.

YOUR SPIRITUAL TOOLKIT

Section A: Spiritual Practice

Section B: Simple Exercises to Develop Your Awareness and Intuition

Section C: A Brief Description of Energy Centers

Section D: Exercises for Developing Psychic Energy Tools

SECTION A

SPIRITUAL PRACTICE

Stay awake.
Watch and reflect.
Work with careful attention.
In this way you will find the light within yourself.

—Gautama the Buddha

The Nature of Practice

Waking up takes practice. And staying awake consistently requires regular practice. In the beginning, our light flickers on and off. We may *know* that the truth is within us, yet we compromise our certainty in our inner Source and place our trust in others we deem more reliable. Or we may suspect that we had as much to do as the other person in creating a misunderstanding, yet we find it more comforting to blame him or her. And, of course, we know *we* have to change and grow, but it seems easier to try to fix others to suit our needs. We awaken for a minute and we find ourselves snoring, but remember: if you become aware that you're snoring, you *are* waking up! And it's time to practice more consistently.

The process of our spiritual growth is akin to practicing for the high jump. What goes up must come down. At first, we can only clear three feet—sometimes. Then, with regular practice, we establish our ability to clear at least that height. Now, we attempt to clear three and a half feet and so on. What seemed next to impossible four years ago is child's play today.

So, what are a few years of practice for an eternity of life? I often meet people who say they don't have the time to practice. They may be thinking that it's a question of whether to practice or not. Yet we are practicing *all the time!* If you're not practicing one thing, then you're practicing another.

Practice means, "to do something repeatedly in order to acquire or polish a skill." Consciously or unconsciously, we repeatedly perform certain routines or habits all day long. For example, some of us practice complaining or being a victim until we are truly world-class complainers and victims. We may have already practiced ourselves into excellent procrastinators, consummate spiritual worriers, or masterful self-thrashers. To practice spiritual awareness doesn't take more time. You merely need to replace some of your other practices that haven't brought you true fulfillment. The choice is not *whether or not* you practice but *what* you practice.

A large part of practice is getting back up. Most of us fall unconscious even after some of the most harrowing wake-up calls. We tend at first to just "deal with" the problem and get it "fixed." Once the disease is "cured," the child is back home "safe," or the relationship is "saved" (again!), we go back to "business as usual." We cleared three feet for the first time and celebrate our sweet victory, only to forget that there might have been an eternal lesson to be learned in all of this. We languish in our complacency of a "safe and sound" life . . . at least until the next wake-up call.

Once we take the initiative in responding to the daily calls of purpose, however, we begin the routine practice of our awareness high jumps. It helps to set realistic goals that stretch our abilities but not pull our self-esteem hamstrings. Then, little by little, we clear greater heights of awareness with regularity and establish our vantage point there. And sometimes, as we practice to consistently clear three feet, we end up clearing four. It lets us know that we can do it even if not quite yet on command.

Always practice with a grateful and compassionate acceptance of how you are now, while clearly envisioning how you would like to be. That is one of the secrets of your soul fulfillment: accepting yourself just as you are now in the world while holding true to your heart's dream allows you to incarnate your divinity through your humanity. So, whatever you practice, always practice in the spirit of giving to your inner being in kindness, good humor, and love.

> *Live right life, worship God. That is all. Nothing more.*
> —Final words given by Shivapuri Baba,
> an extraordinary Indian master who lived for 137 years.
> (Quoted in Blackman, *Graceful Exits*, 106.)

Keeping It Simple

When learning, do not overindulge your intellectual interrogations. Remember, that's just your bruised ego trying to con you out of the truth. Be open instead, like the flower of wonderment of a little child, so that you can be the beneficiary of your trust and discover eternal treasures in the simple.

Most of us have learned to disregard the pure simplicity of life in our struggles to survive in an increasingly complex world. It's funny that we so readily sacrifice the simple for the complicated, with the excuse that we don't have the time for it. Yet it's the simple that doesn't take much time. The simpler we keep something, the less time and effort it takes to have it. Persist with the simple and profound changes, and fulfillment will occur over time.

Also, we frequently associate *simple* with *stupid*. If it's simple, it must be stupid or not worth our effort. Of course, part of simple means it doesn't take a lot of effort. Spirit is simple, but definitely not stupid or worthless. Experiencing spirit and living as spirit takes practice but no effort. You'll find that often the greatest masters are those who keep things the simplest. Keep all your practices simple and enjoy them.

When you read books or attend lectures, practice regularly a few of the most important exercises you've learned. Make them a part of your spiritual toolkit. This is another way to keep it simple. Don't try to do everything at once. Take one or two things and use them regularly for a while and appreciate the fruits of your labor as they progressively ripen. If you take what you learn and use it to the fullest, your next lesson or your next step will always be delivered to your front door. The teacher, in whatever appropriate form, will always arrive when the student is ready. And you *make* yourself ready when you practice your previous lessons well.

When Are We Going to Get There?

When we practice anything, we tend to seek proof of our progress. "Are we there yet? How far have we come?" In order to do so, we may seek out others we respect and compare our experiences with theirs. Unless we keep our perspective and surrender our judgments, however, we can invalidate ourselves constantly because we haven't yet "seen the light," "felt the overwhelming bliss of existence," or "cured ourselves of an illness."

Do not get trapped in measuring your spiritual attainment or progress by certain dramatic experiences. Instead, know that the true measure of your evolvement is in how much you are able to recognize the essence, the truth of Divinity in everything, in everyone, and in *every* experience.

Some of us have experienced instances of awakening to Spirit with all its sound and light shows. Sophy Burnham writes of having such an experience in her book *The Ecstatic Journey*: ". . . I was immersed in a sweetness words cannot express. I could hear the singing of the planets, and wave after wave of light washed over me."

There are many testimonies of those who had a "near-death experience" of physically dying temporarily only to return to life. Many of them attest to variations of being in the light of Spirit. Some of us have learned to enter into this splendor of the spiritual domain regularly through meditative practices. Yet, for most of us, it is difficult to attain a desire for enlightenment, life, or spirit that is as single-focused as the drowning person's want for air. For one thing, the demands of daily living compete for our attention as intensely as children often do for their parents' love. But these are all calls of love beckoning to us in all its myriad forms. Just as we cannot stop the reverberations of the church bells from going through us, we must appreciate the many faces of God smiling through the world to their respective beloveds. It is not for us to take away each one's fulfillment, but to show them the way to grow if they so desire.

In truth, for all of us, enlightenment and awakening to spirit are parts of a gradual process of life, even for those of us who have had seemingly sudden experiences entering into the light. These are occasional "booster shots" to catapult us into the next phase of the adventure. The more dramatic experiences of enlightenment are not necessarily better. Sophy Burnham herself quotes the Dalai Lama as musing in one of his books: "I wish that I had such mystical experiences myself, but no luck!" And we have little room to question the enlightenment and wisdom of the revered Tibetan leader.

Kyriacos Markides writes in *The Magus of Strovolos:* ". . . a close friend of my teacher's was also a master of high spiritual stature but whose psychic abilities had remained dormant." Sometimes, it is the intensity of our desire for enlightenment that brings about mystical experiences but, in other cases, it is those of us who have been most resistant to spirit who receive a greater injection of spiritual medicine.

I once heard Dannion Brinkley, author of *Saved by the Light*, talk about the major wake-up call of being struck by lightning, which forever changed his life. Having heard of all the wonderful contributions that Dannion had made to help others, a woman in the audience told him how lucky he was to have such a remarkable experience and that she wished she could have something like that also. He laughed, shaking his head. "You must be kidding." He went on to describe the horrors of being struck by lightning, the excruciating pain of having the inside of his body "fried," and the years of working to recover from the physical and psychic trauma. He admitted, "Now, I am lucky to have received all the treasures of learning, growth, and understanding through this experience, but you don't have to be hit by lightning to learn these things."

It's there already inside all of us. Some people take more intensive wake-up calls to wake them up. But, if you look in your own backyard, you may discover that you're already heeding some of the calls, and you don't have to have your guts fried in order to experience spirit. As the saying might go, the lightning always seems brighter in the other person's body.

Spiritual growth is neither a race nor a contest. We do not gain extra credits in heaven for suffering greater pain or for putting on a better performance. And instead of asking, "When are we going to get there?" we need to ask, "Where are we already and what do we have to share now?"

I have also learned that we need to approach our spiritual practice not so much as we might some arbitrarily assigned homework, but more as we might a chance for lovemaking. When we do, we welcome the opportunity and instead of moving with reluctance, dreading some expected drudgery, we dance with abandon to our private meeting place, thinking of nothing we'd rather be doing. And as we reach out ever so gently to touch our beloved, we cannot wait to remove our clothing so that not a stitch can inhibit the love between us. As we shed our shame and judgments to stand naked, unafraid before our beloved, we proclaim: "Here I am. Touch me, have me. I am yours!"

Kill me, O my trustworthy friends,
For in my being killed is my life.

Love is that you remain standing
In front of your Beloved.
When you are deprived of all your attributes,
Then His attributes become your qualities.

Between me and You, there is only me.
Take away the me, so only You remain.
I am the Supreme Reality.

—Al-Hillaj Mansoor,
one of the great founders of Sufi mysticism who
was publicly executed by total dismemberment
in the main square of Baghdad in the tenth
century for proclaiming, *Ana'l Haqq*, "I am the
Supreme Reality."

SECTION B

SIMPLE EXERCISES TO DEVELOP YOUR AWARENESS AND INTUITION

Although learning exercises from a book can never replace full instruction from a qualified teacher, the following section contains simple psychic exercises you can learn and practice to help you get on your way in expanding your spiritual awareness. Since it may be awkward to try to practice these exercises while reading them, you may wish to record them first on tape or other audio media and play them back. Better yet, you can practice them with a friend, each of you taking turns reading the exercise slowly as the other's guide. Enjoy!

For more complete instruction, we offer lectures, workshops, seminars, and retreats around the U.S. and abroad. Audio CD and cassette tape versions of these spiritual tools can be ordered from my website as they become available.

Awareness Exercise: Seeking First That Which Gives Everything

This simple awareness exercise can be done upon waking before you get out of bed each morning or at any time of the day, sitting in a chair, lying down, or standing. When you make this exercise a regular practice before you do anything, you will begin to have everything you need to fulfill whatever you were going to do. Whether you're starting your day off, embarking on a new project, approaching a difficult problem, communicating with your children, or practicing your regular meditation, first set your awareness in the correct direction and relationship for you to be able to have what you are seeking.

- First, notice what you are aware of. You may notice the blaring of your alarm clock or the music of the songbirds outside your window. You might notice tiredness, aches, or excitement. The enticing aroma of coffee or breakfast may be captivating your attention. Whatever you're noticing, it's your *awareness* that's noticing it.

- Take a deep breath and stretch to loosen any tension in your body. Be thankful for the day and whatever it may bring. Be thankful for what you have in your life. Set aside whatever you're *not* thankful for in your life along with a mental note that you will explore what it has to offer you or teach you that you can be thankful for.

- Say "hello" to your awareness in your mind, as if it's your friend (it *is* your friend). Know that your awareness will go wherever you direct it. Notice what your awareness is occupied with at the moment. Are they feelings, thoughts of work, worries, aches, or sounds? Notice how many seemingly different things your awareness is aware of all at the same time. It is always being aware, whether you're paying attention or not.

- Observe that you're noticing what your awareness is being aware of. Imagine that you can talk to your awareness and ask it to go anywhere. Now, ask it to "Go toward that which gives me everything." Keep it simple and effortless. Do not try to concentrate on it. Simply ask your awareness, sit back in your mind, and observe.

- Whenever you find your awareness drawn to something—feelings, sounds, images, thoughts, anything—ask it to go toward that which gives you everything instead. Let go of any expectations of what is supposed to happen or preconceptions of who, what, or where regarding what it is that gives you everything. Awareness will completely and exactly follow what you ask it to do. Awareness knows how to get to wherever you ask it to go. It's like asking an experienced cabdriver to take you to a hotel you have no idea how to get to. Sit back and relax. Let awareness go to that which gives you everything. Don't decide it's God or some other preconception. Let it be a surprise.

- Observe the changes you begin to experience. Notice the continual movement of awareness. Observe the quality of your awareness changing. Take a deep breath. Do this for as long as you wish but at least for a couple of minutes.

- When you're ready to get up, take a deep breath and stretch your body gently. Open your eyes. Be grateful for this day. Notice how you feel, and get up.

Getting to Know Your Body Exercise

This is a good body relaxation, awareness, and healing exercise. You can practice this any time you like, and it will help you as a spiritual being to get into your body more fully. If possible, wear loose, comfortable clothing:

- Lie down on your back on a carpeted floor or on a comfortable exercise pad. Take a few deep breaths. Close your eyes. Let go of any tensions in your body with each exhalation. Feel your breath filling up your lungs. Observe the rise and fall of your chest.

- Bring your legs together and gently push them down on the floor. Spread your toes wide. Separate your feet about ten inches apart. Relax your legs and feet and let them fall open.

- Feel your back on the floor. Tuck your shoulder blades under without pinching them together. Let them be relaxed. Relax your arms with your hands one to two feet out from your body. Let all the tension in your body melt into the earth.

- Relax your neck and head. Feel your brain soften. Relax your eyes. Observe where your awareness is. If your awareness is on people, things to do, or worries, let them go. (Imagine you're holding them in your fist and open your hand and watch them fly away like a flock of birds.) If your awareness is out of your body looking down at it or somewhere else, such as in your office, acknowledge where you are and gently bring your awareness back into your body. If it's in some area of your body, just notice what's there and then let it go.

- Imagine that your awareness is like golden air that you can direct to flow anywhere you choose. It's like golden smoke of incense wafting gently and silently through your body. You can feel, sense, hear, and know whatever this golden air of your awareness touches.

- Let this golden air float down through your legs to your feet. Let the fingers of this air float into each of your toes. What does it feel like? What do you sense in each toe? Let the golden air of your awareness expand into the rest of both your feet. Notice the sensations as the golden breeze floats across the different areas of your feet. Can you hear anything? Imagine your feet could talk. Let them talk to you. What do they have to say? Whatever it is, just listen and acknowledge.

- Now, let your awareness expand and float up both of your legs. Let it caress the inside of your legs: the bones, muscles, blood vessels, nerves, fat, skin. Observe how they respond to your awareness. Feel them, listen to them, know them.

- When your awareness comes up to your knees, imagine the golden air forming into hands that scoop up warm, healing waters to pour over your knee joints. Feel it deeply penetrate down through your joints and down into the earth, taking any tension in your knees with it.

- Then, let the golden air of your awareness continue to expand up through your thighs into your hips and pelvic area. Observe as it floats through, gently touching everything along the way. What do you feel? Let your awareness touch and get to know these areas in your body. Let the various parts of your body talk to your awareness. What do they say? Listen quietly, without judgment.

- Let your awareness continue to float up through your abdomen. Let the golden air gently float through and caress every part of your body from the spine through all the organs to the skin. Let it float through at the speed of smoke flowing from a stick of incense. Don't dwell on any particular area for too long.

- As the golden air of your awareness reaches the diaphragm muscle area, let it gently massage it as you observe your inhalation and exhalation of breath. With your next inhalation, let the golden air enter into both lungs, filling them up all the way to the top. Let your exhalation release any stale energy in your lungs, while the golden air of your awareness expands into the rest of your chest area. Let it caress your heart tenderly. Imagine that your heart can talk to you. Listen. Let your heart tell your awareness what it needs, what it wants. Let your awareness give it more space to be. Release the tension there with each breath.

- Continue to let your awareness expand through your body and explore. Let it flow down through your arms and hands. Imagine pouring more of the warm, healing water through your hands, releasing the tensions in all the little joints down to the earth. Sense and know.

- Now, let your awareness flow through your neck and into your head. Let it flow through and gently caress your brain, your inner ear, your sinuses, your mouth, your teeth. Observe.

- Then, let the golden air of your awareness expand through the pores of your skin and surround your whole body. Imagine that every square inch of your body is being gently supported by your golden awareness. Relax. Let all your tensions drain out of your body into the earth.

- When you feel ready, gently and slowly move each part of your body. When you have loosely moved all your joints, slowly roll over to your right and lie face down. Slowly, get up on your knees and hands. Come to a sitting position. Now, gently, get up.

As you practice this exercise, you can make up your own variations. Sometimes, you may wish to pay particular attention to different parts of your body. Always go lightly through the whole body, but feel free to listen more to the muscles of your legs or a particular organ, for example. Get to know your body and make it your friend. Enjoy!

Centering in Spirit

The following is a simple daily practice for centering your awareness in spirit and developing certainty that you *are* spirit. This is an experiential practice, not merely an affirmation exercise. Remember, *how* you practice this is as important as *that* you practice it.

- First, stop yourself from doing the next thing in your daily business for a moment. Disengage from the rushing stream of activity and thinking.

- Close your eyes for a moment. Take in a deep breath and relax your body and mind as you exhale.

- Collect yourself. Imagine that you are gathering back to yourself your energy and awareness from everyone and everything you've been involved with. Decide that any energy you projected into people (in resistance, judgment, attachment, worry, competition, control, etc.) or left in places or situations returns to you neutralized. Imagine that you are sitting comfortably behind your eyes, in the center of your head.

- Open your eyes. You are now ready to proceed.

- Decide: *I am spirit.* Mentally be conscious of each word: *I . . . am . . . spirit* as you decide to tune in to your spiritual nature. Do the same in each of the following steps.

- Decide: *I am*. Experience yourself just being (existing).

- Decide: *I have my being*. Experience that you have your existence within you. Validate any changes in your state of being.

- Decide: *I express my being*. Experience the radiance from within you. Validate any changes in your state of being.

- Decide: *I am aware*. Experience *that* you are aware (not awareness of anything in particular).

- Decide: *I have awareness*. Experience that you have awareness within you. Validate any change of awareness.

- Decide: *I express awareness*. Experience awareness illuminating from within you. Validate any change of awareness.

- Decide: *I am energy*. Experience that you are a field of energy.

- Decide: *I have energy*. Experience that you have energy within you. Validate any change in your energy.

- Decide: *I express energy*. Experience the flow of energy from within you. Validate any change in your energy.

- Decide: *I am spirit. I have a body*. Experience your spiritual self in relationship to the energy of your body. Notice the differences. Validate your new space.

- Stretch gently. Resume your activities in this new space.

Once you learn this process, you can take less than a minute to practice it (you can take as long as you want, however). So, practice often throughout the day. Take a "spirit" break instead of (or in addition to) a coffee or cigarette break. Try it on your walk or in your car before driving off (buckle-up your spirit safety belt!). Regular reminding and validating of your spiritual self centers you in spirit.

Meditation to Ask a Question and Intuit an Answer

This is a good practice exercise to develop your intuitive ability and learn to "know" your answer instead of always trying to "figure it out." It would also serve you to review the material in chapter 6 (Experiencing Your Purpose through Intuition).

- Sit in a comfortable chair, relaxed, with your back upright and both feet flat on the floor. Refresh yourself with a couple of deep breaths; then breathe comfortably. Close your eyes. Be aware behind your eyes, in the center of your head.

- First, be aware of your body. Decide to let your body be where it is, how it is; let it feel what it is feeling. Let go of any tensions and worries for now.

- Ground yourself.

- Now, what would you like to ask?

- Once you have formulated one question, hold the palms of both hands together comfortably on your lap. Quietly to yourself, ask your question clearly.

- Imagine this question circulating throughout your body and being. Let everything else drop off out of your mind as you circulate this single question.

- Imagine being the question. Experience the question with your whole being. Relax with the question as if you are hanging out with your best friend.

- Let go of any thoughts and feelings that pop up as you relax with the question.

- When you feel that you have become the question, unclasp your hands and put them face up on your lap. Relax and be receptive.

- The answer is already with you. Don't try to go get it. Relax and let it reach your conscious awareness. Don't try to concentrate.

- Observe your experience. What do you feel? Do you have a sense of something? Notice any "knowing" of an answer. Do you see or perceive anything? Do you hear a thought in your head? Is there some sort of unexplainable understanding? Don't censor anything. Enjoy. Be patient. Let it mature.

- Don't analyze what you get immediately. Sit with it. Experience the energy. Experience the knowing.

- Let any doubts, self-invalidation, or judgments slip away from you. Give your spiritual self space to be and know.

- You may get instant clarity, or the answer may be nebulous to you at first, but it will grow over the next few days. Sometimes it may be like waking up from a dream and you won't know quite what to make of it but, as you ponder its meaning over time, it will become clear to you.

- Decide to let this answer circulate within your consciousness for a while before jumping in to do something about it (especially while you are practicing and developing this ability).

- If you have another question to ask regarding a different aspect of the same issue, repeat this process with the new question.

As with learning anything else, if using your intuition consciously is a new experience, give yourself some time to practice and become familiar with it. Beginning to access your intuition is the first step; the second is developing enough trust in your spiritual self and intuition so that you can act on it.

A BRIEF DESCRIPTION OF ENERGY CENTERS

A treatise on the major energy centers (chakras) in the body can easily take up volumes. There are many books about chakras already available should you wish to learn more. Here I have included a brief description of these energy centers as I see and experience them for the purpose of helping you work with them in some of the exercises given in Section D of this Spiritual Toolkit.

The Chakras: Sacred Portals

Almost twenty-two years ago, I awoke in the middle of the night and found a bright shining star encircled by a radiant blue light hovering by the ceiling. I knew this soul who was to be my first son. "I'm ready," he said.

A brilliant white light streamed from him into the womb of his mother-to-be. Then, with a flash of light, I saw him enter the womb. Like a supernova I once saw on film, the light expanded out and then closed back into itself. Beautiful beyond words.

A geometric pattern began forming, at once like a geodesic sphere and a snowflake. Into this divine template, the first cells of his body were forming. From the center to the outside, again and again, the creative energy pulsed the first cells into form. These whirling galaxies of energy through which spirit spun out the material world were the chakras forming.

Chakras are energy-awareness centers. They are the revolving doors of creativity and communication between spirit and the world. Often, when you read about chakras, you may find discrepancies in how various clairvoyants describe and categorize them. Some will say there are twelve major chakras. Others will say there are three. Most tend to speak of seven major chakras. It's not that one of them is right and the others are all wrong, it's just a matter of which of the energy centers one interprets as a major chakra.

The best way for you to find out, of course, is to develop your clairvoyance and look for yourself. Then you can tell what each healer or teacher is talking about. There's no need to fight over who's right, or end up confused and ditch the whole thing. Anyway, for the purpose of this book and to help you with the exercises in Your Spiritual Toolkit, we'll briefly describe seven of the major chakras in your body that line up in front of the spinal column from just above the tip of your tailbone to the crown of your head. Although there are many more energy centers both in the body and outside of it, these seven are the ones that you will need to learn about first. Once you learn to really manage these seven chakras, you won't have too much of a problem discovering or working with the rest of them.

Each of the seven major chakras in the body has twelve levels of energy/information functions. Each of these twelve levels contains twelve sub-levels. Thus, each chakra operates on 144 different levels of energy and information. Except for the crown, or seventh, chakra at the top of the head, each chakra is connected on an electrical level to a nerve plexus. The crown chakra is connected to the brain. The physiological function of each of the seven chakras is related to the endocrine glands and controls their operation. Each chakra also manifests on the body surface as a grouping of acupuncture points and meridians.

As you face the chakra, it looks like a spinning disc of energy-colors. The inner part of the chakra spins clockwise and the outer part spins counterclockwise. The energy from the inner portion of the chakras travels through a network of energetic channels and through the cells of the body to manifest around the body as layers of colors called the "aura." The cells that make up our body act as "prisms" to our soul energy as it reflects and refracts through them to create the rainbow-like layers of the aura. When all the chakras are functioning optimally, the energy from the outer part of the chakras shows up as a counter-revolving layer of electric blue light in between each layer of the aura that keeps the layers protected and distinct in their own vibrations.

Levels of Chakra Functions

Briefly, the twelve basic levels of the seven major chakras function as follows:

- *The first level* of the chakra is the psychic level. This is the part that spins clockwise. This is the level where the various psychic abilities are manifested, such as clairvoyance in the sixth chakra behind the forehead or clairsentience in the second chakra just below the navel.

- *The second level* of the chakra acts as the memory bank where information is compared and associated.

- *The third level* of the chakra is the psychological aspect or how the information and energy are communicated to the body.

- *The fourth level* is the filter that is related to the physiological functions in the body. It controls the detoxification processes in the various organs that are related to that chakra. It recognizes pain in that region and sends messages to the analytical part of the brain so that the soul can respond.

- *The fourth through the seventh levels* of the chakra are energy filter/transformers. They refine the dense energies coming in from the body to enable the soul to experience and use them. They also serve to step down the power from spirit so that the body can assimilate that energy.

- *The eighth to the twelfth levels* of the chakra all concern themselves with strictly spiritual considerations of the being and have little to do directly with one's day-to-day existence in the material world. These pertain to the spiritual being prior to any material incarnation.

The Psychic Functions of the Chakras

The following are brief descriptions of primarily the psychic functions of each of the major chakras (numbered 1 through 7, tailbone to crown—see figure 1):

- *The first chakra* is located just above the tip of the tailbone at the base of the spine. This energy center deals with survival, both self-preservation and the preservation of the species (including the beginning of the reproductive/sexual process). The life force (*prana* or *chi*) enters into the body from the crown chakra and travels down as an energy of oneness to the first chakra where it polarizes into masculine and feminine forces.

- *The second chakra*, located about an inch and a half below the belly button and couple of inches in from the front of the body (average body thickness), basically deals with feeling on all levels. It is often associated with emotions and sexuality since this is where emotions as well as sexual desires are felt. (But sexuality isn't limited to any one chakra. It is the dance of the masculine and feminine energies that begins at the first chakra and is experienced and expressed differently in each chakra along the way.) The second chakra also acts as a feeling "radar" and determines the "reality" of what it feels.

- *The third chakra* is located by the solar plexus, just below where the rib cage meets in the middle. The central function of this chakra is energy distribution. It manages how much of what kind of energy goes where. This includes out-of-body experiences and the memory of them; the chakra manages how much of your energy-

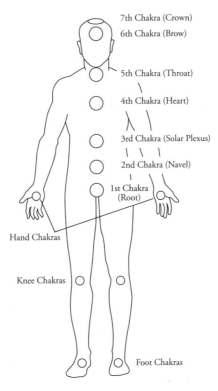

Figure 1: The Chakras

consciousness "goes" to the awareness beyond your physical body realm. The third chakra also directs the energy distribution of your ego states: *who* are *you* in relationship to others now ("shifting gears" / "changing hats")?

- *The fourth chakra,* located in the middle of the chest, is the heart chakra. It is a magnetic energy center of oneness. The basic function of this chakra is affinity. It deals with your ability to be yourself while you are at one with another. It is here that you determine where you are with others and how you feel about them. While the second chakra feels the sensation of things, the fourth chakra lets you feel how *you* feel in relationship to things.

- *The fifth chakra*, located in the area between the cleft of the throat and the back of the neck, deals with all levels of communication:
  - » *Clairaudience*—the ability to hear and communicate with spirit; also, to hear extremely well.
  - » *Inner Voice*—the ability to communicate with your inner self.
  - » *Telepathy*—the ability to send and receive thoughts.
  - » *Pragmatic Intuition*—the ability to intuit matters dealing with practical communication (such as knowing who is about to call on the phone).

  The fifth chakra is also the bridge between the reasoning self and the feeling self. It is a center for discernment. This is where we work out our individual free will in relationship to divine (free) will.

- *The sixth chakra*, located behind the forehead, is often called the third eye. It deals with higher and deeper levels of perception, such as clairvoyance and abstract intuition. This is also where you determine whether what you are seeing is real or not, perceive what is going on, and see where you are going.

- *The crown chakra*, located at the top of the head, is the lotus with the thousand petals. Each degree of enlightenment and autonomy that the soul has attained can be ascertained by how many of the petals are turned on in the crown chakra. This is the center of intuitive knowing and trance-mediumship. At the most complete level, intuitive knowing is cosmic consciousness. At the level of day-to-day experiences, you can tap this ability to know the where, what, how, when, who, and why of things all at once.

EXERCISES FOR DEVELOPING PSYCHIC ENERGY TOOLS

This section contains basic, yet invaluable psychic energy tools as well as several exercises to help you develop them. Each one of these tools and exercises were originally developed and taught by the late Lewis S. Bostwick, who pioneered a new way of training healers, clairvoyants, and mediums. He also founded the Berkeley Psychic Institute in 1972 in order to establish a sanctuary for budding psychics so that they may learn these and other tools for their spiritual growth and enlightenment.

As mentioned earlier, learning these exercises from a book can never replace full instruction from a qualified teacher. Please understand that these exercises are not to be taken as a complete program, but are included here for several purposes:

- To inspire those who are not familiar with them to begin to explore and experience them (a starting point)

- As a companion guide for those who have taken my beginning workshops or are working with my seminar tapes to review the basic steps of the exercises at home

- For those who have already received full training in these or similar techniques to use as notes and reminders

My recommendation on how to use this section is for you to first read through and familiarize yourself with an exercise. Then, record the exercise at a pace that will allow you to practice it without pressure when you play it back. Another suggestion would be to partner up with a friend and take turns leading each other through the whole exercise—and compare "notes" afterward. You may also order audio tape or CD versions of Your Spiritual Toolkit from my website as they become available.

Grounding Exercise

Note: Remember not to use force or effort in any of these psychic exercises.

- Sit in a comfortable chair, relaxed with your back upright and both feet flat on the floor. Refresh yourself with a couple of deep breaths; then breathe comfortably. Close your eyes.

- First, be aware of your body. Decide to let your body be where it is, how it is. Let it feel what it is feeling.

- Become aware of your spine. Follow down along your spine with your awareness until you notice the tip of your tailbone. Sense your first chakra and imagine it as a spot of light about the size of a half-dollar piece.

- Now, imagine a giant tree trunk extending from the bottom of this energy center to the center of the earth. This is your grounding. Imagine releasing the excess energies from others you have been carrying around. Let them all fall down this tree trunk. See the foreign energies as water or particles of sand flowing down the tree into the center of the earth where they are recycled. Just relax and imagine watching everyone else's energy flowing down your grounding. Observe any changes in your energy, awareness, and body.

- Stretch gently, open your eyes, and bend over, letting your head and arms drain out excess energies. Slowly come up and look around you. Get up when you are ready.

Notice how much more you are in your body and how much more grounded you are. With practice, you will become more aware and more grounded. As you go through your day, regularly check your grounding. In the beginning, while getting the hang of this, when- ever you feel ungrounded or inundated with others' energy (expecta- tions, competition, invalidation, emotions, etc.), repeat this exercise to reground yourself. Let all the foreign energy fall out of you. It will only take a few moments and later, once this becomes second nature, all you'll need to do to reground or strengthen your grounding is to become aware of it wherever you are, whatever you might be doing. Also, check your grounding before you begin something such as driv- ing your car, going into a meeting, or performing.

Replenishing Your Space Exercise

Remember not to use force or effort in any of these psychic exercises.

- Sit in a comfortable chair, relaxed, with your back upright and both feet flat on the floor. Refresh yourself with a couple of deep breaths; then breathe comfortably. Close your eyes.

- First, be aware of your body. Decide to let your body be where it is, how it is; let it feel what it is feeling.

- Next, decide to be behind your eyes in your head. Be aware of the space behind your eyes. While aware behind your eyes, decide "I am." You, the spirit-self, will become more present in the center of your head. Notice your body and awareness from there. Decide you can be more in your body.

- Ground yourself from your first chakra to the center of the earth. (Follow the previous grounding exercise.)

- Now, imagine there is a golden egg-shaped energy space about three to four feet out all the way around your body.

- Imagine a golden sun, radiant like the sun on a beautiful summer day, about three feet above your head. See the sun brimming with vital life force. Slowly, bring this golden sun into the top of your head. Let the seventh chakra energy center at the crown of your head absorb as much of the life force as it needs. Just imagine that this life force replenishes, heals, and balances this energy center and each one it fills. Bring the sun into your head to let the sixth chakra behind your forehead absorb its fill of the golden life force. The sun continues down to the throat where it fully replenishes and balances the fifth chakra throat center.

- Next, the sun fills up the fourth chakra heart center in the center of your chest. As you bring the sun down into your abdomen, it energizes the third chakra solar plexus center. Going further down the inside of your body, the sun replenishes the second chakra energy center below your navel. Then, the sun fills up the first chakra energy center above the tip of your tailbone, the source of your grounding. Next, the energy of the sun travels down your legs and arms and fills in the chakras at your feet and hands, knees and elbows.

- Then, let the sun expand inside your body to replenish every cell in your body. Imagine the cells drinking in the life force. Finally, see the golden energy of the sun radiating out of the skin of your body to fill up the egg-shaped energy space all around your body.

- Now, decide that all of this space belongs to you to have, take care of, use, enjoy, and appreciate.

- Take a couple of deep breaths. Stretch and open your eyes. Gently bend over and dangle your head between your knees and relax. Let all the excess energies release out of your head, shoulders, and arms. When you are ready, slowly sit back up and look around. Are you refreshed?

Running Cosmic and Earth Energies Exercise

- First, sit up in a comfortable chair, put both feet flat on the ground, and close your eyes. Take a deep breath and relax.

- Ground yourself.

- Be aware behind your eyes, in the center of your head.

- Then, be aware of the soles of your feet. There is a chakra in the arch of each foot. You may notice a tingling there. If you don't see them at first, imagine them as small energy vortices.

- Imagine earth energy from deep in the planet streaming up through your foot chakras and into your legs. The earth energy flows through an energy channel, an energy tube, running through the middle of each leg (see figure 2).

- The earth energy continues up to a minor chakra about an inch behind each knee. Flowing through the knee chakras, the energy continues along the leg channels through the center of your thighs until it reaches your first chakra. This is the same chakra where your grounding cord is connected. Any excess earth energy simply grounds down the grounding cord.

- Next, be aware of the top of your head. Imagine cosmic energy coming into your crown chakra.

- The cosmic energy flows in through your crown chakra into four energy channels down through the back part of the head and continues down along your spine with two channels on either side (left and right of your spinal column) all the way down to your first chakra.

- As the earth energy from your leg channels and the cosmic energy from your back channels flow into your first chakra, the earth and cosmic energies mix in this chakra.

- Decide that a pumping action in the first chakra will then pump a mixture of about 85 percent cosmic and 15 percent earth energies up inside the front of the body through two energy channels (two to three inches in front of the spine).

- As the earth and cosmic energy mixture flows up the front two channels, it flows through your second chakra. The two channels connect to the right and left sides of each of the disclike chakras up to the crown.

- The energy continues up the two channels to your third chakra (solar plexus).

- Then, the energy continues up to the fourth chakra in the center of your chest.

- The energy goes up the two channels next to the fifth chakra at the cleft of your throat. Once again, the energy flows in, through, and out of this chakra to continue up to the sixth chakra behind the center of your forehead.

- Finally, the energy flows through the sixth chakra and goes up the two channels to the crown chakra at the top of your head. The energy mixture fills the crown chakra and then flows up and out like a beautiful golden fountain.

- Once you have established this flow of earth and cosmic energies, continue to be behind your eyes and observe the flow through all the channels and chakras. Remember to let go of any effort on your part to force anything. Just know that it is flowing as you have imagined. If you don't see the energies yet, practice imagining the complete energy flow each time you practice running energy.

- At the end of your session, replenish yourself completely with the golden sun of life force energy as in the earlier exercise. Then stretch, bend over, and dangle your head and arms to release any excess energy in them and in your shoulders.

- Slowly, come up and open your eyes. Look around the room, be aware of your body, gently stand up, and move around. Notice any changes in your awareness and energy.

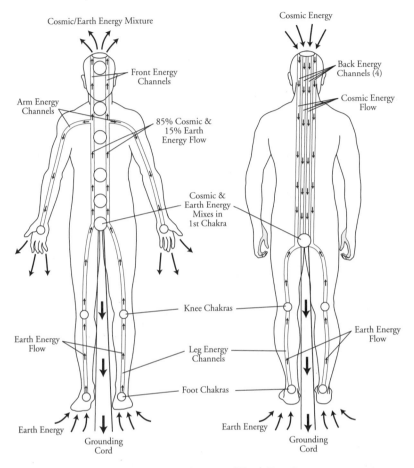

Figure 2: Running Cosmic and Earth Energies

In the beginning, you can practice for ten to twenty minutes at a time. You could start off by practicing once a day, then build up to twice a day when you are comfortable with it.

Creating and De-energizing Mental Pictures

Regularly practicing this exercise will help you develop your ability to create spiritually as well as to reclaim the energy from your attachments to thoughts and feelings, and the mental pictures that contain them.

(Review chapter 12: Mastering Your Memories.) These abilities will be important in further spiritual practices. Before practicing this exercise, be comfortable with grounding yourself, centering in spirit, replenishing your space with energy, and running the cosmic and earth energies.

- Sit comfortably upright in a chair. Have both feet flat on the floor. Close your eyes. Take a deep breath and relax. Let go of the tensions in your body. Become aware of the space behind your eyes. Decide to be there in the center of your head.

- Ground yourself.

- Run the cosmic and earth energies.

- Now, mentally picture a rose about ten to twelve inches in front of your forehead.

- Be aware that you created this picture as a spiritual being. The body doesn't create it.

- Observe this image for a few moments. Let go of any judgments. The picture doesn't have to be "perfect" or be what you might expect. Just let it be.

- Then, imagine exploding the picture. You are releasing all the energy that you had in it. Decide that the energy you released will come back into the crown chakra.

- While grounded and running energy, repeat this a dozen times or more for practice.

- When you decide to finish this practice session, replenish yourself completely with the golden sun of life force energy.

- Then stretch, bend over, and dangle your head and arms to release any excess energy in them and in your shoulders. Slowly, come up and open your eyes. Look around the room, be aware of your body, gently stand up, and move around. Notice any changes in your awareness and energy.

Whenever you find yourself stuck on a thought, feeling, image, a certain kind of energy, a problem, or even a person, take a moment to ground yourself and find some neutrality. Then, mentally create a picture of a rose in front of you, and put the thing that you're stuck on into it. Decide that you don't have to give your seniority and power over to it. Then, imagine exploding the whole picture and letting the energy go. Decide that the energy that was in the thing will return to your crown chakra. Each time you do this, you will find that the charge on the thing will get less. Eventually, you will be able to objectively deal with it if it needs to be managed. Many times, however, you may discover that once you de-energize the picture, there really isn't much of a problem after all.

Working with Dichotomies Exercise

This is a powerful exercise. Practice this after you are comfortable with grounding yourself, replenishing your space with energy, running the cosmic and earth energies, and creating and de-energizing mental pictures. Also, review chapter 13, Choosing Truth at Every Crossroads, especially the section on dichotomies.

- Sit comfortably upright in a chair. Have both feet flat on the floor. Close your eyes. Take a deep breath and relax. Let go of the tensions in your body. Become aware of the space behind your eyes. Decide you are there.

- Ground yourself.

- Run the cosmic and earth energies.

- Imagine your crown chakra turning a beautiful golden light. Be at this gold vibration. After running energy for a couple of minutes, re-establish your awareness behind your eyes, in the center of your head.

- Now, choose the dichotomy you would like to work on.

- When you practice this dichotomies meditation, frame your dichotomies as: I can totally have _____. Examples: I can totally have leaving my job / I can totally have not leaving my job; I can totally have being single / I can totally have not being single; I can totally have being afraid / I can totally have not being afraid. (To "have" here means that you can "accept yourself" regarding something, as in "I can totally accept myself being single.")

- For the purpose of doing this exercise for the first time, use the dichotomy example: I can totally have being happy about _____ / I can totally have being unhappy about _____. Choose some condition you are in, a situation, something that happened, a relationship, etc., to fill in the blank. Later, you can use this same meditation by selecting any dichotomy that you would like to process. Do this entire exercise while you are grounded, in the space behind your eyes, and running the earth and cosmic energies.

- Now, imagine a rose appearing about ten inches in front of your forehead toward your left side that energetically represents "you being happy about _____." As you observe this rose that represents "you being happy about _____," decide that it's okay for you to be happy about it, that you can totally have being happy about it.

- Once you make that decision, observe the thoughts and feelings that arise in your awareness. It could be anything: *I can't be happy about that because that's criminal; if I were really happy, I would lose my job; I can't be happy about it because it was stupid; if I became happy about it, my mate would get upset; how could I possibly be happy about it, I lost my best friend; I can't be happy when I'm in pain.*

- Whatever comes up, no matter how ridiculous or serious or emotionally charged, acknowledge it and then let it pass. Do not engage with any of the thoughts or feelings that come up, but merely let them pass through or imagine them exploding (see "Creating and De-energizing Mental Pictures"). Continue to observe the rose representing "you being happy about _____."

- Notice what else comes up. The reasons why you shouldn't or can't be happy about it will start to rise in your awareness. Let them go or imagine exploding them.

- Next, let that rose representing "you being happy about _____" remain there on the left side and then imagine another rose that represents "you being unhappy about _____" on the right side in front of your forehead. Observe it.

- Decide that it's okay for you to be unhappy about it, and that you can totally have being unhappy about it. Be neutral and observe what considerations and feelings arise.

- What comes up for you may be anything, but here are a few examples: *I can't be unhappy about it, I have work to do. I can't let myself be unhappy, I should be happy for my parents/children/spouse. I can't afford to be unhappy. It's bad to be unhappy. I'll lose my friends if I'm unhappy. If I'm unhappy about it, it means I was wrong.* Notice whatever comes up and let it pass on through or imagine exploding it.

- Now, set that rose aside and be neutral. Go back to the first rose on your left representing "you being happy about _____." Once again, decide that this is fine. Observe the thoughts, pictures, and feelings coming up. Imagine them passing through and dissolving or exploding. What changes do you notice in yourself in relationship to you being happy about _____?

- Once again, set that rose aside and become neutral. Then return to the rose to your right that represents "you being unhappy about _____." Decide that is perfectly fine. See what considerations, pictures, and feelings arise that invalidate you being unhappy about _____. Let them all pass through and dissolve or let them explode.

- Set this rose aside. Now, go back to the other rose. Repeat this several times. Each time, observe and let go of the pictures and energies that come up that go against you having that side of the dichotomy. As you go deeper, you may notice that most of the pictures and thoughts came from other people. You may notice thoughts such as *Wipe that grin off of your face—I'm serious* or *You can't be that happy because no one is,* or you may notice a picture of your mother trying to cheer you up so she wouldn't have to feel guilty about her child being miserable. Once again, it could be anything. The goal here is to release the pictures and energies held in your subconscious that invalidate your ability to have both sides of the dichotomy.

- When you are finished with going back and forth between the two sides, be neutral to both of the roses. Let them be. Let go of any remaining thoughts, feelings, and pictures. Notice where you are with each side of the dichotomy. Is it lighter and easier both ways? Can you be more satisfied with either side? Then, explode each rose and let all the energy go. Decide that your energy released will return to your crown chakra.

- Notice the earth and cosmic energies running through your channels and chakras. Enjoy the experience. Be amused. Let all the thoughts and feelings wash away with the flowing energies. Imagine that all the excess energies fall down your grounding.

- Be aware in the space behind your eyes. Imagine a golden sun of your life force energy over your head. Bring this energy into your body from your crown chakra. Let it bathe each of your chakras with life force. Let it replenish and heal each chakra. Then, let the golden sun expand into every cell of your body and replenish and heal them. Finally, let the sun expand out from your body through your skin into the layers of the aura around you. Let the life force replenish and heal your aura. Let all the excess flush down your grounding to the center of the earth. (For complete instructions, see the "Replenishing Your Space Exercise" earlier in this section.)

- When you're ready, gently stretch your arms and shoulders. Open your eyes, slowly bend over, and let your head and arms dangle toward the floor. Release all excess energies from your head, neck, shoulders, and arms. Slowly sit back up. Look around you. Be right here, right now. When you are ready, slowly stand up and move around. Notice your body and say "hello" to it.

When you've had a chance to practice this process a few times with different dichotomies, write out a list of fifty or so dichotomies that are important to you. These are the ones that keep popping up in your life or in your thoughts. The more you free yourself in relationship to these dichotomies, the more energy and creative freedom you will experience.

When you feel ready to practice with choices you have to make in your life, such as whether to live where you are or move somewhere else, stay with this job or leave, get into this relationship or not, follow the same steps. Each rose would represent one side of the dichotomy. In these bigger issues of life, try this process out in small doses. Take one pair of dichotomies and go through this meditation process for about ten to fifteen minutes. Then, try it again every few days. Notice what happens with your awareness, feelings, clarity, and contentment in relationship to the choices. Ultimately, you'll find that the power is not in the choices, but in you. More and more, you'll be able to experience that you can be happy with yourself no matter the outcome. You'll also discover that "either/or" is never the only choice. Your choice is limited only by your imagination!

In spirit, outside of this physical three-dimensional realm, there is no time or space. Whatever you decide, so it is. In that situation, you are not beholden to a place or time by making a choice. You make a choice now—and then you make a choice now. Now you choose white and now you choose black. Now you could be female and now you could be male. So what's the big deal? You can have both of everything. In your physical body, limited by time and space, however, if you give up your power to the physical restrictions, you give up your spiritual fulfillment in having both sides in oneness. You don't have to split yourself up. If you can't have it, you can't take it or leave it. Only when you can have both sides of the dichotomy can you truly choose of your own free will. Then, whichever way you choose is going to be the right choice. There are no wrong choices.

You might, however, ask, "What about killing someone or not killing someone? Isn't there a right choice and a wrong one?" You will find that if you can have both choices, if you are okay either way with killing or not killing, there is no desire to kill. Killing a human being comes from being stuck in not having a choice. In fact, all negation of life arises from the experience of having no choice and the seeming powerlessness in that experience. When you can truly experience within yourself your freedom to choose, what you choose will prove to be beautiful, good, and true in life.

BIBLIOGRAPHY

Barks, Coleman. *The Illuminated Rumi.* New York: Broadway Books, 1997.

Blackman, Sushila. *Graceful Exists: How Great Beings Die—Death Stories of Tibetan, Hindu & Zen Masters.* New York: Weatherhill, 1997.

Burnham, Sophy. *The Ecstatic Journey: Walking the Mystical Path in Everyday Life.* New York: Ballantine Books, 1997.

The Comparative Study Bible. Grand Rapids, MI: The Zondervan Corporation, 1984.

Harvey, Andrew. *The Essential Mystics: Selections from the World's Great Wisdom Traditions.* San Francisco: HarperSanFrancisco, 1997.

Hodson, Rupert. *Michelangelo: Sculptor.* London: Philip Wilson Publishers, 2003.

Levoy, Gregg Michael. *Callings: Finding and Following an Authentic Life.* New York: Three Rivers Press, 1997.

Markides, Kyriacos C. *The Magus of Strovolos: The Extraordinary World of a Spiritual Healer.* New York: The Penguin Group, 1985.

LLEWELLYN ORDERING INFORMATION

Order Online:
Visit our website at www.llewellyn.com, select your books, and order
them on our secure server.

Order by Phone:
- Call toll-free within the U.S. at 1-877-NEW-WRLD
  (1-877-639-9753). Call toll-free within Canada at
  1-866-NEW-WRLD (1-866-639-9753)
- We accept VISA, MasterCard, and American Express

Order by Mail:
Send the full price of your order (MN residents add 6.5% sales tax) in
U.S. funds, plus postage & handling to:

> **Llewellyn Worldwide**
> **2143 Wooddale Drive, Dept. 978-0-7387-1196-6**
> **Woodbury, MN 55125-2989**

Postage & Handling:
Standard (U.S., Mexico, & Canada). If your order is:
> $24.99 and under, add $3.00
> $25.00 and over, FREE STANDARD SHIPPING

AK, HI, PR: $15.00 for one book plus $1.00 for
each additional book.

International Orders (airmail only):
> $16.00 for one book plus $3.00 for each additional book

Orders are processed within 2 business days.
Please allow for normal shipping time. Postage and handling rates subject to change.

You Are Psychic
Debra Lynne Katz

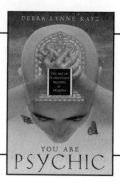

Learn to see inside yourself and others. Clairvoyance is the ability to see information—in the form of visions and images—through non-physical means. According to Debra Lynne Katz, anyone who can visualize a simple shape, such as a circle, has clairvoyant ability.

In *You Are Psychic*, Katz shares her own experiences and methods for developing these clairvoyant skills. Her techniques and psychic tools are easy to follow and have been proven to work by long-time practitioners. Psychic readings, healing methods, vision interpretation, and spiritual counseling are all covered in this practical guide to clairvoyance.

978-0-7387-0592-7
336 pp., 6 x 9, illus. $14.95

Spanish edition:
Tú eres psíquico
978-0-7387-0877-5 $14.95

To order, call 1-877-NEW-WRLD
Prices subject to change without notice

The Secret of Letting Go
GUY FINLEY

Llewellyn is proud to present the revised and expanded edition of our bestselling self-help book, *The Secret of Letting Go* by Guy Finley. Featuring an attractive new cover and fresh material, this Finley classic has been updated inside and out.

With more than 200,000 copies sold, Guy Finley's message of self-liberation has touched people around the world. Discover how to extinguish self-defeating thoughts and habits that undermine true happiness. Exploring relationships, depression, and stress, his inspiring words can help you let go of debilitating anxiety, unnecessary anger, paralyzing guilt, and painful heartache. True stories, revealing dialogues, and thought-provoking questions will guide you toward the endless source of inner strength and emotional freedom that resides within us all.

978-0-7387-1198-0
312 pp., 5³⁄₁₆ x 8 $14.95

Journey of Souls

Case Studies of Life Between Lives

MICHAEL NEWTON, PH.D.

This remarkable book uncovers—for the first time—the mystery of life in the spirit world after death on earth. Dr. Michael Newton, a hypnotherapist in private practice, has developed his own hypnosis technique to reach his subjects' hidden memories of the hereafter. The narrative is woven as a progressive travel log around the accounts of twenty-nine people who were placed in a state of super-consciousness. While in deep hypnosis, these subjects describe what has happened to them between their former reincarnations on earth. They reveal graphic details about how it feels to die, who meets us right after death, what the spirit world is really like, where we go and what we do as souls, and why we choose to come back in certain bodies.

After reading *Journey of Souls*, you will acquire a better understanding of the immortality of the human soul. Plus, you will meet day-to-day personal challenges with a greater sense of purpose as you begin to understand the reasons behind events in your own life.

978-1-56718-485-3
288 pp., 6 x 9 $14.95

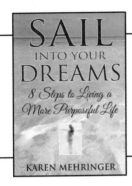

Sail into Your Dreams
8 Steps to Living a More Purposeful Life

KAREN MEHRINGER

Sail into Your Dreams is the perfect book for anyone who's ever asked, "Is this all there is to life?"

Unsatisfied with her busy life in Seattle, Karen Mehringer embarked on a six-month, life-changing ocean odyssey to Australia, Indonesia, Fiji, and, most importantly, toward the joyful, fulfilling life she had always wanted.

You don't have to leave land to make your dreams come true. Karen shares the wisdom and practical tools she learned on her ocean odyssey, showing us how to focus on what truly matters. Journal entries and inspiring stories from Karen and others highlight how to slow down, nurture yourself, connect with others, and tap into your life force energy—the source of infinite possibilities.

This eight-step program will help you assess your life and eliminate toxic relationships, emotional trauma, physical clutter, and debt—making space for new experiences that awaken your passion and spirit.

978-0-7387-1053-2
240 pp., 5 x 7

$13.95

Energy for Life

Connect with the Source

COLLEEN DEATSMAN

Lightning. Water. Sunshine. Apples. All matter is composed of energy, even ourselves. So what happens when our energy dissipates, becomes stagnant, or blocked? Imbalanced energy can jeopardize our quality of life and health—leading to fatigue, depression, or chronic illness. Colleen Deatsman's proven program for energy harmony demonstrates how to reignite and fortify one's vital life force energy.

This guide to energy work is full of easy energizing techniques to clear blockages, seal energy leaks, access universal life energy, and strengthen your energy field. Guided journeys, meditations, and other exercises can help you relax, de-stress, boost your energy, improve flow, and connect with spirit guides and other divine energies. *Energy for Life* also includes a handy audio CD of guided meditations.

Colleen Deatsman (Michigan) is a certified alternative healing consultant, a Reiki master, a shamanic practitioner, a hypnotherapist, and a licensed counselor. She holds a master's degree in Rehabilitation Counseling and owns a private practice in counseling services.

978-0-7387-0774-7
216 pp., 6 x 9

$19.95

Real Steps to Enlightenment
Dynamic Tools to Create Change

AMY ELIZABETH GARCIA

Connecting with the divine is crucial for spiritual advancement, but choosing a spiritual path is anything but easy.

Amy Elizabeth Garcia simplifies the journey to enlightenment into thirty-three spiritual goals, such as finding your life purpose, developing trust in the universe, relinquishing the need to control, recognizing synchronicity, and fostering peace. Focusing on a specific spiritual lesson, each chapter begins with a divine message from the author's spiritual master that includes stories from his human incarnations. Garcia goes a step further in bringing these concepts to life by sharing her own life experiences. Every chapter includes a prayer inspired by angels and exercises for spiritual growth—the perfect complement to this beginner's guide to enlightenment.

Amy Elizabeth Garcia (California) is a Reiki Master who receives guidance from her angels, healing guides, and the Master Jesus as she channels the Christ Force energy. She teaches workshops and conducts intuitive counseling and energetic healing sessions.

978-0-7387-0896-6
336 pp., 5¾₆ x 8 $14.95

Chakras for Beginners

*A Guide to Balancing
Your Chakra Energies*

DAVID POND

The chakras are spinning vortexes of energy located just in front of your spine and positioned from the tailbone to the crown of the head. They are a map of your inner world—your relationship to yourself and how you experience energy. They are also the batteries for the various levels of your life energy. The freedom with which energy can flow back and forth between you and the universe correlates directly to your total health and well-being.

Blocks or restrictions in this energy flow expresses itself as disease, discomfort, lack of energy, fear, or an emotional imbalance. By acquainting yourself with the chakra system, how they work and how they should operate optimally, you can perceive your own blocks and restrictions and develop guidelines for relieving entanglements.

The chakras stand out as the most useful model for you to identify how your energy is expressing itself. With *Chakras for Beginners* you will discover what is causing any imbalances, how to bring your energies back into alignment, and how to achieve higher levels of consciousness.

978-1-56718-537-9
216 pp., 5³⁄₁₆ x 8 $9.95

Spanish edition:
Chakras para principiantes
978-1-56718-536-2 $9.95

To order, call 1-877-NEW-WRLD
Prices subject to change without notice

Spiritual Development for Beginners

A Simple Guide to Leading a Purpose-Filled Life

RICHARD AND JAN POTTER

What exactly is spiritual development? Is it about being happy, becoming wise, finding yourself, finding the right religion, or discovering a deeper purpose? *Spiritual Development for Beginners* clarifies this complex idea and offers friendly guidance to anyone—religious or not—embarking on this great adventure.

Emphasizing spiritual growth as a universal and personal process, the authors offer mystical insight and an array of practices—from a variety of spiritual traditions—to forge a unique path to spirituality. Techniques involving breath, light, sound, and visualization help seekers center their consciousness, refine their auras, open their hearts, master their emotions and impulses, alter their perspectives, and strengthen their connection with spiritual realms. This practical guide also shows how to use meditation, prayer, and dream interpretation as tools to transform consciousness and become a "whole person."

Professors Richard and Jan Potter (Nebraska) are married and have taught at Dana College in Nebraska for over twenty years. Former members of the Sufi Order of the West, a universalist mystical school, they are experienced as spiritual guides and have led workshops and seminars in the area of spiritual development.

978-0-7387-0750-1

288 pp., 5³⁄₁₆ x 8 $12.95

Get Out of Your Way
Unlocking the Power of Your Mind
to Get What You Want

Layton Park

Beliefs, dreams, fears, goals—they all begin in the mind. Hypnosis offers a way to tap into the subconscious mind to produce amazing life changes.

From professional sports to the business world, hypnosis has helped millions achieve their desires. In *Get Out of Your Way*, Layton Park explains how and why hypnosis works, and shares "universal laws of mind" for transforming our belief system to allow our dreams to come true. Readers will learn how to clarify goals, construct effective affirmations, and engage these affirmations for positive life-changing results. Also featured are compelling case histories—true stories from the author—demonstrating the success of self-hypnosis.

Included with the book is an audio CD of easy-to-follow self-hypnosis techniques that can be used for accomplishing career goals, losing weight, quitting smoking, resolving phobias, and fulfilling a wide variety of personal ambitions.

978-0-7387-1052-5

240 pp., 6 x 9

$19.95

To Write to the Author

If you wish to contact the author or would like more information about this book, please write to the author in care of Llewellyn Worldwide and we will forward your request. Both the author and publisher appreciate hearing from you and learning of your enjoyment of this book and how it has helped you. Llewellyn Worldwide cannot guarantee that every letter written to the author can be answered, but all will be forwarded. Please write to:

Michael J Tamura
℅ Llewellyn Worldwide
2143 Wooddale Drive, Dept. 978-0-7387-1196-6
Woodbury, MN 55125-2989, U.S.A.
Please enclose a self-addressed stamped envelope for reply,
or $1.00 to cover costs. If outside U.S.A., enclose
international postal reply coupon.

Many of Llewellyn's authors have websites with additional information and resources. For more information, please visit our website at:
www.llewellyn.com